Palgrave Philosophy Today

Series Editor: **Vittorio Bufacchi**, Univer:

The *Palgrave Philosophy Today* series prc
major areas of philosophy currently bei
around the world. Each book gives a s1
a key area of philosophical study. In ad
distinct interpretation from an outstan
with current work in the field. Books in t.

C000131873

....uucii.s aiiu teacners
with not only a succinct introduction to the topic, with the essential information necessary to understand it and the literature being discussed, but also a
demanding and engaging entry into the subject.

Titles include

Pascal Engel
PHILOSOPHY OF PSYCHOLOGY

Shaun Gallagher
PHENOMENOLOGY

Simon Kirchin
METAETHICS

Duncan Pritchard
KNOWLEDGE

Mathias Risse
GLOBAL POLITICAL PHILOSOPHY

Joel Walmsley
MIND AND MACHINE

Forthcoming Titles

Helen Beebee
METAPHYSICS

James Robert Brown
PHILOSOPHY OF SCIENCE

Neil Manson
ENVIRONMENTAL PHILOSOPHY

Chad Meister
PHILOSOPHY OF RELIGION

Matthew Nudds
MIND AND THOUGHT

Lilian O'Brien
PHILOSOPHY OF ACTION

Don Ross
PHILOSOPHY OF ECONOMICS

Nancy Tuana
FEMINISM AND PHILOSOPHY

Palgrave Philosophy Today
Series Standing Order ISBN 978–0-230–00232-6 (hardcover)
Series Standing Order ISBN 978–0-230–00233-3 (paperback)
(*outside North America only*)

You can receive future titles in this series as they are published by placing a standing order. Please contact your bookseller or, in case of difficulty, write to us at the address below with your name and address, the title of the series and one of the ISBNs quoted above.

Customer Services Department, Macmillan Distribution Ltd, Houndmills, Basingstoke, Hampshire RG21 6XS, England

Metaethics

Simon Kirchin
University of Kent, UK

First published 2012 by
PALGRAVE MACMILLAN

Palgrave Macmillan in the UK is an imprint of Macmillan Publishers Limited,
registered in England, company number 785998, of Houndmills, Basingstoke,
Hampshire RG21 6XS.

Palgrave Macmillan in the US is a division of St Martin's Press LLC,
175 Fifth Avenue, New York, NY 10010.

Palgrave Macmillan is the global academic imprint of the above companies
and has companies and representatives throughout the world.

Palgrave® and Macmillan® are registered trademarks in the United States,
the United Kingdom, Europe and other countries

ISBN: 978–0–230–21946–5 hardback
ISBN: 978–0–230–21947–2 paperback

This book is printed on paper suitable for recycling and made from fully
managed and sustained forest sources. Logging, pulping and manufacturing
processes are expected to conform to the environmental regulations of the
country of origin.

A catalogue record for this book is available from the British Library.

A catalog record for this book is available from the Library of Congress.

10 9 8 7 6 5 4 3 2 1
21 20 19 18 17 16 15 14 13 12

Printed and bound in Great Britain by
CPI Antony Rowe, Chippenham and Eastbourne

Contents

Series Editor's Preface

It is not easy being a student of philosophy these days. All the different areas of philosophy are reaching ever increasing levels of complexity and sophistication, a fact which is reflected in the specialized literature and readership each branch of philosophy enjoys. And yet anyone who studies philosophy is expected to have a solid grasp of the most current issues being debated in most, if not all, of the other areas of philosophy. It is an understatement to say that students of philosophy today are faced with a Herculean task.

The books in this new book series by Palgrave are meant to help all philosophers, established and aspiring, to understand, appreciate and engage with the intricacies which characterize all the many faces of philosophy. They are also ideal teaching tools as textbooks for more advanced students. These books may not be meant primarily for those who have yet to read their first book of philosophy, but all students with a basic knowledge of philosophy will benefit greatly from reading these exciting and original works, which will enable anyone to engage with all the defining issues in contemporary philosophy.

There are three main aspects that make the Palgrave Philosophy Today series distinctive and attractive. First, each book is relatively short. Second, the books are commissioned from some of the best-known, established and upcoming international scholars in each area of philosophy. Third, while the primary purpose is to offer an informed assessment of opinion on a key area of philosophical study, each title presents a distinct interpretation from someone who is closely involved with current work in the field.

Metaethics is arguably one of the most demanding areas in philosophy, requiring dexterity not only in ethics but also metaphysics, philosophy of mind, epistemology and of course logic. Mastering metaethics demands coming to terms with an increasing array of 'isms', something that has hitherto made this subject impenetrable to many undergraduate students of philosophy.

In this text for the Palgrave Philosophy Today series, Simon Kirchin has succeeded in a task that many thought was unfeasible: how to make metaethics accessible (and fun) to undergraduate students, while also being innovative and thought-provoking to the more seasoned philosophers. Starting with a detailed account of G. E. Moore's *Principia*

Ethica (1903), a text that sets the scene for all subsequent debates in contemporary metaethics, Kirchin goes on to explain the conceptual architecture underpinning the major contenders in contemporary metaethics – moral realism; naturalism; error theory; noncognitivism – as well as up-and-coming theories which are attracting much attention in the literature today, for example sensibility theory. At the end of the text Kirchin also provides the reader with a clear, scholarly analysis of the key issues regarding moral motivation.

Kirchin's book is that rare creature in the philosophical landscape: a single text that will teach advanced undergraduate students all they need to know about metaethics, while at the same time making an original contribution to the discipline.

Vittorio Bufacchi
General Editor, Palgrave Philosophy Today
Department of Philosophy
University College Cork

Preface and Acknowledgements

This textbook covers a lot of ground, but I have decided not to cover every aspect of modern metaethics. For a start, that would be impossible unless the book was at least five times the length. But, also, this book is not a conventional textbook, although it can be used in that way. I think of it more as an 'argumentative essay', tying together many of the key ideas in metaethics in, I hope, an informative and engaging narrative. It is designed to introduce people to metaethics as well as argue for a particular view and certain ideas. I hope it encourages people to read many of the key articles and books on metaethics; indeed, this book is designed to be read alongside those other writings. Whilst I do not skimp on details, at times I merely introduce and sketch an idea or argument, inviting readers both to discover what metaethicists have argued for and to think through the idea or argument for themselves with initial help from me.

Metaethics, as it is often written about and discussed, has a number of set questions. Further, it has a number of set positions that offer answers to these questions. This book details many of the main questions and positions. Three further thoughts follow from this. First, readers should be aware that whilst there is some compartmentalisation in this book, I believe strongly that one can understand one metaethical position only if one understands all the others. So, many ideas are returned to every so often, and if one starts at, say, Chapter 4 to read about error theory, not everything will be understandable right from the start. After this preface, one needs to read from Chapter 1. Secondly and following on, I note a strong belief of mine. Part of the understanding that needs to happen across positions has the following character. Every metaethical position has its strengths and weaknesses, with the strengths of one being reflected in the weaknesses of others. Often people pick a general position and try to defend it as best they can. (Of course, some metaethicists might disagree with this idea and think their position is pretty much perfect.) At the end of Chapter 1, I list the main things we want a metaethical theory to talk plausibly about.

Lastly, for many reasons we should applaud concentrated focus on questions and detailed examination of arguments. Yet, I think that metaethicists, as other philosophers, are often too caught up with the standard questions themselves. (I tar myself with this brush, I hasten to add.) At the end of this book I bring out one sceptical thought about how metaethics is often debated.

Readers should note that what I find key are the questions themselves and our responses to them. As far as possible I ignore jargon, labels, and even prominent metaethical thinkers. However, metaethics employs *a lot* of jargon, so we will not have an easy ride in this regard. What I do try to do is bring to the fore the questions and responses themselves and why they are interesting. Philosophy has at its core ideas, and it is these that I put at the centre of this book's philosophical story. Each chapter ends with some recommendations for further reading, and it is there where I tie ideas to various writers. Note, lastly, that when I first give the main characterization of a philosophical position, I typically italicize and put in bold the position's label.

Writing a book is hardly ever done in isolation. I am grateful to Vittorio Bufacchi for inviting me to write this book, and to the Philosophy editor at Palgrave Macmillan, Priyanka Gibbons, for helping me to see it through. Both Vittorio and Pri have been enormously patient with me and, if possible, I both hang my head in shame and salute them at one and the same time. I received comments on earlier drafts from Tim Chappell, Ray Critch, Antti Kauppinen, and Pekka Väyrynen. Also, many cohorts of my students have been subjected to lectures that I have turned into this book. To all of these good folk I give thanks. Some of this book started life many years ago as my PhD thesis when I was a student at the University of Sheffield. I learnt a huge amount from my supervisors, David Bell and Richard Joyce, and this book seems meagre repayment in comparison. I am also grateful to those friends whose names I have borrowed for my examples. I owe two large debts to the couple of anonymous reviewers who read the penultimate draft of this book and who both provided helpful and extensive comments, as well as spotting a few howlers. Lastly, and most importantly, I could not have written this book unless I had had both *some* isolation *and* something wonderful to think about and return to when I was not staring at a flickering cursor on a blank computer screen. Penny, Freddie and Molly have contributed greatly to the writing of this book, and have suffered both my absences and presences. To them I give my heartfelt thanks.

1
What Is Metaethics?

1.1 Starting thoughts

There are plenty of things that happen in this world that people think are morally right and morally wrong, morally good and morally bad. As you sit, now, reading this book, we can imagine that somewhere in the world someone is sharing their sweets with someone else. Similarly, some adult is binding some child's feet in very tight and uncomfortable ways, causing the child (muted) distress. Someone else is putting their elderly parent into a care home so they can go and live in a different country. Someone else is dumping chemicals poisonous to humans into the sea. Someone else has taken the day off work to go and read at their child's school. Someone else is testing drugs on various animals in a laboratory to make sure they are safe for humans to use. Someone else is helping to decide whether a country should invade a neighbouring state. And so on.

We often pass moral judgement on these and many other sorts of activity and action. We may do so when chatting in a pub or bar, when reading a news story, or when watching the television. And, when we pass such judgement, our minds might wander in various ways to think about the things we are judging and what our judgements amount to. For example, we might become very interested in the issue of research on animals and think hard about whether this is justified. Similarly, we may ask whether a war can ever be just and, if so, what conditions have to be fulfilled for it to be morally permissible. These and many other questions are of great practical concern and have a quite specific point. They are good examples of questions asked in *applied ethics*.

As we think through such issues, our minds might wander and we might ask questions of a more general and abstract nature. For example, perhaps we note that many actions are morally wrong and we want to work out what it is about these actions that makes them so. Perhaps, we may think, there is something that all of the wrong actions have in common – some aspect or feature of them that unites them and justifies our classifying each and every one of them as morally wrong. Perhaps we think there is something about the effects and consequences of the actions that makes them wrong, and from that we choose to focus on specific types of effect. Perhaps, alternatively, we ignore the consequences entirely and think about the various action types there are. From that, we might devise a set of ideas to show why it is that *these* sorts of action – stealing, lying, killing – are wrong, whilst *those other* types of action – sharing, caring, aiding – are morally right. Alternative to all of this, we might wonder why we should be so fixated on deciding what should be done rather than working out what sort of moral person we should be in general. These and other questions in the neighbourhood are the lifeblood of *normative ethics*.

(I have done something already that a few writers may think controversial: I have seperated normative ethics from applied ethics. There is clearly some link between the two, for some writers might try to defend the wrongness of war, say, from within a certain normative perspective such as consequentialism. I use this division only for convenience's sake here; I am not wedded to it. Indeed, I am about to introduce a third main area of ethical enquiry. Although I am more wedded to its distinction from the other two, I am not going to discuss how distinct it is in this book.)

This book is not concerned with either applied or normative ethics. Instead, our focus will be on a different set of questions and ideas, questions and ideas that constitute *metaethics*. Imagine that two people – Duncan and Helen – are discussing something they have heard about, such as a country's policy to limit severely the numbers of children any family can have. Let us also imagine that whilst both acknowledge that there are good reasons to favour this policy – worries about overpopulation and environmental sustainability being obvious ones – both think that it is, in the end, morally wrong. Duncan and Helen both agree that families should have some freedom from the state to decide how many children they can have, at least within reason. However, then their discussion takes an interesting turn, revealing some disagreement. Duncan thinks that this sort of policy is always wrong, no matter what the country and governmental structure. He might be prepared to relent on his view if the environmental situation got a lot worse. But, as things stand on that score, he thinks that any government that had this view would be wrong. Crucially, he thinks it would be wrong no matter what the government and, indeed, their citizens decided. Helen takes a different view. She reiterates that *she* thinks the policy is wrong. But, she also worries that it is odd to claim that this policy is wrong no matter what the people in a different government have decided. Her focus is on the thought that whilst she and Duncan might find this policy wrong, their judging in this way might be caused by various local factors, such as how they have been raised, and the values and ideas currently found acceptable in their society. Whilst they might privilege the moral importance of the freedom of the family and individuals, for example, other people in different locales may prefer to privilege the strength of the state and the moral importance of the country-wide communal unit, for instance. In short, Helen might say that whilst she thinks the policy is wrong, she acknowledges that some other people might think the policy is right. And – here is the disagreement with Duncan – she thinks that neither of these views about the policy has authority beyond the country or the tribe or the group. What people in this other country think is morally right is fine and 'right-for-them', she thinks, and her judgement that the policy is wrong has no universal authority: she and Duncan cannot justifiably criticize the view that the policy is right, only note that they do not agree with it.

Duncan, meanwhile, seems to think that there is such a thing as universal authority. (For argument's sake, let us extrapolate from this example to all moral debates and questions.) As far as Duncan is concerned, there are, as we might colloquially put it, correct and incorrect answers full stop. Just because you, or your group, or your country think that something is right or kind or cruel or just, this does not make it so. And for Duncan, it appears, that applies even when you are deciding what you should do in your own country. There is something beyond people's judgements that makes it the case that their judgements are correct or incorrect, true or false, and these classifications apply no matter what people themselves think of their views and their society.

The debate between Helen and Duncan sets us to thinking about metaethical issues: we are thinking not about first-order ethical issue, but are instead thinking about the status and nature of our moral actions and moral judgements. Helen and Duncan's debate is often the sort of everyday discussion that people who are new to formal metaethical study reflect on as being the experience that connects them with the academic debates. Throughout this book there are going to be many ideas and positions introduced that complicate how I characterize Helen and

Duncan's debate and which take us beyond it. Nevertheless, it is a good starting point.

Let us put a couple of labels on Duncan and Helen's thoughts. Helen we can call a ***moral relativist***. She thinks that the authority of moral judgments is a local affair. There is nothing beyond what we think that can give authority to our judgements, nothing beyond them that makes them 'really true' rather than just 'true-for-them' or 'acceptable-for-them'. A little while later we will think harder about moral relativism, particularly what we mean by 'we' and 'our'. But this will do for now.

Duncan is clearly a sort of ***anti-relativist***, for he denies Helen's claim. He may acknowledge, as a matter of fact, *that* people make different moral judgements. But, he thinks that there is such a thing as some universal authority: we *can* talk in terms of some standard that makes some judgements true and some false no matter what people in fact think. Now, often people call Duncan's position a type of ***moral realism***. They might reason thus: 'Duncan thinks there a moral judgement is correct or incorrect "globally", as it were, that there is universal authority to moral judgement, and a very natural way of explaining this is that Duncan thinks there is some moral reality independent of human judging that people are trying to represent with our judgements.' This is an understandable thing to say I think, but there are a few ideas to pick out from this train of thought. (Independence? Reality? Truth?) As we will see, I don't think it too controversial to think of Duncan's stance as *involving* a *type of* realism. However, it may be too extreme for us to say that 'realism' should be used *exclusively* for those positions that state that there is some moral fact and truth of the matter for every moral debate and where such truth exists independently of what any and every human believes.

Indeed, in setting up the debate I focussed on truth and falsity, and standards of correctness and incorrectness: Helen is concerned with judgements being (at most) 'true-for-us' and 'true-for-them', whilst the sort of realism Duncan espouses exemplifies the idea that the truth and falsity of moral judgements is independent of what anyone thinks. However, whilst undoubtedly useful to understand the debate in these terms, some – but by no means all – writers understand our contrast differently. Instead of focussing on truth and falsity, one could focus on resolutely metaphysical or ontological questions and focus on the thing to which judgements should conform in order to be true. So, for example, one could say that for Duncan there is a moral reality to which judgements should correspond if they are to be true, and this correspondence and the reality are things that are independent of any human being and their thoughts. When it comes to relativism, things are trickier. For we might say that there is *something* that makes judgements true, but given that we are dealing with 'true-for us' and 'false-for-us' then it seems odd to say that there is some reality. Still, writers sometimes talk of relativists thinking that there are moral properties, even if that may jar a little because, intuitively, we might think that only realists believe in moral properties.

I will sort out some of this later on in this chapter as well as return to these ideas throughout the book. Three things are clear. First, what matters in metaethics is not so much the labels and jargon that are used. What matters in metaethics is asking in a deep way what ideas the words are being used to stand for. Talk of 'moral properties' when it comes to relativism may jar, but it might be where we are led if we follow through on some ideas. Secondly, there is a possible debate to be had about how best to construe metaethics and its questions: as metaphysical enquiries, as enquires focussed on language and on the truth and falsity of judgements, or as enquiries focussed on something else (something from epistemology or from philosophy of mind). In this book I do not discuss this metaphilosophical issue. All types of question will be discussed, although the metaphysical will be more obvious than the others. That said, no decent metaethicist can focus just on one, I think. We need to be alive to the interplay between, say, metaphysics and concerns about language.

Lastly, the debate between Duncan and Helen gives us an inkling of the terrain of metaethics, but there is a lot more to uncover. It's time we thought about the whole area.

1.2   The main questions and some standard positions

As just mentioned, I run many of the thoughts in this section in terms of metaphysics, although our use of language will make an appearance at the end. I often talk in terms of moral 'properties' that are part of moral 'reality'. We could use alternative terms such as 'features', 'aspects', or 'facts'. I stick with 'properties' for the most part. Similarly, right now I use 'moral', although I use 'ethical' also across this book, and I treat these two terms as synonyms.

With those notes in place, I can state what, to my mind, is the chief initial question of metaethics: Do moral properties exist? Those that answer in the affirmative are **moral realists** and those that answer negatively are **moral anti-realists**. These two labels cover many different positions and, indeed, there are some anti-realists who try to make room for moral properties understood in particular sorts of ways. That seems plain strange: moral anti-realists who believe in a (sort of) moral reality! We'll come to that move in Chapter 5. For now, I'll keep things simple and say that moral realists believe in a moral reality and moral properties whilst anti-realists do not. After all, this question is the chief *initial* question: it gets us thinking and from this interesting ideas develop.

(a) *Moral realism*: So, do such properties exist? In order to answer this question, we need to understand what sort of thing we are after and, hence, we need to consider a second question: What *is* a moral property? This second question can be understood in a variety of ways and will have a variety of aspects to it that are important in metaethics. For a start, we might be talking about values or evaluative properties, such as kindness, badness, and so on. Or, we might be talking about reasons, demands and prescriptions, such as a demand for you to help an old lady with heavy shopping bags, or a reason to give to charity. It has to be said that often in current metaethics, whilst recognizing that evaluative properties and reasons are different, many writers do not focus too much on this difference when considering the issue of realism. It is taken for granted that if you are a realist of any sort, then you will be a realist about both evaluative properties and reasons. However, we can note that there is an interesting debate to be had here about whether the one type of thing is more conceptually basic (or more metaphysically basic, or more epistemically basic) than the other, or whether neither is. I leave this debate aside in this book.

With that said, there is still something else important to reflect on when thinking about the nature of moral properties, something that *does* occupy a lot of metaethicists' time. We need to think hard about the relationship – the three-way relationship – between the moral properties that seemingly exist, the nonmoral, natural world in which we live, and the humans for whom things have value and to whom reasons are said to apply. Think about it like this. A stabbing has a number of aspects to it. It might happen on a certain day. A blade of a certain length might be used. The metal might enter someone's body at a certain speed. And so on. We also normally want to say of many stabbings that they are morally bad and wrong, and some of them are further thought to be cruel and wicked. Now, whilst we are normally confident that the nonmoral properties exist – after all, we can see and measure the length of the blade – we might be less confident that any supposed moral properties exist. After all, we cannot touch them or smell them.

We might not even literally see the property of badness, for what we might literally see is a blade going into someone's stomach, and we categorize that as morally bad. This prompts us to think more grandly about the subject. In our current age modern science is taken by many to be the prime standard, if not the *only* standard, of what exists and what we can discover. Whilst science can make sense of the solidity of a blade and the speed of a hand, it does not really deal with demands to act and things such as kindness. Biologists might talk of a plant 'demanding' certain nutrients to grow, but that is just loose, metaphorical talk. When it comes to metaethics, on the other hand, philosophers are trying to talk and think non-metaphorically. How does the moral perspective that we have of the world fit with how science explains and characterizes it?

There are a number of answers. First, some realists embrace **moral naturalism**. Moral naturalists say that moral properties exist. To show this, they are (typically) content to say that the moral claims we make about the world are true or false, and that there is something about the world, a moral property or properties, that makes them so. The key move, according to naturalists, is to realize that moral properties are in fact best understood as being natural, nonmoral properties. We then get a variety of moral naturalisms. Some naturalists say that moral properties can be reduced to various sorts of natural properties. Wrongness may turn out to be some complex organization of brain states, such as various sorts of pain, which we can isolate and use to produce moral-to-natural 'maps': 'if some action is *this* natural sort of way then we know it will be *this* moral way'. Other naturalists are nonreductionists, but still maintain that moral properties are natural properties. We will sort out this difference concerning reduction later in the book. For now, it is important to realize that naturalists are *not* saying that moral properties exist and that they have their own unique nature, but are in some way *connected with* some other properties. This implies that there are two sorts of properties in the end, with moral properties being very different from natural ones. As the label implies, naturalists do not think that. We will develop naturalism and lay out its varieties in Chapter 3.

Some people wish to be moral realists but do not like naturalism. They embrace **moral nonnaturalism** instead. For them moral properties of whatever sort are metaphysically and conceptually *sui generis*, at least with respect to the natural world. (*'Sui generis'* is Latin for 'of its own kind'.) We cannot identify moral properties with other sorts of properties, such as natural properties. This position has some appeal if one does not wish to be a naturalist and one wishes to support realism.

But, why would one want to be a realist in the first place, and what is so bad about naturalism? And, if one does adopt nonnaturalism, how does one conceive of the relationship between the nonmoral world and the moral properties that are said to inhabit it? I explore and answer these questions in Chapters 3 and 6.

Recall that I said there was a three-way relationship to be explored. So far we have thought about the relationship between the moral stuff that seemingly exists and the nonmoral world. Another issue that occupies realists and others is the relationship between the moral stuff that seemingly exists and human judges. In particular, realists might ask, and be forced to answer, why it is that certain moral properties come to exist and what role human judges have in their existence. We might think that moral properties, whatever they are, come into existence, stay in existence, and have the character they have independently of anything to do with human thoughts, feelings, commitments and the like. (Recall the use of 'independent' in my initial characterization of Duncan in the previous section.) Or, we might say that things have the moral properties they have partly or wholly because of how humans judge things to be. This last idea might seem a little odd, particularly with the insertion of 'wholly'. For it seems that we are assuming that human judgements concerning the moral nature of an action can create the property of goodness, say, that the action has. We are not picking out things that *already* exist, but are imposing views onto a (nonmoral) world. That might be a defensible position, but why call this a version of realism? Indeed, if we are saying that human judges help to create these moral properties, and if we assume some differences between humans, are we in danger of returning ourselves to something like Helen's relativism: these moral properties 'exist-for-us' but they may not exist for people with different responses.

This is a good worry to raise. But as we will see, this sort of position – or something more sophisticated – is quite popular in metaethics. The alternative realist position, that properties are not *at all* dependent on how humans judge and feel, is clearly deserving of the label 'realism'. (I characterized Duncan's view in this way.) It faces other problems though. Many commentators find it rather extreme and implausible. We will discuss this issue further, again primarily in Chapters 2 and 4. What I emphasize now is that we have two issues on the table: the relationship between the moral and the nonmoral, and what we can for now think of as the amount of 'creative input' that humans have with regards to the existence and character of supposed moral properties.

There are important links between these two issues, but it is also vital to keep them apart, as I occasionally show in the rest of this book.

(b) *Moral anti-realism*: Let us move away from moral realism and think about its opposite. Many writers find it implausible to say that moral properties exist. Moral anti-realism comes in a number of forms. In this book I consider two main types: error theory and noncognitivism. In order to introduce them let us consider some more labels. Realists often embrace two further ideas: cognitivism and descriptivism. *Cognitivists* claim that moral judgements or beliefs are (wholly or primarily) representing states: there is some moral stuff and our judgements are attempts to represent it correctly. If they do that, they are true, and if they fail they are false. (There is a theory of truth – the correspondence theory – smuggled in here. Whether it is essential to cognitivism is moot, I think, but we'll let that point pass.) The focus here is, strictly, on how best to interpret the moral mental state. To 'cognize' something is to have a belief about something, and if one is correct (and other things hold), then one can be in a state of knowing something. This is to define cognitivism primarily in terms of a type of mental state that is reflected in, or expressed by, one's moral judgement. However, sometimes writers use 'cognitivism' to indicate something about everyday moral language and truth only, not about any mental state. If we do distinguish between mental states and language – as some other writers do – then we need another term. *Descriptivists* claim that moral language's (whole or prime) function is to describe stuff in the world. And, from this, descriptivists will typically say that judgements can be true or false, that is they are 'truth-apt'. Here are some examples that indicate both cognitivism and descriptivism. Just as we might believe that the stabbing happened on a Tuesday and has the property of being swift, so we believe it is wrong. This belief is reflected in the language typically used. Just as we say, 'Today is Tuesday' and 'The blade is sharp', so we say, 'The stabbing is wrong'.

The realist-cognitivist-descriptivist triumvirate is a neat package. People who sign up to all three parts can tell a nice story. They believe in moral reality. They believe that everyday moral judgements are attempts to represent that reality correctly. We have mental states that are attempts to cognize the world and give us knowledge, and our moral language reflects that in the way in which it tries to describe the world. Despite the neatness of this position it can be attacked. Not only can the whole part be attacked, but some theorists pick and choose which parts to accept and which to attack. So, now for those anti-realist positions.

Moral error theorists are, typically, cognitivists and descriptivists. They believe, along with moral realists, that everyday moral judgements are representations of something, and typically that 'something' is assumed to be moral reality of some sort. But, error theorists deny moral realism. They think that people are profoundly mistaken in their beliefs and judgements. There are no moral properties or moral reality, and hence everyday ethical thought and language has, at its core, a great, fatal falsehood. Well, that is what some error theorists say. It is open to an error theorist to pick on any claim or claims they think are rotten, not just a claim about the existence of moral properties. There will be more on this in Chapter 4.

Moral error theory is much like atheism, at least as normally understood and when directed at traditional Christianity. Traditional Christianity has, at its core, a belief in a miracle-performing, creating, omniscient, omnipotent, personal God. Atheists argue that there is no such being and so the whole of traditional Christian thought and language built around it is erroneous. Such sincere thought and language should go the way of sincere belief in witches and literal magic.

Notice that although metaphysical issues are still in the air, we have shifted to focus on what people believe and say morally. Many moral anti-realist positions think hard about everyday moral language and thought and use this as a way to reflect on the metaphysical assumptions and arguments we might make. This is very clearly the case with our next position.

Error theorists are quite negative about everyday moral thought and language, yet some other anti-realists are more positive. *Noncognitivists* (typically) agree with error theorists that there are no moral properties, but wish to vindicate our everyday activity. They do so by reflecting on what moral judgements are.

Moral realists and error theorists are both cognitivists and descriptivists, remember? But, there are different sorts of mental states and many ways in which language can function. For example, imagine that instead of being stabbed – that example is getting gruesome – Bob presents Jenny with a bowl of strawberries. 'Mmmmm!', says Jenny, licking her lips. Well, 'Mmmmm!' does not describe anything. A good test to see if an English utterance is attempting to describe anything is to see if it can replace *p* in the following sentence and if the resulting sentence still make grammatical sense: 'It is true [or false] that *p*.' We can readily see that 'It is true that "Mmmmm!"' doesn't make sense at all, at least in standard English. When Jenny says 'Mmmmm!' she is expressing her liking of strawberries. (We assume she is being sincere and really does like the strawberries; she isn't acting, for example.) Similarly, 'yawns' normally expresses boredom rather than describe that one is bored. The sentence 'Oh, I'm bored!' typically does the job of reporting you are bored. Likewise, we can presume that Jenny's mental state, as she licks her lips, will not be a belief that she likes strawberries. Rather she will be in a state of desiring the strawberries or she may be anticipating eating them.

Well, that is a fair presumption. But, note now that our language and our mental lives are complex. Imagine that when Bob walks in Jenny exclaims, 'I love strawberries!'. Strictly speaking this is a description or a report, a report by Jenny of her love of strawberries, and if we wished we could find out whether Jenny's claim was true. This utterance has descriptive 'surface grammar', as it is sometimes put. However, we know from experience that when people say this sort of thing in this sort of circumstance they are not reporting, or not *just* reporting, their love of strawberries. They are also expressing their desire to have some. Similarly, 'Oh, I'm bored!' can be used quite naturally to express boredom. Perhaps, then, this is how moral language works and how moral mental states should be construed. Whilst a lot of moral language has the surface grammatical form of being descriptive, on reflection we might conclude that it is doing a different job. Its 'depth grammar' is to express our desires and attitudes towards things, or (a possibility we have not yet considered), perhaps it is a way to issue prescriptions, commands and orders. So, when I say 'That institution is just' perhaps what I am really doing is saying something such as 'Hooray for that institution!', or perhaps I am ordering you to respect and protect it.

So, noncognitivists wish to show that moral language and thought can and does do more than just describe some supposed moral reality. Indeed, noncognitivists think that description is not its main function. And, so, although they typically do not believe in moral properties of the sort that error theorists also attack, noncognitivists are not committed to taking a negative stance towards everyday moral thought and language. In Chapter 5 we will think more about noncognitivism, the reasons for adopting it, and two problems it faces. We can also note, lastly, one more thing. Although it is traditional to think of noncognitivist theories as being anti-realist, it is open to noncognitivists to adopt the language of 'properties' and 'reality' in the hope that they can further vindicate everyday moral thought. Perhaps the best conception of a moral property is not along traditional realist lines, but is instead something that can be built upon the insight that moral language can be perfectly in order and do useful work, and yet not be primarily in the business of straightforwardly describing anything.

So, as the reader may have seen with that last thought, the terrain is already getting messy. This section is supposed to be introductory, but already *a lot* has happened. We have started with metaphysics and moved onto language (and mental states). We have thought about the places of moral properties in a natural world, and also canvassed a different but seemingly related distinction between the moral properties that may exist and human judgement about the world. We have had positions that seem to be anti-realist, but which can make room for moral properties of a sort, and positions labelled realist that seem to make a lot of room for humans' views of the world, helping to create the moral properties that seem to exist. And, we haven't even begun to think about epistemological questions, such as 'How do we know that moral properties exist?'

The main conclusion to draw from this is not just that metaethics can seem messy, but that it often is. We will have to stay alert.

Right now I turn to another set of questions that occupies a lot of metaethicists' time, and has really interesting connections to the ideas just canvassed.

1.3 Moral psychology

We have already encountered the idea of moral mental states. I used the word 'belief' a fair bit. In everyday language people might reserve the idea of a belief for those commitments and ideas that are very important. We might speak of a politician's belief in justice or liberty, for example. But in metaethics, as in other areas of philosophy, 'belief' is used in a more wide-ranging and mundane manner. 'Belief' is a catchall term for any sort of mental state that aims to represent the world correctly. So, one can have a belief that a table is brown or that today is Tuesday, as well as having a belief that liberty is a good thing. And, of course, such beliefs can be correct or incorrect. Perhaps today is Thursday, not Tuesday.

So, a big question in metaethics – one that has direct bearing on issues about moral language – concerns whether the mental states that typically accompany ethical utterances should be construed as being beliefs, as aiming to represent the world. When I say that the giving of some strawberries was kind, is it correct to construe my state of mind as being one that is attempting to represent the world in a certain way?

My judgement that ten strawberries were shared seems to be a report of what has happened. Is the judgement that the action was kind the same? Many people think that is the best way to construe matters. After all, if you think that moral stuff really is there, and if you are optimistic about us and our faculties, then you will think that the mental states people have are in the business of representing that stuff. However, as we have seen, we might construe things differently. No matter what the grammatical form of the utterance, perhaps moral mental states are best construed as wants, or commands or – a word we will use a lot – desires. Again, 'desire' is liberally used in metaethics as a catch-all term for any sort of mental state that is a want, an urge, a commitment, a plan, an intention, or a yearning. (We will not focus on these other things too much, but a lot of what can be said for desires goes for them also.) Desires are assumed to be non-representing states. Think about what happens when Jenny licks her lips and says, 'Mmmmmm!' as Bob enters with the strawberries. There are reasons to think that moral judgements are accompanied by or express desires. Desires are all about preferences and likings. Furthermore, they seem to express or embody how we are motivated to act. (More on that in a moment.) Preferences, likings, and inclinations all seem to be an important if not an essential part of our ethical lives. When we are stating that some action is generous, say, it seems that we are not merely reporting, in a cold and detached way, what it is. We are expressing our liking of the strawberries as well.

So, there is a battle to be had: What sort of mental states are moral judgements? Further to that question, more interesting questions lie ahead. Why think that these two states – beliefs and desires – are the only options? Many modern writers seem to suggest, if only by implication, that these are our only options. However, not only might there be many different sorts of mental states out there (and that the sly 'this is only a catch-all' move disguises and misleads far too much), it could be that the mental state that typically accompanies moral judgements is both a representing state and – at the same time – a state of being motivated. Perhaps there are some states that combine the two aspects and we can have the best of both worlds.

There is another prominent debate surrounding moral psychology, linked to the previous point. What is the link between making a moral judgement and being motivated to act appropriately on that judgement? Imagine I make a moral judgement, of whatever kind, no matter how plausible, and no matter whether it is true or false. Often there is some motivation, of some strength, on my part to act appropriately in accordance with the judgement. So, if I think that giving to charity is kind, I will feel some motivation to give. (And if I think that stabbing this person would be wicked, I will feel some motivation to refrain from doing so.) The motivation we feel may even be our strongest desire, and thus we act accordingly. Some people think it is a necessary part of making a moral judgement that motivation of some strength be present. Some other people disagree. It is clear that sometimes motivation is present, but it is not always, and when it is not that does not mean we should regard the moral judgment as bogus and a case of merely parroting words. There are things to say in favour of both sides. We will see that this debate is intimately connected with the previous one concerning beliefs and desires, and we will also see how these two debates about moral psychology are bound up in the earlier metaphysical debates. I discuss issues of motivation throughout the book, and bring them to sharp focus in Chapter 7.

1.4   Moral relativism again

There is no chapter devoted to moral relativism in this book. But this position pervades much of what we will consider and it is a crucial part of the background against which modern metaethical discussion takes place. Some professional philosophers may explicitly snub relativism, and introduce the relativist into their discussions as a sinister bogeyman, designed to scare innocent young philosophers and trouble their dreams. Other philosophers seem to accept that there are relativistic versions of many metaethical positions. And, outside of academia, we may find people who are resolutely against relativism, as Duncan is, as well as others who have an attitude just like Helen's across many issues.

To explain why relativism is crucial and why we might have these different reactions, let us return to Helen. I introduced the terminology of 'true-for-us' and 'false-for-us'. This is very important. It seems natural to say that relativists believe that there is no moral truth when it comes to moral judgements and that absolutely anything goes when it comes to morality. But, there are many varieties of relativism beyond this. Think about the name: *relativism*. The idea is that a moral judgement is seen as being decent, correct, acceptable, kosher or, indeed, true, *relative to* a certain standard/idea or something. As part of this, the standard is assumed to be something that is local and, typically, this local thing is essentially something to do with human judges. When it comes to Helen in the debate above, it seems that the standard is her country or social group. The key relativistic thought is that the something that acts as a standard will be different for different people, and that all such standards are equally authoritative, authoritative to a certain local set of judgements. In contrast to all of this, Duncan also has a standard for moral judgements. But for him this seems to be a sort of moral reality that is conceived to be independent of humans and, thus, this reality has universal authority.

We may get different sorts of relativism depending on the standard. Helen could choose her social group as the standard. But, we might ask, how homogenous is her group? What *is* the social group? If people within her social group disagree about something, for example some governmental policy, then it is doubtful that her group can then act as *a* standard, for there is no such thing. Helen and people within her group may have the same *general* values and ideals in common, but then such a standard may not give us enough detail when it comes to a particular case. For example, perhaps people in Helen's group favour both family freedoms *and* environmental protection. Some cases, such as the one we considered, will expose a tension between these two general stances.

The obvious way out of this difficulty is to narrow what counts as the standard. One of the most narrow standards for a judgement to con-form to is 'what the particular judge [e.g. Helen] believes'. And, more narrowly than that, relativists might add that the standard that mat-ters is a particular person at a certain age of maturity, on a certain day. This will give a *very* extreme sort of relativism: what is morally right or wrong depends on what *you* believe (at a certain time). This seems like a very implausible account of morality. At the very least, we will want to account for people being wrong about moral matters, and this seems difficult if not impossible to do within this position. This is probably the reason why some people are averse to relativism *per se*, since they have this extreme version in mind. These people may continue to be averse to relativism as we turn our back on such narrowness and widen out so that the standard (again) becomes one's social group and tribe. After all, there are plenty of examples of whole societies going wrong. But, even if this less narrow position is still worrying, it may be harder to shake off.

It is particularly hard to shake off because, as we have seen, there are a number of positions that, whilst wishing to avoid the extreme sort of relativism just encountered, base the correctness and incorrectness of moral judgement on human judgement, sentiment and reasoning abil-ity. I do not wish to get into the details of these positions now; we will do so in Chapter 6. However, three quick points will suffice here. First, often the standard used in such positions is human beings and their responses and reasoning abilities generally rather than some particular social group. Second, whilst accepting that their position has some limited relativism, such theorists will use the label 'relativism' only for the more extreme views just introduced. Because their position seeks to encompass humans generally, they will prefer to emphasize the general nature of their account and how wide the authority of the standard is. Such theorists also work, quite consciously and sincerely, with notions of moral truth and moral property. As part of this, and third, they will say that it is enough to tie the authority of the moral standard to human beings. There is no sense in trying to justify all of our moral judgements such that they have authority over Martians as well, for example.

I started by presenting a big clash between Duncan and Helen. This clash remains, as I show in Chapter 2. But, there are many types of relativism. My contrast between the social group and one person is blunt, but I hope it gives a flavour of what one could say. Indeed, it seems that the varieties of relativism come in a sliding scale, from the less extreme to the more extreme versions.

As I have said, there is no distinct chapter on relativism. Yet the position, and the desire to avoid extreme versions of it, will be something we return to every so often. Seeing how some people try to reconcile a desire to avoid extreme relativism with an attempt to make humans' judgements central to the story of how moral value gets into the world will be interesting.

1.5   Concluding remarks and a plan

In this chapter I have set out some of the main questions and positions that occupy modern metaethicists. There has been a fair bit of terminology already. Matters on this score will get worse. But, the key thing to remember as I said in my Preface is that it is the ideas and arguments that are important, not how we label them.

To summarize, here is a plan of the book. In Chapter 2, I lay out what realism is and the motivations for it. I focus our attention on one of the relationships I have introduced, that between the moral properties that seemingly exist and human judges. In Chapter 3, I explain, in detail, about the relationship between the moral properties that seemingly exist and the natural world. I concentrate on naturalistic forms of moral realism, ultimately arguing against them. As I said in the Preface, I believe that one understands a metaethical position fully only by understanding its opponents. Thus, having thought about realism for a while I think it is crucial that we think about types of anti-realism. In Chapter 4, I discuss error theory: what it is, its attractions, and its problems. Further, one of the most famous arguments for error theory will cast light on the issues about realism we have already discussed. In order to continue the anti-realist story, I discuss noncognitivism in Chapter 5. I end that chapter by introducing a problem I believe is fundamental to it. This problem takes us directly to the concerns of Chapter 6. In this chapter, I return to moral realism and cautiously defend a nonnaturalistic version of it. In Chapter 7, I augment my defence of that position by elaborating on the two topics introduced earlier concerning moral psychology. In Chapter 8, as advertised, I explain briefly about what it is to engage in metaethical enquiry and consider one of the key assumptions of the whole debate as it is normally carried out.

In the Preface I promised to list matters about which metaethicists need to speak plausibly. So: we need an account of how humans and (seeming) moral properties are connected; an account of how (seeming) moral properties are situated in or relate to the nonmoral, natural world; an account of how everyday moral language and thought works; and lastly, an account of the relationship between moral judgement and psychology. In each case, of course, a metaethicist might tell us why such an account is *not* needed or not so important. But, they can't ignore any of these issues altogether, I reckon. And, finally: recall that earlier I said that the strengths of a position will be reflected in the weaknesses of one or more of its opponents. We will see this clearly if we keep the ideas just listed in mind.

Further Reading

There are a number of places to start reading about metaethics. Miller (2003) is a recent, comprehensive and, in my view, great textbook. It is more technical than this book, but consequently gives more detail. The first few chapters of Chappell (2009) and the whole of Fisher (2011) are both gentler introductions than the Miller. McNaughton (1988) is also very readable and standardly referenced, although some recent debates are not included. Smith (1994) set a lot of recent metaethical debates in motion, especially those surrounding moral motivation and reasons, but it is also an excellent introduction to many metaethical topics. Wong (2006) is the best modern defence of moral relativism. Gowans (2012) is a good summary of the position, and Kirk (1999) is a good introduction to the issue of relativism generally. Copp (2006) has a number of great chapters on different metaethical positions, a few of which I pick out in other 'Further Reading' entries later in the book. Similarly, see Skorupski (2009). There are two recent collections of metaethical articles worth investigating: Fisher and Kirchin (2006), and Shafer-Landau and Cuneo (2006). Two other collections that are still valuable and which have excellent introductions are Sayre-McCord (1988), and Darwall, Gibbard and Railton (1992). Finally, the Stanford Encyclopedia of Philosophy – http://plato.stanford.edu – has a number of excellent entries on metaethical topics.

2
Moral Realism: Mind-Independence

2.1 Introduction

In Chapter 1 I introduced moral realism. I also introduced the idea of a three-way relationship that exists between humans as valuing and reasoning creatures, the natural world we inhabit, and the moral properties and reasons that seemingly exist. This chapter introduces us to the relationship between moral properties and humans, whilst Chapter 3 – which is far longer – considers the relationship between the natural world and moral properties.

I stress that this chapter *introduces* us to something. We will not have a final discussion of all the things in this chapter until Chapters 6 and 7, but that is because we need to discuss other things first. However, this present chapter is important because it sets us on our way.

Although I concentrate on moral properties, we will have one eye on evaluative properties generally. So aesthetic properties such as elegance and ugliness, and certain epistemic properties such as wisdom and naivety, are also in play.

2.2 Why realism?

In the following sections I detail different sorts of realism and motivations for adopting them. In this present section I detail why people are inclined towards realism first of all.

Recall that realists believe that moral properties exist. Stabbings and sharings, and institutions and people, can be good and bad, kind and cruel, just and inappropriate. Why believe that properties such as goodness and kindness exist? A key reason for thinking so is simply that in our everyday lives we supposedly think and talk as if there are such things. We act on the basis of moral properties, whether we explicitly reason and refer to them before we act, or whether our actions are instinctive. This is just like many nonmoral cases. We may choose one knife over another because it is sharper. We may choose one form of transport over another because it is faster or more reliable. We may choose one hat over another because its shade matches the colour of our shoes. Similarly, we often choose one action rather than another because it is just or kind. And, to switch to aesthetic values, we may choose one tie over another because the alternative is both gaudy and old-fashioned.

We can dwell a little more on this phenomenon. Some people think there is a distinct sort of phenomenology associated with our moral and evaluative lives. 'Phenomenology' is used here as a fancy word for 'felt experience'. Ordinarily we seem to experience the world as containing evaluative properties, just as we experience the world as containing fingers, chairs and clouds. A moment's reflection, in even the most philosophically disinclined, will probably result in the thought that evaluative properties are not the same as chairs. For example, we can touch chairs and literally see them. We can measure their height and weight. We may not be able to investigate clouds in the same sort of way, but we can still empirically investigate and measure them in some fashion. Not so evaluative properties that *seemingly* exist. (I italicize to note the doubt that may have crept in.)

However, this itself may do nothing to show that we cannot speak of their existence. After all, electrons are thought to exist and, true, they can be measured in some way, but they cannot be seen by the naked human eye or touched by us. Quarks are even stranger. We should be open to the possibility that things can exist and yet be different in their nature from other things that exist. We may not be able to see evaluative properties literally, but some people still talk of being able to perceive them. Some people think it obvious that some stabbings are wrong. 'Can't you see how wrong and cruel it is?', they might say, in a puzzled fashion, to those that take a different view. Similarly, although some trains may be reliable and their seats comfortable, it is not so clear that properties such as reliability and comfort can be investigated by conventional science even though we would be prepared, ordinarily, to think that such talk was perfectly straightforward.

But, this is to get ahead of ourselves. We are already on the road to considered reflection about whether evaluative properties exist. We are concerned right now with the attractions of realism and many philosophers – realists and non-realists alike – agree that evaluative properties *seem* to exist, at least initially. Indeed, some realists are so enamoured by our value phenomenology that to them this is the main or even only way in which one can argue positively for realism. Any other positive arguments are arguments for a particular brand of realism, not for realism as such. Indeed, some realists go further and say this isn't really even an *argument* for realism. It is just a reporting of what seems natural. Metaethical argument and debate start only when people begin (perhaps with some justification) to doubt what seems naturally fine. Whether or not realists take this line, for many of them a description of our moral phenomenology is the first move in metaethics. The fact that evaluative properties seem to exist is something against which non-realists have to argue against, and this is a task they need to take on immediately, as soon as they join the debate.

It should be pointed out that it is not just phenomenology that matters to many realists. Recall that at the start of §1.2 I said that I preferred to run our debates – at least initially – in terms of metaphysics and here we are talking about which things seem to exist. But, recall that the issue of language was also important. Are moral judgements typically expressed as if they are attempts to describe the world and state facts about it? Are they the sorts of thing that can get to be true or false in the first place? (Recall from §1.2(b) the examples of the strawberries and the stabbing, and the language used about them.) Many metaethicists, of all stripes, agree that moral judgements appear to have some descriptive function and are the sorts of thing that can get to be true or false, that is many people agree that their surface grammar is descriptive. Many realists think this is no accident. For them it reflects our 'pretheoretical' inclination to assume that values exist. So we say that blades are sharp and that ties are brown and purple. We also say that some stabbings are wrong and that some ties are gaudy. It seems, initially at least, that we pick out evaluative properties in the world just as we pick out objects and their nonevaluative, nonmoral properties.

The various sorts of realism have their own attractions, and we will look at one brand in a moment. But, we can draw our discussion of the initial attraction of realism to a close. Its attraction can be stated simply: many moral realists are realists because in our everyday lives moral properties are experienced and talked about as real.

As it happens, I worry about whether our moral language is as descriptive as some realists think it is. Others think along the same lines, and this will become apparent in Chapter 5. Not as many people worry about the pretheoretical intuitions, but I worry about them also. In Chapter

8 I have detailed about this. However, right now we need to investigate an important brand of realism.

2.3 Moral properties and humans

In Chapter 1 we encountered Duncan. Duncan seemed to think there really is a moral reality and, in some vague sense thus far, it appears that he thinks this reality is untainted by human influence. As I mentioned earlier, some realists think differently from this. I will introduce them a little in this chapter, and discuss their view in Chapter 6. In short, such realists claim that moral properties exist but that they somehow *depend* on humans. So, we have different conceptions in play of what moral reality and moral properties are.

In order to nail a view at the start to run our thoughts, we will explore Duncan's view further. This view is often described simply as 'realism', but because of the range of realisms on offer I call this view **Independent Moral Realism** ('IMR' for short, and its supporters 'IMRealists'). At their core, IMRealists believe the following:

> *Thesis IMR*: The existence of moral properties and moral reasons is a mind-independent matter. That is, the existence of such properties and reasons is not dependent on what human beings, either individually or collectively, think, desire, are committed to, wish for, etc. Similarly, the 'type' or 'character' of value or reason that they are – e.g. goodness, kindness – is a mind-independent matter.

We have two things distinguished: the existence of values and their type. The former idea is meant broadly and covers both the creation of such things and their continuation. The latter idea refers to the fact that some actions are kind rather than being cruel. The fact that some actions have *these* moral properties rather than *those other* ones is also something independent of humans. Further, note that IMRealists may offer an account of how it is that humans come to know that moral properties and reasons exist. There will be a little more on that epistemic issue later. For now we can concentrate on this metaphysical claim.

It seems that if any position is deserving of the label 'moral realism' then it is this one. But, is it so clear exactly what it means? The idea of mind-independence can be a little confusing and needs sorting. Consider, first, a case easy to understand. Imagine we have a deer dying in an earthquake in some place remote to humans. Imagine that humans had no part in causing the earthquake, they did not cause the deer to be there, and so on. Now imagine that for whatever reason we want to say this was a bad thing, rather than a thing that just happened. (I mean here just that it has some general value of being bad; it does not necessarily have to be morally bad.) We can now ask the question of what it is that grounds this badness. The deer's death is bad, but is it bad because humans – if any were there to judge it, or us considering it now – judge it to be bad? Or, is it bad no matter what humans say or could say about it? If you take the latter option, you are saying that this badness is a mind-independent matter. This is clearly so because we have specified that human judgement plays no part in why the action is bad.

Now consider a second case. Deers dying in earthquakes are all very well (in a manner of speaking), but most if not all of the situations and actions that supposedly carry moral value involve humans doing things or saying things, often to other humans. Consider this case. Alan and Edward are at a birthday party – Edward's – and are talking together with a group of other people. Edward has been given a truly hideous jumper by his Aunt Julia, and is wearing it. Unfortunately, Edward thinks it is a lovely jumper. Alan, finding it impossible to miss a trick, makes fun of his friend and produces a truly delicious but wicked putdown of Edward's sartorial tastes. Silence falls. Edward is obviously hurt, and leaves so as to change his jumper, returning a little later, embarrassed and muted. Alan has obviously done something wrong and, if we filled in the details, we could say that he had acted in a mean manner, for example.

So, clearly we have some moral properties in play here. (Or, if we are imagining the moment before Alan opens his mouth, we can think of the various reasons that seem to exist for him to perform, or refrain from performing, a variety of actions.) We can ask the same question as before: Is Alan's action wrong wholly or partly because of what humans think and desire, or wrong independently of such things? The issue is slightly more complicated than the deer case because part of the reason why Alan's action was wrong is that Edward felt hurt and embarrassed, and such feelings are obviously, in some sense, dependent on Edward's 'mind', that is on his general personality-cum-psychology. (Imagine instead if Edward had laughed off Alan's remark and traded friendly insults by making some quip about Alan's exotically coloured tie.) Does the fact that we have now referred to Edward's emotions and thoughts in our story as to why the remark was wrong rule out the possibility that Alan's action was mind-independently wrong? No. The issue of mind-dependence and mind-independence is whether the action or situation or whatever *as a whole* is wrong or kind or whatever. We can count Edward's feelings of hurt as part of the situation to which value is supposed to attach. Indeed, imagine if we had the situation as described and then, later on, Edward said to us that he was wrong to have felt hurt and embarrassed at what Alan said. We might wish to say – if we are IMRealists – that Edward's new view is incorrect; it was wrong of Alan and, perhaps, it is mind-independently wrong, wrong no matter what anyone thinks, and that includes Edward. There is a moral reality that is fixed, and it is fixed independently of what anyone believes. So, although this case is a little more complicated than the deer case, in the end IMRealists will say that the evaluative properties that exist in the situation are both mind-independent.

In short, 'mind-independent' is not synonymous with 'humans not involved': a matter can be mind-independent and, in some sense, it can exist because of the presence of humans and their views. But, if we ascribe value, for example, to that situation, that value can still be mind-independent because we are asking whether the goodness exists even if no human would or could think it does when asked to sum up the entire situation. Similarly, 'mind-dependent' is not straightforwardly synonymous with 'humans involved'.

Back to IMR. When IMRealists put forward their view, they claim that whatever it is that has evaluative properties has such properties no matter what any human believes or how they react. And these 'whatevers' include situations and possible courses of action, which themselves may be partly constituted by human thoughts and responses. In one sense, then, IMRealists can say that moral properties depend on human beings, because many of the things that have value are things created because of human interaction and response. But, once those things are in place, we can always ask a further question about the nature of the evaluative properties of those things, and for IMRealists such properties are independent of humans. That's what is meant when we are debating the issue of evaluative properties' supposed mind-independence.

Of course, things can get complicated. So far we have imagined that moral reality is fixed: Alan's comment is either right or wrong, and Edward is either correct initially or comes to be correct, just as any other judge might be. But, think again about what happens when Edward changes his mind about what Alan says; he was over-sensitive before. Previously we assumed that Edward would then come to be correct or not. But now we introduce a twist. If Edward had not changed his mind,

Alan's remark would have counted as morally wrong precisely because Edward had felt hurt. But, now that Edward thinks he was being over-sensitive, and sees Alan's remark as harmless fun, Alan's action changes its ethical value. It transforms from being mean to being playful. Does this more complicated scenario see IMR in trouble? No. Even if human reactions can change the ethical reality that is being judged, and so in some sense value is dependent on human responses and thoughts, IMRealists will still view Edward's change of heart as being *part of* the situation to which value is supposed to attach. The key thought for them is that whatever the situation, and however it changes and expands because of human responses, at the end there is a *further or final question* to be asked about whether the 'thing' in question has a value and what it is. For IMRealists, whatever evaluative properties a situation or action has is a mind-independent matter, influenced in no way by any human judgement about the situation or action, where we may explicitly note that such situations contain within themselves judgements by humans about other humans' actions, say.

At this stage, two words – 'objectivity' and 'subjectivity' – often make an appearance, both in the minds of those new to metaethics and in the writings of seasoned commentators. So, before we ask why one might wish to adopt IMR, let us briefly think about these two terms.

2.4 Objectivity and subjectivity

The words 'objectivity' and 'subjectivity' (and 'objectivism', 'subjectivism', and the like) can refer to a bewildering variety of ideas, and sometimes cause confusion. I do not detail all of the ways in which they can be used, but I hope this brief survey gives a decent guide.

First, consider:

O1: Something (a property or object, say) is objective if its existence is independent of what anyone does or could believe, desire, be committed to, and the like.

O2: Something (a certain subject matter and discourse such as ethics or aesthetics, say) is objective if it admits of correct and incorrect judgements, answers, and the like. Relatedly, judgements made within such a domain can be described as being objective.

O3: Some person is objective if they are unbiased about a matter in question. Such a person's views will be objective if they are produced without the person being so biased.

O1 is just (part of) *Thesis IMR* in different words. It is very natural to think of IMRealists as espousing an 'objective' account of morality. O3 is something we may often hear in everyday contexts, I think. It has some links, however vague, with O1. The subject matters are different – the existence of properties, the views of people – but the core idea is the somewhat vague 'lack of human, personal involvement'. Despite this link, we will not worry at all about O3. (I introduce it for contrast and list it third as we will care far more about O2.) More interesting is the contrast between O1 and O2. Again, the subject matter is different; this time, the existence of properties on the one hand, and the subject domain, and the judgements which partly constitute it, on the other. But, as should be obvious from Chapter 1, we have some subtle inter-play in various positions between the properties that exist and their nature, and the judgements about them that people make.

In metaethics, sometimes O1 and O2 are combined, and sometimes they are not. IMRealists naturally want to add O2 to what they say. Duncan believes that there are correct and incorrect answers in moral matters. These judgements seem to be correct or incorrect no matter what your social group or culture or view. What makes these judge-ments true or false is whether they correctly represent moral proper-ties, which are conceived to be mind-independently existing things. As we can see in this little description of Duncan's view, O1 comes in at the end. But, we could conceive of moral properties differently. Some people try to have a conception of moral correctness and incorrectness as applied to moral judgements, yet eschew O1 and try to combine O2 with something else.

That brings us to three senses of 'subjectivity'.

S1: Something (a property or object, say) is subjective if its existence is somehow dependent on what humans (or an important subset of humans), do or could believe, desire, be committed to and the like.

S2: Something (a certain subject matter and discourse such as eth-ics or aesthetics, say) is subjective if it does not admit of correct and incorrect judgements, answers, and the like. Relatedly, judge-ments made within such a domain can be described as being subjective.

S3: Some person is subjective if they are biased about a matter in question. Such a person's views will be subjective if they are pro-duced by a person so biased.

S3 is listed just for contrast with O3, S1 and S2. Speaking from personal experience, I sometimes hear 'subjective' used as an attempt to indicate S3, although the overwhelming number of cases I hear are attempts to indicate S2. This happens when people say things such as, 'Well, morality / art / sport / cooking / etc. is all just subjective, isn't it?'. Of course, there are certain claims we can make that *seem* to be ethical or aesthetic claims that clearly *do* admit of correct and incorrect judgements. For example, 'This is a painting' and 'He killed her'. But, as should be obvious, the sorts of judgement we are interested in are not judgements about whether things that support (supposed) moral and aesthetic properties exist. We are specifically interested in judgements about whether these properties exist (and how they do so), judgements such as 'This is tasty', 'This is elegant', and 'This is cruel'.

S2 indicates a certain sort of relativism, in my view, and a fairly extreme sort at that. There are things to sort out here. When talking about Helen we introduced the ideas of, for example, 'true-for-her' and 'true-for her-society'. There is some standard that helps to make things true – Helen's general views, the views common in Helen's society – and we can readily identify the idea of truth with the idea of judgements being correct. Given the explicit wording of S2, with its rejection of correctness and incorrectness, it appears we have a mismatch. Helen's position does not seem to fit with S2. But, as should be obvious, that mismatch is only apparent. An extreme relativist will say that there is just a very local standard, perhaps Helen's views alone. We might then talk of 'true-for-her'. But, in everyday thought, when faced with someone who really believed that this was a good way of characterizing their view, a person might ask what use the word 'true' has in this case. It seems superfluous, since something important about truth, for many people, is that it has quite a wide if not universal application: if some judgement is true, then it is true for everyone. The standard is something about how things are, not just how things are according to some local group or single person.

Well, that gives us a link, despite the wording, between S2 and more extreme (i.e. highly localized) forms of relativism. But, we have a delicate matter. We could adopt far less extreme versions of relativism – but which some may still think are relativistic (or relativistic-like) and as we do that, our confidence in describing certain judgements as correct and incorrect may increase, so much so that we leave behind S2. This delicate matter will be mentioned again at the end of this section and reappear in Chapter 6.

For now, let us consider other things. First, what does it mean to adopt something such as S1? An example often given in this regard is the example of colour, which many writers – but by no means all – think fits with the idea encapsulated by S1. We typically think there are colour properties: that roses are red and that grass is green. But, say many people, objects and items get to have the colours that they have partly because of the reactions that humans have towards such objects. If we did not make references to how humans experiences roses or grass, then we would not be able to give a full characterization of their colour properties.

There is far more to unpack about the idea of colour, and how evaluative properties may differ from them. Again, this is a matter for Chapter 6. For now, it is enough that we have this suggestive example on the table.

Second, unlike the case of O1 and O2, I think that a combination of S1 and S2 is slightly awkward, if not downright contradictory. S1 states that there are properties. If there are such things one would think that moral judgements are or should be attempts to represent and capture them. And, if we admit that, then surely some judgements will represent and do so well, and some will fail completely. There is a clear pull to say that we can talk of correctness and incorrectness, or at least a pull to talk of the slightly less stark 'better' and 'worse'. But all of this clashes with the extreme relativism that is at the heart of S2. After all, we do not adopt an extreme relativistic view of colour. Even if we admit that some people experience the world and its colours in different ways – just think of colour-blind people – we think there are better and worse way of experiencing the world. The colour-blind are labelled thus, they are not labelled 'colour-different'.

Third, that it may be hard to think of real-life cases where S2 can be said to apply uncontroversially. Think about everyday discussions of ice-cream flavours and our evaluations of which is better and worse. We sometimes enjoy discussing, even arguing, about whether chocolate is better than vanilla, say. But, on reflection we might – *might* – think that such arguments are a bit silly. There is no one best tasting ice-cream flavour, nor any sensible way to rank all of the ice-cream flavours that has universal application. There are no correct and incorrect judgements here. Well, perhaps. Anyway, if you think this then you are likely to be applying S2 in a clear, straightforward manner to the question of which flavour is best. As I indicated above, some people think that S2 applies to more than just the rival merits of ice-cream flavours. Perhaps it applies to works of art: if you think that the latest piece of manufactured bubblegum pop is as good as Beethoven, then that's just fine. And, of course, some try the same move when it comes to ethics.

For illustration, we may worry whether S2 can be applied thoroughly to evaluative judgements about ice-cream flavours, let alone art and ethics. Even if we can agree that it is silly to debate which of chocolate and vanilla is better, we would surely blanche if someone sincerely said they preferred ear-wax flavour, or that they fancied bleach and garlic ice-cream with a ripple of dust. We would not think these people just different, but would also think them odd and peculiar at the very least, if not just wrong. But, if we applied S2 thoroughly, such judgements about these tastes would be ruled out. Tastes are simply different, not odd or strange or wrong.

This is not to argue against S2, but merely to talk through one example to illustrate what it amounts to. Our example shows us one thing, however. Even if we think that it is odd to argue about the best tasting ice-cream flavour, then we might say that there are standards and that certain flavours can be ruled out as odd and, well, wrong. To widen things somewhat, just think about restaurant reviews and cooking competitions on television. Cooks can receive high praise and heavy criticism. There are clear standards that are taken to operate by many practitioners.

This allows us to think hard about S1 and O2. O2 can go along with O1, but it need not always. And even though S1 is opposed to O1, we need to see clearly that S1 can be combined with O2.

In the case of ice-cream flavours just sketched we seemingly have some standards that operate. On what are these based? Some mind-independently existing set of properties? Well, possibly. But, it seems initially highly plausible that such standards are in some way influenced by human judgements: immediate tastes of the various ice-creams and comparative, reasoned judgements about them. This takes us straight into the territory of S1.

Many metaethicists try to combine O2 with S1, the idea being that within the domain of ethics there are correct and incorrect answers, but that what underpins these correct answers has something essentially to do with human judgement, desire, reason and the like. Within this framework there is a lot of possibility, as we will see throughout this book.

Here are three reminders to end this section. First, as I mentioned earlier, the fact that we have the mention of human judgement (and reasoning, desire and the like) means that we could well have a certain form of relativism if one is inclined to be broad about this label's use.

The question is how extreme or weak the relativism is: many modern metaethicists make all human response the basis of the standard, rather than some local group. So, there is still some 'relativism', but it does not appear to be Helen's view from §1.4

Secondly, the notions of 'correctness' and 'incorrectness', let alone 'truth' and 'falsity' may be elastic here when thinking about O2, simply because of what our judgements are supposed to conform to, and for other reasons as well. Lastly, many people will call the positions they develop that combine O2 with S1 types of realism. But, these are crucially different from IMR, as we are about to see. After all, our main task in this chapter is to understand IMR, so we should return to it now.

2.5 Why be an IMRealist?

There are, I think, two main motivations for being an IMRealist. I spend more time on the first because I believe it is more important and also because I have indicated it already.

(a) *Bias, etc.*: IMRealists are IMRealists because they are worried that any adoption of a position that has any hint of S1 will lead, inevitably, to accusations of bias. As such it will be merely a type of localized justification where, in fact, a key part of our concept of morality is that it has universal authority, free from the constraints of anything human. We have come at this idea a few times now. I explore it more over the next few paragraphs.

Imagine we think that human responses and judgements are essential to actions and situations having the (seeming) moral properties they have. We are trying to make sense of the idea that there are things we can call moral properties but do not like the idea that such things are just brutally there, attached to some complex situation. It must be that things are good or cruel because, in the end, humans in some way judge them to be so. If we think like this, we immediately face a question, one that leads to some worries. Which humans' views count? Perhaps we decide to pick a particular person – Edward, you, me, some saint or other – and claim that this person is the person who determines the moral values of everything. First, it is important to realize that this is *not* a form of relativism. We are talking about indexing the correctness of *all* judgements to one person, and it is this one person whose views create and determine the supposed moral reality. This person alone has authority. (This view is often described as a type of realist-subjectivism, because we have only one subject or person involved.) So, with that made clear, it should be apparent that this looks implausible as a moral theory, if not downright dangerous. Remember: this person is not just working out whether something is cruel or kind. They are *determining* or *stipulating* whether it is. We could pick a truly dreadful judge, and even the best of us have our off-days.

Instead, we could say that a particular group of people determine what the moral properties are. That may seem better, but only for a very short time. First of all, history is littered with examples of groups, tribes, and societies that have made value judgements that have turned out to be wrong. Just think of the many people who have voted for politicians with abhorrent policies, and who then victimize and even kill others. We met this worry before, when thinking about Helen. Likewise and secondly, it is all very well saying that a 'group' should determine what is morally right or wrong, but groups are composed of people, and people's views differ, over time and over issues. How homogenous are groups in their ethical views? Often, not very. We could just demarcate a group simply because of the moral view they hold, not because of any accident to do with geography or history. But, then all the work is being done by the moral view itself, and we want to pick on something that itself will vindicate a set of moral views, not begin with the views themselves.

Perhaps we could go back to individuals – or groups – and instead of picking on people seemingly at random, or picking on them because of their particular views about certain issues, we pick on them because of their *general* judging characteristics, and supply reasons why certain characteristics are to be favoured. Indeed, we may not worry about any actual judges, but just concentrate on hypothetical judges and their characteristics as a way of understanding real-life judges. Perhaps our favoured judging characteristics are: being knowledgeable, wise, calm, disinterested, and patient. Here we face another question. Do we specify these best judges in wholly nonmoral terms? (Although it comes in various forms, this sort of view is often called **ideal observer theory**.) That may seem attractive: we want people who are knowledgeable and calm. But, there is a big worry. In many real moral debates people can be equally knowledgeable and equally calm about an issue yet disagree. They cannot both be correct. Furthermore, having lots of knowledge isn't always a good thing. It can cripple us and lead to inaction and indecision. It seems that we may want a judge to have just relevant knowledge. But relevant to what? Relevant to the case in hand, which will be a moral case. So, we might think that the judge has to have some appreciation of morality already in order to discern which knowledge to employ.

Often people say that it is those who have and exercise moral attributes who are the best at appreciating what should be done: those that are kind are best at picking out the kind action. This is not just a problem with the attribute of being knowledgeable. We can worry about a characterization of the best moral judge that specifies just a few attributes such as calmness and patience. Such attributes – any attributes – are not always good things. Sometimes, in the face of outrageous social injustice, for example, we want immediate and angry responses. Often, the best moral judges are people who know when, where and how to exercise a whole range of character traits. They know when to be calm and when to be angry (and when to be grumpy, and indifferent, and incandescent). Perhaps we need to introduce this sort of 'second-order' faculty. But, crucially, this sort of faculty is often classified as a moral faculty, given that it directly concerns how we act towards ourselves and others.

Hence, there seems good reason to favour the view that we should specify the best judge in explicitly moral terms. We probably wouldn't say they were to be characterized only in moral terms. Being knowledgeable about all aspects of the world seems important. So, we'd probably want a mix of moral and nonmoral attributes.

However, there are at least two worries here. A minor worry returns us to an idea we have just sneakily accepted. Can we really assume that people who are kind are the best judges of which actions are kind? Does the ability to give the correct moral judgement flow directly to and from the ability to act morally? Kind people may act instinctively only, and people who are indifferent might still be very good at working out what they should do. But, although these are interesting points, to my mind it seems a fair bet to assume that in general kind people are the best at picking out when and where to be kind. There is a more important worry, however, which also returns us to a previous thought. What exactly is meant by kindness? People will have different views about exactly which things are kind. We need some more specific conception of what kindness is in order to specify the judges to such an extent that we can be sure that these figures are decent determiners of the moral world. But, it seems we can get these specific ideas of various moral qualities only once we have specified the judge. It seems we are caught in a circle that is highly and hopelessly vicious. We are assuming a notion of kindness in order to characterize the judges who, in turn, determine what it is to be kind.

We can go back and forth on many of these points. Indeed, I revisit the issue of circularity in detail in Chapter 6. There are defences for many of these ideas available. The point over the last couple of pages is to reveal a certain way of thinking, and to articulate a certain pull that some people feel quite strongly. Lying behind the worries in the previous paragraph is a worry about moral relativism, be it extreme or moderate. As soon as we say that human thoughts and responses to the world determine or influence in any way the evaluative properties we think exist, then we are in a position where we have to adjudicate between different human responses. We have to specify which human views are the best ones, or the decent ones, or the morally okay ones, and in doing so we can be accused of moral bias. It *seems* perfectly acceptable to say that giving to charity is good, or that giving to *this* charity is morally good, but perhaps we are saying this because it is what we are comfortable and familiar with, not because it is true. Think back to Chapter 1. You might agree with Duncan that the governmental policy is wrong. But, other people – people who are geographically and socially close to you and Duncan – disagree. And, once we go down this route, we should worry whether anyone's view, no matter how knowledgeable and calm they seem to be, is better than anyone else's. If we cannot secure the idea that some people's views are better than others', then we are not securing something we want to secure.

But what, exactly, are we trying to secure? Think back to O1 and O2. In order to avoid relativism we need to say that judgements of a particular domain – in this case moral judgements – admit of correctness and incorrectness. There is an assumption behind this idea, namely that the correctness applies to all people, not just some people in some locale. People can go off and do their own thing, and they often do, but they cannot simply choose to deny that moral standards and rules apply to what they do. The big philosophical question is whether we can secure the standard applicable to all by basing what is morally right and wrong wholly or partly on what humans think and feel. It seems not, for we will always have a suspicion of bias and of locality.

So, we get a pull towards objectivity conceived along the lines of O1. In order to secure the idea that moral judgements can be correct and incorrect we need to base such correctness on something that is free from all human influence, untainted by anything to do with the variety and messiness inherent in human judgement. In which case we need to make morality mind-independent. In short, we need to embrace *Thesis IMR*. This is the key motivation for being an IMRealist.

There is more to be said about many points raised here, and as I've said, we'll do that in later chapters. The past few pages have been an exercise in trying to get under an IMRealist's skin and working out what the broad and deep pull is towards IMR. Although I respect the motivation for its adoption, I do not like this view at all. This is partly because it faces problems, problems of a similarly broad and deep manner. The main problem – or entangled problem*s* – with IMR will be aired in Chapter 4, but it is worth sketching now.

Some commentators think that the conception of moral properties that IMRealists put centre stage are odd and strange. How can something be a moral property or a moral demand, how can something be the sort of thing that has relevance for human valuing creatures that respond to demands, and yet not have its existence grounded in and dependent on something human? Further to this, how do such moral properties fit within the natural, nonmoral world? And, indeed, if there are these strange properties, how would we find out about them? Perhaps the ontology is so strange that we need special epistemological equipment to know about them.

In Chapter 4 I argue that these questions are probably fatal to IMR. But, all of this remains a suspicion for now.

(b) *Progress and agreement*: Let us briefly think about some positive claim that IMRealists make in favour of their view. They might postulate that there has been moral progress. People's lives may have got better as a result of changes in moral judgement and motivations to make things go better. Or, even if people's lives haven't got better, perhaps people's views about how the world should be have got morally better.

Or, perhaps IMRealists might postulate something slightly different. We could take a number of people from different parts of the globe and ask them what they think some basic moral judgements should be, or ask how they think we should order a society. The supposition is that we may be surprised at the amount of convergence there was, not just between these people, but between this group and other groups whom we tasked in the same way.

In all of this, IMRealists might play up the idea of agreement in moral judgement and outlook. We have similar ideas and ideals, even if we do not always live up to them. IMRealists argue that the best way of explaining all of this agreement is that people are picking out the same moral reality.

Now, all realists who give themselves this label may wish to say the same thing. IMRealists may, however, stress that the more we based the correctness of judgements on human beings, the more local we make things and, hence, the more we are likely to find divergence and disagreement. If you are confident of there being a fair amount of agreement on basic moral issues, no matter what the culture and background, then this is good evidence for IMR's truth.

Obviously, much of the strength of this argument is based on the empirical claim about agreement. We could ask, in relation to this, what sort of judgement we are after. There is likely to be more agreement if we have general ideas in play – for example, 'Stealing is typically bad' – than if we have more specific ideas in play – for example, '*That* sort of sexual activity is permissible'. And, anyway, we might worry about the link between agreement (of sorts) with mind-independence. All realists may wish to rely to some extent on agreement, not just IMRealists.

That said, there is something interesting about agreement and its link with realism. As with the other motivation, we will discuss this again in Chapter 4, and beyond.

For now, we can conclude that IMR draws on, indeed encapsulates, a decent and understandable worry, a worry about relativistic ideas. It remains a serious option at the moment. Further to this, we will find echoes of it in other positions, simply because other positions want to have the comfort and security of O2 in some fashion, an idea which naturally goes with an adoption of O1.

2.6   Concluding remarks

In this chapter we have considered IMR and advanced two reasons why people are attracted to it.

I started by noting that we have two relationships on the table. So far we have not discussed in any great detail the relationship between moral properties that seemingly exist and the natural world. It may appear as if there is no difference. IMRealists espouse the mind-independence of moral properties. Moral naturalism, which we have yet to investigate, is the claim that moral properties are natural properties and, initially at least, we might think that natural properties, such as those things studied by the natural sciences, also exist mind-independently. This, I think, is a very confused way of thinking. In the next chapter we will sort it out towards the end. In order to build up to that, we need to think about what naturalism is and we need to consider a very important challenge to it.

Further Reading

IMR is my terminology. One of the best modern articulations of IMR is Brink (1989), which also serves as a useful introduction to many other debates in metaethics. Brink also articulates nicely why one would want to be a realist. Sosa (2001) is also well worth reading, particularly in connection with the position I discuss in Chapter 6. A more recent and sophisticated defence of this sort of view is Enoch (2011). The debates about moral experts that I touch on in this chapter has a long history. Firth (1952) is a classic discussion of this, where he puts forward his ideal observer theory.

3
Moral Realism: Naturalism and Reductionism

3.1 Introduction

This chapter has a number of aims. First, I explain a little about what naturalism is and why someone might wish to be a naturalist. I then discuss a hugely influential argument given against naturalism. We will see that it faces a number of problems, one of which sets the scene for modern naturalism. In doing that we will see that naturalism comes in a number of varieties: one important distinction is between reductionist and nonreductionist types. I offer arguments against both. At the end I return to the material in the previous chapter and show why we have two relationships in play: that between moral properties and humans, and that between moral properties and the natural world.

In case it is not clear, all of the positions discussed here are types of realism. The key issue concerns the characterization of moral properties in relation to the natural world.

3.2 A naive naturalism and the motivation for adopting it

(a) *A naive naturalism*: Modern versions of naturalism have become very sophisticated. They have done so partly in response to the argument I canvass in the following section. In order to introduce that argument we need to think about the type of position it was attacking. I resist the urge to give a definitive characterization of naturalism right now, simply because it will spoil the power of the argument, and destroy the narrative of this chapter. Definitive characterizations will come later.

Despite those opening words, we can say that moral naturalists think that one can, in a sense of the term to be explored, 'identify' moral ideas with natural ideas, or recast the former in terms of the latter. For example, imagine we note that an action – such as the licking of a lollipop – is pleasurable. Further, we note that its pleasure is the main reason why it is good. Here I mean 'good in general', not just 'morally good', although a next step for hedonic utilitarians would be to say that if handing the lollipop to a child maximizes pleasure in a certain case, then your act of sharing *is* morally good and, further, morally right. From this sort of case and our speculation, we might then become confident and claim that we have some idea of what goodness is in general, namely the maximization of pleasure. When we want to find out whether an action is good, all we need to do is find out whether it maximizes pleasure.

We would, of course, have to supply arguments for this identification. Beyond any worries with specific arguments, there is an obvious worry with this specific proposal as it stands. One can imagine actions that maximize pleasure but which do not seem to be good. A commonly given counter-example is one where we kill someone whom no one cares about, and in doing so we generate much pleasure for ourselves, so much so that this action maximizes pleasure. That action cannot be morally good, surely?

This worry is a good one. But, in the next section I discuss an even grander worry with the whole idea of trying to recast moral notions as wholly natural notions.

For now, this gives us a sense of what naturalism is, namely the claim that moral ideas can be recast as natural ideas. But, what is meant by 'natural' here?

(b) *Natural?*: 'Pleasure' is a good – and classic – example of a natural phenomenon. Pleasure might be understood in a moral or evaluative way, but here we understand it naturalistically and nonmorally. We can define pleasure (loosely) as the positive feeling and/or idea one gets when something happens. That doesn't seem to be a moral or evaluative notion, although it is the sort of thing that can be morally significant, as we saw in the lollipop example.

Would we want to leave things there? Pleasure may be slightly amorphous and vague, but increasingly scientists – psychologists, neuroscientists, and the like – are finding ways to study it that are characteristic of their disciplines. Such scientists put people in situations designed to arouse pleasure, ask them to record whether they are experiencing any pleasure, and at the same time look at the electro-chemical reactions happening in their brains. In doing so they seek to fit pleasure clearly into the natural world. They can find ways to measure it, predict when it will occur, and do all of the things that scientists typically do with many other phenomena. So, instead of identifying goodness with (just) pleasure, we get it recast as some more complex phenomenon, seen as some collection of types of brain state. This is just an example. But, it does expose the ambitions of some naturalists, which is to try to locate moral notions within the world of natural science, since natural science is taken by many as the main if not only way in which to investigate phenomena that exist. In this way it helps to define what it is to exist: something exists only if it can be studied by scientists. Not all naturalists think along these lines, as we will see below. But, some do.

With that said, how exactly should we define 'natural ideas' and natural phenomena? We could choose to say that these are the ideas and phenomena with which *current* natural science deals. But, that definition on its own is too vague: we require some idea of what counts as key phenomena, with some illustrative examples. Perhaps the example of pleasure will help, but we will need more examples than that. And, anyway, talk of current science may be too narrow a definition, for two reasons. First, we might need to broaden 'the natural' to include phenomena studied and measured by the social sciences, phenomena such as unemployment and human migration. Indeed, once we start thinking like this, some socio-cultural objects such as knives and money might also make it onto the list of natural phenomena. We may have to decide where to stop, but that on its own may not be very problematic; we may just have to think hard.

A second issue prompts more thought, however, about the whole definition. As we know, science and the phenomena that it takes to be part of its remit have changed over the years. We have split the atom and we have started to make inroads into investigating the mind. Who knows what discoveries are over the horizon? Perhaps various 'alternative' medicines may be shown not to be so alternative. Maybe there really is something that causes (seemingly) *super*natural phenomena that can be studied using methods similar to those employed in current science? So, perhaps we should not focus on current science, but on *possible* science.

For many people, including some naturalists, those previous few lines leave things still too vague. Some of them think that characterizing the natural explicitly in terms of the discipline of science – a 'disciplinary' characterization – invites all sorts of problems. They prefer to leave behind this sort of definition and try to characterize what is natural, and hence 'real', by picking out an idea or two that serve as marks of the real, freed by certain disciplinary understandings. We can call this a 'criterial' understanding of the natural. For example, one important thing that seems to be a mark of the 'real' and which has become an important idea over the past few centuries (partly because of science) is whether something can *cause* something else to happen. So, something gets to be a natural something, and hence a real something, if it has the capability of effecting other things. One can put this idea in different words, so as to tease out another idea: perhaps we notice a phenomenon, and something gets to be real if it helps to *explain* why this phenomenon exists. We will return to these ideas below.

So, we have thought about what naturalists very generally say – that moral ideas can be recast as natural ideas – and also introduced the question of what might count as natural. Now for one final introductory discussion.

(c) *Why should we adopt naturalism?*: Naturalists worry about the place of moral properties in the modern world. Being realists, they want to make the case for there being such properties and for moral judgements being true and false. They want people to be taken to account for being wicked, say, where wickedness is a real phenomenon. So, if one thinks that modern natural science (and social science) is the mark of what is real, or at least the beginning of an understanding of what is real, one will want to be able to say that moral judgements really can be true or false because they are about things, things we can readily make sense of and understand as being real. Even if it may at the start be difficult to agree on the details – current *or* future science? natural *and* social science? – we should strive to ensure that moral ideas are seen to fit comfortably within the natural world.

I now draw a few things together. Naturalists believe, loosely, that moral ideas and notions should be (wholly) recast as natural ideas and notions. In opposition, nonnaturalists deny this: it makes far better sense to think of the moral as being *sui generis* and as different from the natural. (We will see why later on.) In order to see what this amounts to, we need some starting idea at least as to what a natural idea is. Lastly, even if naturalists do not define 'natural' wholly in ideas derived from or inspired by the discipline of science, undoubtedly many of them start with this notion.

We have not yet pursued the very important distinction between reductionist and nonreductionist accounts of moral naturalism that I have mentioned, although it was in the air when I was talking through the pleasure example. Right now we need to think hard about an even more important idea. I have left the notion of 'identification' and 'recasting' very vague, and also spoken loosely of moral ideas being recast as natural ideas. What, exactly, are we recasting as what? Is there some special difference between natural ideas and natural phenomena? In investigating a key argument, we will begin to answer these questions across the next few sections.

3.3 The open question argument

In this book I deliberately mention particular philosophers sparingly. One person who I do name, however, is G. E. Moore. His *Principia Ethica*, published in 1903, in many ways sets the scene for the metaethical discussion of the twentieth century that continues to this day. His ideas have much-publicized flaws, and arguably they exist in one form or another in the work of his philosophical ancestors. But his thoughts are a touchstone for many metaethicists as they get to the heart of much of the subject and they are expressed in a forceful, attention-grabbing way.

Consider the following question: 'Barry is a bachelor, but is he an unmarried male?' That seems like a silly question to ask, even if it is grammatically fine. If one understands what 'bachelor' means, then it doesn't make sense to ask the question for the answer is obvious. Of course Barry is an unmarried male, that is just what 'bachelor' means. We might say that this question is 'closed', at least to mature users of English. There is no sense that one could disagree and go another way. The question is not an open one.

The issue at the heart of things is definition, or characterization, or analysis. (I use these terms interchangeably for now.) And we are thinking about defining or characterizing concepts and ideas, plus associated words, in terms of other concepts, ideas and their associated words. In the case of 'bachelor' we can easily define what it means or characterize the concept in other terms. The key issue is whether we can do the same for moral concepts such as good and goodness.

Moore was concerned with attempts to define or characterize the concepts of goodness in naturalistic terms. 'Naturalism' covers a host of different ideas, as has been intimated in the previous section. Moore has the empirical methods of his day in mind, although he thinks quite broadly. The example of pleasure (or 'being pleasurable') from the previous section is his.

So, consider this question: 'This action will maximize pleasure, but is it good?'. This is a sensible question to ask. Indeed, Moore noted, it seems open in the way that other examples, such as my bachelor example, is not. It seems as if we could answer either way on this question, at least in the abstract case when thinking generally.

Those last few words bring out a key point to make right at the start. Commentators often forget that Moore carefully distinguishes his target in *Principia Ethica*. He says at various points (for example, chapter 1, section 6) that we should distinguish the question of what goodness is (the one he is interested in) from the question of which things are good (for example, *this* pleasant thing, *that* pleasant thing, *that third* pleasant thing... and so on). So, if we have a particular pleasurable action in front of us, we might well answer positively to the question posed above. Indeed, we might say that something is good precisely because it is pleasurable. But, Moore's point and task is different. He is thinking about a general definition or characterization of the idea of goodness. He says that one cannot define it in terms of pleasure. This is shown, directly, by the fact that our candidate question has an open feel to it. If we had hit upon a correct characterization or definition of good, there would not be that open feel. The question would be closed.

In fact, Moore concluded that one cannot define goodness in other terms at all. The point about pleasure generalizes to any sort of proffered characterization of goodness. As many people point out, Moore's target is any sort of naturalistic definition of good, but in an important way he misnames his target. His target appears to be *any* attempt to define or characterize goodness, naturalistic or otherwise. So, if one tried to define goodness in *super*natural terms, such as being the work of God or of Merlin, then that would receive the same sort of treatment from Moore. 'This action is the work of God, but is it good?' is, for Moore, open in the same way that the question concerning pleasure is open.

From this we can introduce Moore's positive view. He thought that the idea of good was a simple idea, and could not be defined. From this claim about the *idea* or *concept* of goodness, he makes a claim about the *property* of goodness. Because the idea of goodness is simple and cannot be defined in other terms, particularly natural terms, Moore thought that the referent of 'good', namely the property of goodness, was also special in an important way. It cannot be conceived to be natural, it cannot be conceived in 'other' terms. For this reason, Moore was a non-naturalist about the property goodness. Goodness – the concept and property – is *sui generis* for Moore, it cannot be understood in other ways, particularly natural ways.

This is a very simple version of Moore's position, and a simple version of his argument against naturalism. As is often the case, the argument gets formulated and cast in a number of ways, with various commentators suggesting different things about what Moore's point really is.

Furthermore, there is a lot of textual analysis of *Principia Ethica* and Moore's other ethical writings to be done. I will not pursue every twist and turn regarding Moore's argument. But I do consider three worries with it, two in the next section, and a third in that which follows. Earlier on I drew attention to the question of what exactly we are trying to recast as what. Just now we have seen a distinction introduced between ideas and concepts on the one hand and properties on the other. This distinction is key for the third argument. But, for now, we have two other issues to talk through.

3.4   Two problems with the argument

(a) *Begging the question*: It is routinely mentioned that the argument may beg the question. This worry, along with others, is articulated by William Frankena in a paper from 1939, which is itself a standard reference point. What is Moore's reason for thinking that naturalistic analyses are impossible? It seems to be that, for example, it is an open matter as to whether something that is pleasurable is good. Yet, we can maintain that this is an open matter only if we assume that any pleasurable thing need not be good. We should make *that* (previous) assumption only if we assume that we have no analysis of goodness in terms of pleasure in the first place. But, this last point is what Moore is trying to establish. He is just begging the question. This point generalizes to other potential analyses.

This worry has itself generated a healthy literature. One counter-response is to focus on what it is for a question or matter to be open. In order for some matter to be open, it need not be that we have to assume straightaway that the analysis *is* wrong-headed; this would indeed beg the question. Rather, it would be sufficient just for us to *entertain* that the analysis *could be* wrong. Mature and competent users of concepts cannot do that in the above bachelor example, for example. In contrast, it is supposed, we can entertain that the identification of goodness with pleasure *could be* wrong. And, this supposition – this possibility – is enough to show that the question *is* an open one. Or, in other words, the fact that mature users of some ethical term could have *some* doubt about the matter is itself significant. Mature users do not have to assume that the matter is *definitely* open, in order for us (observers, perhaps) to conclude that because there is some room for doubt, then the matter is open in some significant sense.

It is important not to misunderstand this move. It is not a direct argument against naturalistic analyses, for it is certainly possible for us to entertain something to be open, and yet be wrong. Rather, the point is quite specific: we can formulate Moore's challenge such that it does not obviously beg the question. That is, we can say that something is open on the basis that it could *appear to be* open (to mature users), not on the basis that we have already shown it to be open.

This is a subtle and complicated move against Frankena's thought. It may well work against the challenge that it begs the question. But, it also reveals something important and, possibly, negative about Moore's argument, namely how much it may rely on the phenomenology of what mature users of moral concepts and terms can entertain and what can then be concluded about the analyses that can be assumed to hold. After all, are we really happy to say that just because a matter seems to be open to many, then it *is* open and we can draw conclusions that Moore draws about the indefinability of the concept and irreducibility of the property?

Some people – in support of Moore – make a distinction here. Imagine we make some claim within mathematics that relies on complicated terms: for example, $\sin 2x + \cos 2x = 1$. We then ask whether this is the case. We can imagine that many people will think the matter to be open. But, let us also imagine, the matter is definitely not open and that the equation we are considering is an important truth of mathematics. (It is, in fact.) In this case, then, the appearance of openness does not guarantee that the issue is open, as some might imagine.

However and in contrast, what about questions involving moral terms? Some commentators think we are far more prepared in the moral case to allow that the appearance of openness *is* a very good indication of real openness. The example of pleasure and goodness shows this most obviously. In the moral case we are more prepared to defer to everyday, majority opinion, the thought being that many people have some knowledge, however implicit, about how moral terms can and should be used. In contrast, the mathematical case relies on a lot of specialized knowledge. Indeed, this brings into full view what counts as a 'mature user' of a certain term. For some people, Moore's argument does not fall at this hurdle.

There is no more doubt to think about in this matter. We can leave it here though, partly because a second issue probably bites deeper.

(b) *The paradox of analysis*: When an analysis is proposed, we want someone to be putting forward something that has some point. We want the analysis to provide real knowledge by connecting one thing with another thing and telling us something interesting about how those two things are connected. And, of course, because we want knowledge, we want the analysis to be true.

Human history and knowledge is littered with such examples. Philosophers have tried to analyse knowledge itself in terms of 'justified true belief' and, when this didn't work, they developed ever more interesting proposals. This brings us directly to the so-called 'paradox of analysis'. When we try to develop definitions or conceptual analyses of terms, we want to be able to find a new term or characterization that means exactly the same as the old term. But, we are also pursuing a conceptual analysis because we want to be able to say something new and informative. These twin aims seem to be in conflict: we want to say something that is the same and that is also new and informative.

This paradox has itself generated a lot of literature. Our concern is just with Moore and the open question argument. Many think that it is this paradox that is powering the argument: 'we want some correct analysis of goodness, but Moore has a strong presumption that only goodness can be goodness: anything else will simply not deliver a true analysis, no matter what the merits of the individual proposal'. If we can show that the paradox is no real paradox at all, that may tell us that Moore's argument is not as powerful as he thinks it is.

On that, two points, the second of which will take us to the next section. First, the paradox can be construed in terms of what we know. We know or have a good idea of what a word and concept mean. Indeed, we can make this assumption since it seems necessary for us to be able to say that a proposed analysis is true. However, if we already know what a word means, we will then not gain any (more) knowledge with the new analysis. Thus, the paradox.

But, if we put things like that, some think, we can challenge whether the paradox is a paradox. There seem to be plenty of things that we know and understand without being able to articulate them. For example, we may know how to write correctly and we may know how to drive a car. We may even know how to use a word correctly. But, in these and other examples, we may not be able to articulate very well what is going on: the rules of grammar, the sequence of tasks when driving, or the detailed meaning of the word. So, we might well be able to recognize true (and false) analyses of words and ideas, whilst at the same time gaining a certain sort of knowledge, for the detailed articulation of our understanding may be illuminating.

Indeed – to finish things – who is to say that that could not happen when it comes to goodness? We may find it hard to articulate what goodness is, but once we find a good analysis, we will realize that it is good analysis and gain knowledge. It seems open and indefinable only because we haven't hit on the right analysis yet.

That is an interesting point, but a second is even more telling. Thus far we have characterized Moore as thinking in terms of words and concepts. He drew a claim about properties towards the end of his argument, but he does not make an important move that would have revealed a great deal more about the whole debate. Perhaps an analysis can be informative because we identify one concept with another quite different concept, and perhaps it can also be true because the referent – the stuff in the world that the two concepts are used to pick out – turns out to be the very same stuff.

This takes us to the next section and a challenge to Moore that forms the bedrock of much of modern naturalism.

3.5 A third problem with the argument

Many people think that Moore's argument ignores the crucial distinction between, on the one hand, words, terms, ideas and concepts, and, on the other, properties, reality and stuff.

To explain this, think about a much-used example:

$$\text{Water is } H_2O$$

The concepts 'water' and 'H_2O' are different, with the associated terms having different meanings and associations. Water is that clear, colourless stuff that we wash in, drink, splash about with, and put on our gardens. H_2O is a formal way of presenting a material, involving two elements, fused in a way that most non-scientists do not quite understand exactly. One is everyday, one is scientific. However, the majority of adults know that water is H_2O. (I would be surprised if anyone reading this book didn't know this.) And this is not some coincidence. It is not as if we have two distinct things that happen to be linked. Rather, as most people know and even if they rarely articulate it, water *is* H_2O. We have two concepts and associated terms to represent the very same stuff.

In the example of the bachelor we have an *analytic identification*: we have one term identified with another term, and we know this is true because it is just what the terms mean. Many commentators worry that Moore thought – although he didn't put it in this way – that it was only this sort of identification that counted when trying to analyse (the concept of) goodness. But, as we know full well, the concepts and associated terms 'good' and 'pleasurable' are different. What Moore didn't see, according to many commentators, is that one can have a successful identification even when the two concepts are different, even very different. One discovers through empirical investigation that two concepts in fact refer to the same stuff. This is a type of *synthetic identification*, one that does not depend on an analysis of the concepts themselves. This is exactly what happened in the case of water and H_2O, and many, many other types of scientific discovery.

We can fill out this idea with a story. A few hundred years ago we all knew about water and its various properties: it was runny, clear and so on. However, humans did not know much more than that. We did not really understand the essence and basic nature of water. (Or, perhaps we thought we did. If one goes back to the Ancient Greeks, the working assumption was that water was one of the basic elements of life and the universe.) But, as part of the rise of modern science, humans investigated many materials, including water, and we made an interesting advance in knowledge: we discovered that water is in fact H_2O. To us the identification is unsurprising, but at the time it would have been a revelation.

Consider now the question, 'This is water, but is it H_2O?'. At some point in human history we could not have posed the question since 'H_2O' would have been meaningless gibberish. At some time when modern chemistry was taking shape this question could have been meaningfully asked, and it would have appeared genuinely open: it would have appeared to have been a possibility that water was something other than H_2O. Indeed, young children, when being introduced to chemistry, might be in a similar situation, and experience a similar feeling. (However, it is probably *not* the same since the idea that water is H_2O may be used to explain to children what hydrogen and oxygen are, rather than them understanding hydrogen and oxygen and *then* being asked our target question.) Lastly, by way of contrast, mature educated Western adults do not perceive this as a startling revelation. The question is closed.

But, it is closed in a way different from how our question about bachelors is closed. Again, we have the difference between an analytic, a priori identification of the concept of a bachelor with the concept of an unmarried man, and a synthetic identification of the concept water with the concept H_2O.

So, we have two concepts, but they can be used of the same stuff. Many people think Moore got things very wrong. It may appear as if the familiar question concerning goodness and pleasure is open. But, at a certain point when modern chemistry was developing, a similar question concerning water and H_2O would have been open. Yet, we discovered an identity. Why could the same not be true of a naturalistic identification of goodness? Or, to widen things, why not say the same about any sort of identification, not just a naturalistic one? There is no principled reason why this sort of thing could not take place.

So, many people think Moore's argument fails to establish that goodness is not a natural property. Some naturalists begin their position directly from this failure and argue for a synthetic, naturalistic reduction of goodness. Other naturalists offer different sorts of naturalism, and think that Moore's argument shows us other things, things that link with their particular brand of naturalism. I will sort these links in what follows.

3.6 A summary and two definitions

There has been a lot going on, so let us pause to summarize. Moore's argument was officially targeted against naturalistic positions that sought to offer analytic identifications of the concept of goodness in terms of natural concepts. Many people now think that Moore's more general target was any sort of redefinition of goodness, and many take the most interesting philosophical target to be any sort of nonmoral analysis. Moore's argument may beg the question, and it may worry us as to exactly what an analysis is. An important worry for many modern commentators is that Moore failed to appreciate that two concepts and associated terms can differ in meaning, and perhaps be quite radically different, whilst still referring to the very same stuff.

I think that Moore's argument might still bite in an interesting way. We will return to that later. For now, we need to realize that a number of naturalisms may be on the cards.

We first need to distinguish clearly between naturalism and reductionism in metaethics. They are often run together, but it is important to separate the two ideas. Consider these two definitions which, although right, will receive elaboration over the next few pages. Note that for the moment I run things in terms of properties. We will return to concepts and terms later.

> **Moral reductionists** believe that moral properties are properties that
> can be identified as being other, nonmoral properties, where such an

identification involves us picking out exactly which other properties the moral properties are.

Moral naturalists believe that moral properties are natural properties.

The characterization of moral reductionism requires immediate clarification. By saying 'picking out exactly' I mean that reductionists will typically claim that we can isolate exactly what property or collection of properties each moral property is. Call such isolations 'one-to-one' or 'one-to-many' mappings. So, for example, the claim might be that the property of goodness just is the (natural) property of being pleasurable. Or, we might find that there is a far more complex story to tell about goodness that is so complex, in fact, that there are a number of different nonmoral properties that goodness turns out to be. (More on this below.)

In my definition of moral reductionism, I used 'nonmoral' property. One could be a reductionist and *not* be a naturalist. One could identify moral properties with religious or magical properties. The property of goodness might turn out to be 'the work of God' or 'the work of Merlin'.

Of course, one could be a reductionist and be a naturalist. We just saw that example when thinking about the property of goodness just being the property of being pleasurable. Theorists who occupy this position may disagree amongst themselves about what the moral properties are: being pleasurable, or some brain state understood in purely biological terms? There are lots of other ways in which they can disagree, as we'll see below.

A third sort of possibility rears its head: Can one be a naturalist and not be a reductionist? Yes. In fact, this had proved somewhat popular. The idea can be given in a number of ways, but essentially the thought is that moral properties *simply are* natural properties, already as it were. We do not have the assumption that moral properties are distinct from the natural world, and then we have to seek how to fit them in, as perhaps Moore and indeed some reductionists might think. Moral properties are simply a species of natural properties. And, in saying that, these naturalists do not wish to reduce them to, or understand them in terms of, other sorts of property, natural or otherwise.

There is more to say about both naturalism and reductionism. To start, I focus on the sort of nonreductive naturalism just introduced.

3.7   Nonreductive naturalism explained

The main version of this type of position – possibly the only one discussed much at all – is often referred to as Cornell Realism. This title is
due to the fact that many of the main protagonists in the development
of this position in the 1980s either taught at or were educated at Cornell
University. There are differences between its various supporters. I glide
over these here. See Further Reading for an indication of where some
of my ideas stem. However, although I have the writings of Cornell
Realists in mind, I aim in this section and the next to say something
about the possibilities of a nonreductive naturalism *in general*.

For nonreductive naturalists, as just indicated, moral properties are
natural properties. Furthermore, moral properties are irreducible, irreducible with respect to other natural properties. Consequently, moral
terms and concepts are unanalysable in other terms. One charge nonreductive naturalists often make against Moore is that his open question
argument assumes that because goodness is a moral property (or moral
concept) it *therefore cannot* be a natural property (or concept), and the
whole point is to see if we can find a natural property (or concept) to
identify with it. But, there is the possibility, overlooked by Moore, that
goodness is (already, as it were) a natural property, as well as being a
moral property. We may not be able to identify it in terms of *another*
natural property, but that does not mean it cannot be natural. (This is a
variation, perhaps, on Frankena's charge that Moore begs the question.)
In short, such naturalists agree that Moore may well have been onto
something in saying that goodness – the concept and property – are *sui
generis*. But, that does not mean that goodness is nonnatural. It is just a
special sort of natural property.

This is a very interesting idea. First of all, we need to ask why we
might think that moral properties are natural properties. We then need
to indicate a further distinction that, I think, is crucial. In the following
section I discuss problems for the view.

(a) *Why are moral properties natural properties?*: Cornell Realists and other
sympathetic realists stress empirical investigation and observation a
great deal in their writing. Scientists observe that certain things happen in the world. They develop various hypotheses about what might
be happening to cause the phenomena we see. That is, they postulate
various features, properties, and things which both exist and cause
other things to exist. They may have to go through a number of obser-
vations, and conduct a number of experiments, with controls built in,

in order to test their hypothesis and work out, with some justification, what is happening or likely to be happening. For example, through careful observation, astronomers were able to work out and explain the placement and movement of the stars in the night sky, plus the movement of the Earth in relation to the moon and the sun. Scientists are often prepared to be proved wrong and some philosophers, at least, will stress that the scientific method is particularly good at showing which things can't be the case and in helping us as we develop inferences to the best explanation, that is judgements about what it likely to be true because of how such judgements explain what we experience and what we already believe.

Cornell Realists think that, by and large, moral judgement and moral explanation work in much the same way. There are various moral phenomena that we notice around us all the time. For example, we might observe someone performing a cruel action that results in a victim experiencing pain, or we might form a judgement that someone is being kind. We can test out ideas to try to explain why such phenomena – the cruel action, the pain, moral judgements – exist. The supposition is that the best explanation of why such things exist is that there exist moral properties that cause them to exist.

So, for example, we can relate all of the terrible and wicked things that Hitler and the Nazis did in the build up to and during the Second World War. Such things involve pain, suffering, death, misery, and the like. What could be the cause of these things, and what could be the cause of our judgements that they were so morally terrible? The answer is simply that Hitler and the Nazis really were evil and terrible. If Hitler had not been so wicked, many of the things that he did – both the moral effects such as other individual wicked actions, and the nonmoral things, such as the death and the pain – would not have happened. It makes sense to say, with some justification, that the cause of all of these terrible things was Hitler's wickedness.

Some people are unimpressed by this sort of move. When it comes to explaining our judgements about these events, perhaps what explains them is just a fact about our psychology: humans are programmed to see things such as death and pain when caused in certain ways as being wicked. There does not need to be an *extra* (as critics might think) property of wickedness that explains the death and pain. The best explanation might rely on fewer, outlandish properties and just deal in terms of the psychology of typical judges. In response, Cornell Realists might ask whether we can imagine the pain happening and our judgements that Hitler was wicked being made if Hitler had not been wicked. One could perhaps say that part of the process of judgements being formed depends on the psychology of judges. Indeed, sometimes people form false judgements, and there is no reason for such judgements to occur. But, to think that such judgements could be formed often without the presence of wickedness, and to think that such pain could occur without wicked intent seems far-fetched. After all, there has to be *something* in the world that such judgements are about. (More on this below, in (b).)

This debate can run and run, with each side trying moves to show that their explanation is the better. What I wish to draw from this debate is something about the characterization of the natural in the first place. Recall from above that we had two broad ways or strategies for deciding whether something is natural: a disciplinary way and a criterial way. Although they may often look fondly at the natural and social sciences for inspiration, in much of their writings Cornell Realists focus on some criterion for something being natural that is not simply 'is part of the natural and social sciences'. In my brief discussion just now it seems as if the chief mark of something being natural and, hence, real comes in two parts: something is natural just in case it can cause other things to exist *and* is part of the best explanation of phenomena we see, the assumption being that it has caused such phenomena to exist.

There is something nice about this two part criterion. For a start, as I have already mentioned, in §3.2(b), the rise of natural science has led some people to think that the mark of the real is whether the supposed real thing can hold its own in the natural (and social) sciences. Moral properties may look somewhat dodgy in this way, for they are not the sort of thing that scientists typically study. However, one of the chief things that scientists study, as I have expressed, is causation: what does what to what, if you like, and what is required to explain phenomena. And so, if we take this as the criterion of the real, moral properties look as if they can count as real and we can be more liberal than the disciplinary strategy suggests.

However, we will not be able to leave things there. For example, on certain theological views, God causes certain events to happen in the natural realm. The same is true of Merlin. But, would we really then want to say that God and Merlin are natural things with natural properties? Is magic a *natural* phenomenon? Our labels have surely gone haywire here, for if anything counts as supernatural, then it is God, Merlin and their doings.

So, realists who wish to argue in this manner will probably need a more fine-grained idea of causation and causal power that excludes the works of God and Merlin, yet still lets in moral properties. Details on this have been forthcoming. (See Further Reading.) However, I do not dwell on these partly because I think this debate leads us to a more interesting, general discussion.

(b) *Two sorts of nonreductive naturalism*: There is a distinction that often goes unnoticed, but which I think is crucial. The distinction is one that can, in theory, be drawn within the nonreductive naturalism as thus far developed, although both ideas can be found in the writings of Cornell Realists even if it is not emphasized at all and drawn out. In this sub-section, and the next, I am concerned only with the theoretical possibility of drawing the distinction.

When we say that moral properties are natural properties, understood as outlined above, we have to think about them in relation to other, recognizably, kosher, natural properties. In doing so, we have two different ways of relating them. (There may be more, but these two will do for our purposes.)

First, when we say that moral properties are natural properties we might look at the whole set of natural properties and choose to say that all moral properties are part of the set. Recall that we think that moral properties cannot be reduced to other natural properties, so clearly they will be a *special subset* of this set of natural things. Call this nonreductive naturalism 1, or just **NN1** for short.

NN1 might well be indicated and supported by the emphasis on the criterion of causal power and explanation that Cornell Realists typically give. If we think that we have a criterion of what it is that makes something a natural property, then we can say that anything that satisfies this criterion goes into our set. Causal power, say, is just the defining mark of all and only all the things in the set. We seek to support moral properties as being natural properties, but also support the idea that they cannot be reduced to other (accepted) natural properties. The key point about NN1 is that we can justify moral properties being natural properties, so we need some definition of 'natural' that gets them in. A 'disciplinary' criterion may also be put to work in this way, although this may prove harder simply because, at least, *current* science doesn't study moral properties and demands.

Secondly, one might say that all moral properties are *completely constituted* by (other, accepted) natural properties. Yet, there is no one or no finite set of natural properties that constitutes what any individual moral property is. Call this **NN2**.

That may be hard to understand, so let us take things slowly. Think about all of the morally good things there are. There may be very, very many. Opening doors for people, telling the truth, telling a lie to save someone's feelings, waging a war, protesting against a war, mowing the lawn for a friend, preventing a robbery, carrying an old lady's shopping bags, and so on. There may be no natural or natural-scientific property, or set of such properties, that is common to all of these and the many other morally good actions we can imagine. Yet, they are all still good. Often this idea is characterized by saying that goodness is 'multiply realizable'. There are many, many collections of natural, nonmoral properties (and features, and the like) – many naturalistically different types of goodness – that constitute the property of goodness, and there may be no common nonmoral, natural connection between them. The same will be true of all the other common moral properties.

Just so we keep it in mind, note that we have a naturalistic position, supposedly, because any individual instance of the property of goodness is nothing over and above the natural properties and features that constitute that instance. (More on that claim below and in Chapter 6.) But, note also that there is no sense that we can reduce goodness *as a whole* to something or – better – some *thing* natural, for goodness itself is multiply realizable. Remember, there is no one natural thing or small set of natural things that goodness is. This goes for both the concept and property of goodness.

That last idea can be examined in a few ways. Here are two notes. First, note, this might be why Moore's open question argument, be it asked about concepts or properties, was so powerful: we attempt to find *the* natural thing that goodness as a whole is reducible to, but there is no one such thing. Goodness can be realized in many natural ways, although whenever it is realized, it can be reduced to or identified with a set of natural features. Secondly, it is worth noting in the narrative here that just now I have slid from one natural thing to a small set of natural things, say five or fifteen. So, we might be able to say that some action is good if it has one of these five natural properties. If we can do that, perhaps we will have reduced, or analysed, the concept in some naturalistic fashion, thus negating the whole position of nonreductive naturalism. That is an intriguing possibility. It will come up again below.

Before I end this section and move to consider worries with NN1 and NN2, I offer four thoughts.

(c) *Four thoughts*: First, NN1 can be augmented in a number of ways. One popular way is as follows. Assume one thinks that goodness does play some causal and explanatory role. It is understandable that one might wish to reduce this property in naturalistic ways. But, one important factor stopping this reduction is the limited natural-scientific vocabulary available to us. There is no reason to think that we will have the required naturalistic words and concepts to pick out the property of goodness in an *obviously* natural way. After all, the progress of science has been accompanied by, and achievable only because, we have developed new terms and ideas. Terms and ideas are being developed all the time, and correspondingly some existing terms and ideas are dismissed and left behind. Why think that our naturalistic terms will be able to keep pace with our discoveries? This idea has real power if one allies it with the supposition that the universe is potentially infinite. So, if we buy these ideas, then why should we think that we could form an obviously naturalistic word and concept that could help us 'rename' or recharacterize goodness? We may never get such a word or words. Thus, moral properties may be part of the natural word, but no one-to-one or one-to-many mappings are available because we do not have the necessary natural-reductionist conceptual resources. So, we can combine naturalism with nonreductionism.

Second, let us nail the difference between NN1 and NN2. NN1 is the claim that moral properties are natural because they are part of the set of natural properties. Things get into that set because they satisfy a certain criterion, say. NN2 is the claim that moral properties are natural because any individual instance of a moral property is constituted by properties that are recognizably natural. What about concepts? Supporters of NN1 can maintain that moral concepts are *sui generis* simply because no other concepts are like them. Of course, having said that moral properties are a type of natural property, one could say exactly the same thing about moral concepts: they are a type of natural concept. They would still be, of course, *sui generis*. Supporters of NN2, I think, can naturally say that moral concepts are *sui generis* in the more familiar sense: moral concepts are quite different from natural concepts. They can say this simply because the way in which they motivate their naturalism is in terms of the property – which can remain quite different – being multiply realizable. There is no 'merging' or 'reimagining' of categories here.

Third and carrying on, how distinct are NN1 and NN2? They are, I think, different strategies for aiming at the same goal, different ways of supporting a naturalistic but nonreductionist view of moral properties. I think that one could combine them if one wanted to: we pick a criterion that is the mark of the natural – such as causal power – and note that moral properties get in, and they get in because what plays the causal role are the properties that help to constitute any particular instance of goodness. So, for example, Hitler's wickedness caused him to give some orders and create an atmosphere in which other people gave orders which resulted in many millions of innocent people dying and suffering. But, as well as this, lower-level natural properties, such as Hitler's desire for a better German race and his attraction to power, helped to constitute his wickedness and were part of the causal story.

I, myself, am no naturalist. But, even if I were a naturalist, I might be uneasy with this current suggestion, especially if causal power is the mark of the real. In the toy explanation I have just given, there may be 'causal overdetermination'. What is causing the pain? Is it Hitler's wickedness or his desire for power and domination (amongst other things)? Some philosophers are uneasy about a number of different things at different conceptual or ontological levels causing the same thing. And, in relation to our specific question concerning the relation between NN1 and NN2, if we say that it is Hitler's wickedness that is causally important, then why bother saying that it is constituted by other natural properties? That is, why bother advocating NN2 in the first place? Similarly, if we advocate NN2 and say that Hitler's wickedness has no causal involvement, with only the lower-level natural properties causing things, then we cannot support NN1. That little dilemma seems to favour the claim that it is difficult to combine these two strategies.

I leave this thought here as something for the reader to think through. But, because of this and because it will keep our narrative cleaner, in what follows I assume NN1 and NN2 to be separate strategies and provide thoughts against both.

Fourth and lastly, how does all of this relate to Moore's argument? Recall the charge commentators lay at Moore's feet: if he had been explicitly clear about the difference between concepts and properties he would have seen that two concepts can be quite different and yet refer to the very same property or thing. How does that connect with nonreductive naturalism, for such naturalists are seemingly not interested in defining goodness in terms of a natural concept at all?

Although often not mentioned in discussions of Cornell Realism, I think that the example and subsequent morals drawn from the example of 'water is H_2O' are beside the point as far as supporters of NN1 are concerned. They are not interested in defining goodness in terms of some further natural concept, and then showing that these two concepts refer to the same (natural) property. For them, goodness *is* a natural property already. However, with that said, we can see the possibility of their position by reflection on the 'water is H_2O' case and others like them. Once we see that Moore failed to distinguish concepts and properties, we can see the possibility of the referent being the same for two concepts, and perhaps *then* question why the concept of goodness has to be identified with a naturalistic concept in order for the property of goodness to be seen as naturalistic. Why not just cut out the middle man?

In contrast, there is a *more* direct connection between NN2 and this worry with Moore's argument, although it may not be completely obvious. True, say supporters of NN2, goodness *overall*, both concept and property, cannot be reduced to a natural concept or property. However, we can see that an instance of goodness – the goodness of a particular action, say – can be exhaustively analysed in natural terms. Although nonreductive, part of their 'constitutive' insight develops from thinking hard about how a concept applies in the world, to properties and to other things.

However, it is clear that certain reductive naturalists that gain most direct support from Moore's supposed failure.

There was a certain deliberate vagueness in the above paragraph but one. In the end I find it hard to make sense of NN2 as a naturalistic position for reasons I will come to, despite it appearing to be naturalistic. This is just one of the problems that face nonreductive naturalism.

3.8   Three problems for nonreductive naturalism

(a) *Moral Twin Earth*: There is a really nice argument that affects many different forms of nonreductive naturalism. It stems from a thought experiment concerning 'Twin Earth'.

Two points of background. First, we have to ask what it is that fixes the meaning of moral terms such as 'good'. According to many Cornell Realists, and others, what fixes the meaning is that there is some natural kind – goodness – to which the term 'good' refers and which cannot be reduced to anything else. I'll sort out NN1 and NN2 below.

Second, the Twin Earth thought experiment was originally developed to think about the meaning of terms quite generally, but it has been applied to moral matters. So, for example, we might ask what it is that gives us the meaning of 'water'. We could say that 'water' refers to that substance that has particular, obvious, superficial qualities such as humans' ability to drink it, wash with it, and water their gardens with it. But, that seems wrong, or so some people argue. Imagine we travel to some distant part of the universe – Twin Earth – which is exactly the same as our planet aside from the fact that the stuff that has the same obvious, superficial qualities as our water has a different molecular structure. Our water is H_2O, whilst the stuff on Twin Earth is composed of something we can label XYZ. What happens when an Earthling lands on Twin Earth and points to some watery-like stuff and says, 'That is water'? We should think – supposedly – that she does not speak correctly. She thinks, understandably, that the stuff is water, but really it is Twin Earth water, which we can label twater or water*. Our speaker has made a mistake, albeit probably a blameless one. Our intuition, so the argument goes, is that this stuff is not water. This is explained by the fact that we have two natural kinds – H_2O and XYZ – that fix the descriptions of two *different* things, even though the appearances of those two things, and the label we (or, rather, us and the locals) give those two things, is the same, namely 'water'. Furthermore, in this case we can imagine that, when all was revealed, speakers would realize that we have two different natural kinds. This factor will result in there being little pressure for an argument. That is, we cannot imagine someone saying, 'Yes, but what really is *the* thing that is water', for there is no *one* thing that produces watery properties.

So, with those two pieces of background in place, let us think through a Moral Twin Earth problem for naturalism. In order to get the argument going, we need to introduce some twists.

Supporters of both NN1 and NN2 think that moral properties are natural properties. Furthermore, all such theorists think that the meaning of moral terms such as 'wicked' is fixed by some natural kind. Further to this, they also think that this is something to be discovered empirically: we have a synthetic not an analytic claim. We discover that Hitler's wickedness is a natural property; we do not discover this from analysing the concept of wickedness.

Yet, despite these clear similarities, the case of moral naturalism is not quite the same as the water-H_2O case. For a start, think about NN1. Supporters think that wickedness, for example, is just a natural property. There is no identification of wickedness with *another* natural property. But, that is exactly what happens in the water case: it is identified with another thing. We can get around that by introducing a twist. We just acknowledge for argument's sake that there can be such a thing as self-identity. What we discover, empirically, is that wickedness is itself a natural thing and, furthermore, that it is a natural kind that fixes the meaning of the term 'wickedness'.

What of NN2? The wrinkle here is that supporters of NN2 do not think that moral properties can be identified with any one natural property, or any one set. Such properties are natural but nonreductively so. In order to get the Twin Earth case going – as we'll understand in a moment – we have to imagine that we can at least begin to narrow things down. Perhaps the meaning of a moral term is fixed by goodness being multiply realizable by, for example, the consequences of actions alone, where these are understood naturalistically. Or perhaps consequences are not included at all and we are concerned with naturalistically characterized action types. Whatever account we give, the idea is that such naturalized general ideas fix the meaning of our moral terms.

So, now for the worry. Imagine that on Earth 'good' stands for natural properties. In the case of NN1 it will be the natural kind of goodness, whilst in the case of NN2 it will be some set of naturalized consequentialist properties, albeit given in such a general way that one cannot give a precise reduction of good. In both cases, the supposition is that natural stuff fixes the meaning of 'good'.

Opponents then imagine what would happen if we ran a Twin Earth scenario. Imagine, for NN1, that when Twin Earthlings use 'good' it picks out a *different* natural kind from the one that Earthlings pick out. That is easy to see in the case of water, for we can name the two kinds in the example differently, H_2O and XYZ. In this situation, both are named as 'good'. But you just have to imagine that although Earthling and Twin Earthlings employ the same word, we have two different kinds here, perhaps $good_E$ and $good_{TE}$. In the case of NN2, it is easy to see the clash. Imagine that Earthlings define goodness as having something to do with consequences, whilst Twin Earthlings say that goodness has to do only with action types.

Now, imagine further, that Earthlings and Twin Earthlings meet and are discussing a particular action. If one group calls the action 'good' and the other says it is not, then we have an issue. Recall that when it came to natural terms, it is supposed that there would not be an argument: same word, certainly, but different natural kinds. Do moral terms work in the same way? We should imagine that if goodness really is a natural kind, then it should do. When all was revealed we would say that, in fact, even though we have one word in play, really there are two concepts – 'good-Earth' and 'good-Twin-Earth' – and no possibility of disagreement for the groups would be talking at cross-purposes. (This goes for NN1 and NN2.)

However, say opponents, we – that is, most of us – do *not* have the same intuition in the moral case. We want to say that, normally, the moral Earthlings and moral Twin Earthlings *are* having a real disagreement. We hold to the idea that some unified theory or account of goodness is possible. In the case of NN1 we think that there should be just one natural kind that fixes the meaning of a moral term. Either the Earthlings or the Twin Earthlings have got things wrong. In the case of NN2 we again think there is just one broad natural way in which goodness is multiply realizable, one that plumps for consequences, or action types, or something else. And so there must be some crucial difference between the moral case and the water case. And, many such critics think that the crucial difference is that there is no natural kind of goodness.

More specifically, we may want to say that any suitably worded question connecting 'good' with some Earthling definition will remain open, since it may be the case that the Earthlings have not got the right definition. 'This has the best consequences [understood naturalistically], but is it good?', can still be a reasonable question to answer in the manner already discussed. The worry, put differently, is that the natural cannot be used to characterize exhaustively what the moral is. The moral should be determined on its own terms. This should make us think again about Moore. The original open question argument was just about concepts, as we saw. But something like Moore's argument still seems to stand: if we think that a result about the meanings of moral terms has implications for what we say about moral concepts, we should doubt whether the referents for moral concepts can be natural properties.

This line of argument has received a lot of publicity, and there are more twists and turns than I have presented. Here is one way continuing the discussion, one that still results in nonreductive naturalism being in trouble.

Imagine this defence of nonreductive naturalism. Some people go back to the whole discussion of Earth and Twin Earth. Should we really have the intuition that the Earthling on Twin Earth is speaking falsely when she calls XYZ 'water'? Perhaps we might want to say that the term and concept 'water' come in two parts: water is [definition] *'either* H_2O *or* it is XYZ', where the 'or' signifies that if either part is satisfied, then the thing is water. In which case, the Earthling *does* speak truly when she points at XYZ, for the stuff she points at satisfies one of the parts of our definition, even if she may not have a complete grip on what she is pointing at. Some might therefore think that this helps to preserve the analogy between the moral and the natural case, such that the line of argument cannot get going. Why not allow that good can be similarly characterized?

Although interesting, I do not think this idea works well, even if one accepts the intuition about the water case (as I do, in fact). It seems odd – at least as moral philosophy stands and is likely to stand – that moral goodness could be defined in this way, as being composed of two different things where goodness, say, is picked out by rival natural kinds that are quite different (in the case of NN1), or rival normative theories (NN2). H_2O and XYZ are not rivals in the same sense: they do not stand opposed. They are just different things that could both be water. But, to take NN2 as our example, yoking consequences and action types together as parts of the definition of goodness is not as innocent since for many more theorists goodness (the concept overall) is one thing completely, or the other thing completely. In fact, the two cases employ different 'or's. In the water case, any particular instance of water is either H_2O or XYZ, but both sorts of stuff can be water. In the goodness case, for most ethical theorists goodness as a whole, and not just individual token instances of it, is only ever one sort of thing: it is either consequences or action types (or some other thing).

Of course, a naturalist could give in and bite the bullet here: there could well be two different types of natural kind which fix the meaning of any moral term. But, that would be a big concession. Why? Well, it would give us a sort of relativism: we now have two sorts of goodness (and any other moral concept and term) in play, both of which were locally authoritative. Indeed, we can easily see that there may be more than two planets. We may have far more natural moral kinds than those on Earth and its twin. And, further, it might introduce a moral relativism just on Earth. Most contemporary naturalists will not want to go down this route for we could easily threaten the realism they are trying to support by introducing a potentially rampant sort of relativism.

So, the obvious move for any naturalist *realist* is to say that there really is just *a* natural kind that *should* fix the meaning of various moral words, and anyone who diverts is just wrong. There is much to say about this proposal, but the main one to my mind is that it may take us back to IMR, and this will come under pressure in the next chapter.

Aside from various moves, we can see that the general strength of this whole objection is that it encourages us to think about how evaluative concepts such as goodness work, and how they may be different from natural concepts. We will pursue this more in the third objection below, which is the objection I think really bites.

(b) *Is NN2 naturalistic?*: Before we get to that, let me focus on NN2. I have deliberately expressed it in a vague manner. This is because, frankly, I find it hard to make sense of whether this is a naturalistic position. In short, I do not argue that the position described is false. Rather, I present advocates of NN2 with a dilemma: either their position is a form of reductionism (which contradicts their nonreductionism), or their position is nonnaturalistic (which contradicts their naturalism). This dilemma may appear to be a point about labelling. But, I think it important because assuming that this position can rightfully be described as both nonreductive and naturalistic can cloud our judgement.

Recall that in explaining the idea of a moral property being multiply realizable, I gave a number of examples of good things, such as opening doors for people and carrying old ladies' heavy shopping bags. Given this sort of level of description, we can imagine that any particular example of a good action can be redescribed in nonmoral, natural terms. No one can deny that shopping bags and doors are *prima facie* natural as opposed to moral things. And, further, we might be able to redescribe some of the features crucial to the situations being as they are in terms in which scientists are happy to deal, such as the chemical compositions of bags and doors. We can say this not just of the situations and objects I have just listed but, we can imagine, of any situation and object we might think of. This will then aid the supporters of NN2, it seems.

But, let us now nail the idea of irreducibility. We can grant that there may be no one or small set of natural properties that every instance of goodness has in common. Instead, then, why not imagine a disjunctive list that helps us to characterize goodness naturalistically? So, perhaps we say the following. Imagine X is any particular situation. We then say that:

> X is good if and only if X has the following properties: (*a*, *b*, *c*) or (*d*, *e*, *f*) or (*a*, *b*, *d*) or (*b*, *e*, *f*, *g* but, if *h* is present, not *i*) or (*g*, *f*, *h*) or…. and so on.

All of the italicized letters stand for natural properties or features, properties or features that are relevant to the goodness of the situation. Each bracketed set is called a disjunct.

What we have here is a characterization which gives us a way of summing what goodness is, in natural terms. If we come across a situation we are supposedly able to tell, just by looking at its natural features, whether or not it is good: if it is on the list it is good, but if it is not on the list, then it is not.

Well, that is how it is supposed to work. But, there is a big question mark. Our attention should be drawn immediately to the '…and so on' that comes at the end. What does that mean?

It means that we can carry on imagining that the list will continue into infinity. First of all, is that true? Well, there is good reason to think it true. Imagine two of the examples I have given. Imagine we think it morally good to open the door for Peter. Then we introduce another natural feature or two. Imagine that Peter said something to someone else, Delilah, which caused her to cry. (We might, in normal circumstances, say that Peter was rude, but that seems an evaluative rather than a natural feature.) So, it turns out that opening the door in this case would not be morally good, or at least not morally right. What would be better would be to slam the door on Peter so as to teach him a lesson. But, then imagine we introduce a further feature. Yes, Peter said something to Delilah that made her cry, but she had previously done something to him that was more painful. So, it is now morally good to open the door.

The thought is that we can keep on adding features – and subtracting, and changing features – all day long. We may, in fact, never get a definitive characterization of goodness in natural terms. If we did, then we should represent that with a full stop, not a '...and so on.'.

And this is a very important result. If we had a full stop, then it would show we had completed our naturalistic analysis. We could also count the number of disjuncts and conclude that goodness is multiply realizable and that it is, say, 436 realizations, or 50,436. But, if we have a complete analysis, it seems that we have a complete reduction. We have fully specified what goodness is in wholly nonmoral, natural terms. Goodness just is some complex thing that is captured, completely, by all of the disjuncts taken together.

This would obviously contradict the nonreductionism that was supposed to be being defended. So, it is crucial for NN2 that we never get a full naturalistic characterization. In case it isn't clear, all of the foregoing applies whether we think of goodness as a concept or a property.

So, nonreductive naturalists need to keep the '...and so on'. But, now the other horn of our dilemma comes into view. Is this really a naturalistic position? It may easily seem to be. After all, each of the disjuncts is specified only in natural terms. But, the key question we are asking is whether goodness as a whole – the concept or property overall – is naturalistic. (Recall that this was Moore's concern.) To my mind, there is very good reason to resist the label 'naturalism' here. There is no characterization of *the* naturalistic property of goodness for, in a very important sense, there is no single property. What we have are various exemplifications or instantiations of goodness, and we assume that in each case we can give a wholly naturalistic characterization. But, we cannot nail the naturalistic characterization of goodness; for that would just give us a reduction and take us back to the first horn.

A different picture is surely more inviting. When we list all of the disjuncts we think that they have something in common, namely that there are all exemplifications of goodness. Further, there are presumably many sets of features that are not on our list. All of these sets – both the ones on the list and the ones not on the list – are parts of situations. We have to ask, I think, how it comes to be that some situations are united, and are also different from other situations. The answer seems straightforward: they are united because they are good. Similarly, *those other* situations are not included because they are not good. We do not include a situation on the list because – primarily – it has particular configuration of natural features. Rather, it is included on the list because it is good, and its goodness receives exemplification in a certain, natural way. The goodness of the situations seems to be in pole position here, not the natural features that constitute the goodness of any good situation or action.

I do not – at this stage – wish to plump for a mind-dependent version of realism as against a mind-independent version. (That will come later.) But, for the moment, imagine you do prefer a mind-dependent version. (Recall that, as yet, naturalists can choose either.) We can ask why it is that judges decide, in no matter how complex a fashion, that certain things are good, certain things are kind, certain things are elegant, and so on. From a wholly natural, nonmoral point of view, there may be absolutely nothing in common between all of the various things judged to be morally good, say. However, when we judge from within the moral or evaluative point of view, the set makes sense. There is a pattern that is easy to discern and reason about. Indeed, think again about that crucial part at the end. When we say '... this and this and this. ... and so on.' we are indicating that there is a pattern to the individual parts that can extend across many other situations. Will you be able to continue the sequence, that is will you be able to pick out all and only all the other good things, if you adopt only a naturalistic, nonmoral point of view? It seems not. What is absolutely key is that one has a moral point of view that allows one to see which things are good and which are not. The noting of which natural features are the good-making features of any situation comes after this move, not before.

So what? The point is that it is becoming less and less justified that we call this position naturalistic. What seems essential is that some moral point of view comes before any naturalistic recharacterization of the situations, or before any noting down of the good-making features.

We will return to this idea some more, both when we talk about reductionist realism below, and in Chapter 6. For now, we can see that this dilemma is strong, I think, and that NN2 is difficult to maintain. To repeat, this is not just a point about labels. It is really a point about whether the idea standing behind this sort of nonreductive naturalism is coherent.

We could of course ask a further question relating to the second horn of the dilemma I have discussed. Is there any more to say about why it is that the moral point of view seems prior? Is there anything that sets it apart from the natural? I think there is, and setting that out challenges both NN1 and NN2.

(c) *Evaluation and normativity*: Let us start with a specific point about NN1. We have the set of all natural objects and properties (and relations, and whatever else goes in). Within that we have all the moral properties. From this we can note something important. Within the natural we have a large number of different sorts of property. Something can be both natural and a special something. So, for example, we want to mark subsets of the biological, the physical, the chemical and – if we are letting in social-cultural things – we mark the subset of the sociological, the economic, and then various cultural objects such as knives and lollipops. So, presumably, we would want to mark a special subset of the moral.

But, this then raises some philosophically interesting ideas. Some people think that the moral is different – very different – in character from the other things with which it is put. Even if one admits that moral properties are to be conceived as playing a causal role, for example, the types of things they cause and how they do it marks them as different from chemical properties. As we saw, anyway, God and magicians may cause things to happen, but we may not want them in this set. At the very least, we need to specify the sort of causation we think important that does not depend on some prior notions of the natural, nonnatural and supernatural, for this is what we are concerned with defining.

But, this is just to cast doubt on the criterion by which things get into the set. We might also worry that there is something about the moral such that we should not be putting it into a set with accepted natural things. The moral collects together much that is normative and evaluative. Roughly – *very* roughly – the normative involves or concerns demands, suggestions, requests, enticements and the like, whilst the evaluative involves goodness and badness, and more specific things, such as the properties and ideas of kindness, elegance and wisdom. Natural properties, and even social scientific properties, do not belong to either camp.

First, saying that something is a result of photosynthesis or finding out how many people are unemployed does not itself mark out anything as good or bad, kind or elegant. These things can support and have such evaluative properties, but are not those evaluations themselves. Secondly and similarly, photosynthesis or unemployment figures on their own are not demands. Again, it seems commonplace to think that such things can support demands, but are themselves not demands. As it has been put by some (in various ways), unemployment figures can be and often are normatively significant because they can result in us having a reason to act. But what is normative are not the unemployment figures themselves. What is normative is *the fact that* these unemployment figures are significant or, if one prefers, what is normative is the significance of the unemployment figures.

Evaluation and normativity seem as if they are different from one another, although sometimes the fact is forgotten by some writers and they are lumped together. In recent times some writers have put normativity centre-stage and leave evaluation to the side or perhaps cast its significance only in terms of how it can service the normative: the idea being that values and evaluative properties are important in this debate only in so far as they generate reasons and demands. I think this treatment of the evaluative is profoundly wrong-headed, but I won't argue the case here. What is important to realize is that concentrating on either, but especially both, seems to create a worry for naturalism: natural things seem very different from moral things.

At this stage, a third sort of idea is often mentioned, but not by all writers. When some people judge that unemployment is at certain sort of level or that a pear tastes a certain way, they may not be motivated to do anything. It seems perfectly reasonable to imagine that people can make a legitimate judgement and feel no appropriate motivation at all. But, say some, this is not so with moral and other evaluative judgements. If we judge that the unemployment figures are morally bad in some fashion, or that the pear is delicious and tasty, it seems an important part, even a necessary part, of that judgement that we are motivated to some degree to act appropriately on the judgement. We have met this debate before in §1.3, and we will consider it in detail in Chapter 7. Right now, we need to note that part of the importance of this debate is that it shows there is some presumption, at least on the part of some writers, that the moral, and the evaluative and normative more generally, are different from the natural.

Let us return to the specific issue of NN1 to make things clear. Are we justified in placing moral properties within the set of natural properties? Even if we can make out some notion of causation that allows for moral properties to be causally efficacious, for many the moral is seriously different from the natural, so much so that putting it into the set of natural things seems very wrong. Indeed, putting the moral into a widened category of the natural may dilute the category of the natural so much that it is rendered meaningless. If this set is to include, for example, both normative and nonnormative things – things that demand and suggest, and things that do not – then this seems to be too wide a category to prove useful when thinking about metaethics and issues of what is real.

What of NN2? This issue returns us to the ending comments of the previous problem. We asked there what it is to see things from a moral point of view. We can, perhaps, pick out the natural properties that make a good action good. But one will be able to do that only once one sees things from an evaluative and a normative perspective. It is this perspective that allows the grouping. The difference in style between the moral and the natural means that one cannot easily name or rename what one sees as moral as something natural. We need to put it in the category of the nonnatural.

Naturalists might at this stage protest. Many of them take this challenge very seriously, and there are a number of proposals to try to capture the normative and the evaluative in natural terms. For example, perhaps goodness is something we would desire to desire, all things considered. Perhaps the morally good actions are what people like us but with more knowledge and more patience would advise us to do. The problem with all of these analyses, it seems to me, is twofold. First, we might be able to note that people with more knowledge advise us to do something, but why should we care about that? Some critics – and this is now getting boring – think that we get caring and normative import only if we have normative terms. Perhaps if the judges were specified as being better than us, perhaps morally better than us, then we would have a good analysis of goodness. But that defeats the idea of a non-moral analysis. Secondly, there are all sorts of (natural) responses we could use to provide our analysis of goodness. In making our decision as to which response to use, we need to employ some sort of reasoning, assumed to be free in some sense. This itself may be a normative and evaluative matter, and this decision process will also need to be naturalized. That may not capture in the right way at all the character of the decision. I return to this idea in §6.4.

By way of drawing things to a close, I make a small point about Moore. Recall again the flaw in Moore, about his failure to note the difference between concepts and properties. There is undoubtedly that flaw. Yet, for some writers, he was onto something, even if he didn't articulate it well. For these writers it is thoughts in this sub-section that help to make sense of what Moore was trying to get at. The reason why moral concepts cannot be identified with natural concepts is that the former, but not the latter, have evaluation and/or normativity built in or, better, they just are evaluative and normative concepts, whereas natural ones are not, seemingly by definition. From this thought, some writers make a further leap. We use concepts and terms to mark differences in the world. Moral concepts and natural concepts are so different that we should be reasonably sceptical – or strongly sceptical, perhaps – that they could ever refer to the same sort of thing. This thought is especially strong in those who think that the carving of 'things' in the world is largely a matter of which concepts are employed. If the concepts are radically different, there is little hope of finding there to be *a* thing that both refer to.

Those speculations at the end are designed to provoke, although I happily admit being friendly to them. Suffice it to say, the three problems articulated in this section – particularly this last one – convince me that nonreductive naturalists have much work to do. But, we here reached one of the themes of this book, that concerning the strengths and weaknesses of each position. The strength of naturalism is that it conceives of moral properties as existing things that fit into our natural world. Its weakness is that it may have a tough time in accommodating evaluation and normativity. And these strengths and weaknesses are treated differently by writers. Some writers just cannot imagine jettisoning the idea of normativity from our conception of the moral. To do so would be to change the subject. Other writers believe it is not so important, or believe that the normative can be naturalized in a perfectly acceptable way. On this last point, see Further Reading.

Right now, I think we should conclude that nonreductive naturalism faces a number of strong challenges, and we need to think about a different sort of position.

3.9 Reductionist realism

(a) *Opening comments*: The position I call 'reductionist realism' can get worked out in various ways. I focus on just one of those ways in this section, although I mention another.

This position is realist for it says that moral properties exist and moral judgements really are true or false. But, moral properties turn out to be reducible to other properties. As such, we can give a 'reforming definition' of moral terms because we can say which other, nonmoral things moral terms and concepts apply to. However, no one I discuss here thinks we can find nonmoral synonyms for moral terms; no one thinks we will find nonmoral terms that mean the same as moral terms. As I mentioned above, some reductionists leave it open as to what the moral reduces to, although combining naturalism with reductionism is popular.

Why believe this position? Some argue for it because they think they have found a good reductionist characterization. Some hedonic utilitarians come to mind here. Aside from any worries Moore had, we might worry that this position and any other raises problems because of the thing to which goodness or rightness is supposedly reducible. But, some reductionists are keen to develop their view for other reasons.

Some naturalist-reductionists assume that we typically think there are moral properties in the world and that the world is natural. If we think that, then it seems strange to think in addition that there is no link between the moral and the natural and, indeed, that we could not translate moral talk into natural talk, and that with some cunning we cannot find out which moral properties are which natural properties. They set themselves against NN1 because, broadly, they think that there is some difference between moral talk and natural talk, and they do not want to say that moral properties – as we normally think of them – are a type of natural property in the way that supporters of NN1 do.

(b) *Two positions*: I put aside supernaturalistic reductionism. Even so, naturalistic reductionism can take a number of forms. Here are two.

Synthetic natural reductionists believe that we can reduce properties and work out which natural things moral concepts apply to in the manner just described. According to them, there are one-to-one and one-to-many mappings available and, if they are optimistic, they think we can discover them. Furthermore, they think that we find out these mappings by empirical investigation. Any sort of identification we make will be a synthetic one. This sort of position can be seen as flowing directly from the third worry we raised against Moore's argument: if he had just realized the significance of the difference between concepts and properties, then he would have seen the possibility of this position, perhaps, and realized that he needed to do more to argue for his conclusion.

To make it clear, the focus is normally on the properties being natural: many writers here think that moral concepts can retain their *sui generis* nature, although it is open to any theorist to argue against this.

This is an interesting position. But, concerns of space mean I do not write much about it. In brief, however, my worry with this sort of position is reflected in the 'evaluation and normativity' worry we saw above, and some of my worries with the next position, which I do spend more time on.

Analytic natural reductionists believe just as synthetic natural reductionists believe, only they think that we can establish the mapping by nonempirical methods such as conceptual analysis, not by empirical means. So, any identifications we come up with will be analytic. In what follows, I concentrate on a specific proposal of this type.

(c) *Analytic naturalist reductionism*: Here I concentrate on two parts of the specific version of this position in which I am interested. I criticize each in turn.

(i) First, think of the world, that is the entire universe, we inhabit. Call it W_1. We can assume that W_1 contains nothing but natural stuff. Now imagine another world, W_2, that is naturally exactly the same as W_1. We can assume that if there is any moral stuff in W_1, then there is exactly the same, and only the same, moral stuff in W_2. Why? Because, if we take (ordinarily, aside from this thought experiment and any discussion of reductionism) any good action, it seems we can break it down into natural parts, as we saw above. We can talk about shopping bags, doors, and the like. In short, what we have described thus far is part of what it means to say that the moral *supervenes* on the natural. If we say that the moral supervenes on the natural then we are saying that if there is the very same sort of natural stuff, then there will be the very same sort of moral stuff, and if there is a change in the moral stuff then there *must* have been a change in the natural stuff. That is, the moral stuff cannot change if the natural stuff does not change, and the moral stuff cannot be different across two possible worlds if the natural stuff in both worlds is exactly the same. If you think these ideas hold for the moral and the natural, then it looks as if you think that the moral supervenes on the natural. (There may be further constraints as well, and there are distinctions between different types of supervenience, but I ignore them here for simplicity's sake.)

So what? Imagine we fully describe in natural terms a particular good action, such as the action of helping an old lady with her shopping bags. If we assume that there can be nothing other than natural things, then this must be possible. Now, imagine that our task is to describe goodness in total, naturalistically, that is describe all of the good actions in a naturalistic way. This will be a huge list, full of many disjuncts, just as we saw earlier. This is no doubt possible to do.

If we do that, we will have reduced the moral to the natural. How come? We will have two claims 'Action X is good' and 'Action X has (naturalistic) features *a*, *b* and *c*, or (naturalistic features) *d*, *e* and *f*, or....' And – for argument's sake right now, unlike earlier – assume we have a full analysis, one with an end point. So, there will be no '...and so on.', we will instead end with a disjunct and then a full stop. We can then say that the first claim, about X being good, entails the second, longer claim. And, because we have included and recharacterized *all* of the good actions, then we can say that the entailment runs the other way. That is, something is good if it is one of *these* things (has features represented by one of *these* disjuncts), and, furthermore, if something is one of *these* things then it is good. Thus, because of this, we will have fully captured goodness in natural terms.

It is important to see what this conclusion amounts to. We will have fully captured goodness in terms of the natural; the same goes for all other moral properties. The conclusion is that moral properties simply are natural properties. Each and every distinction about and in the stuff of the world made with moral terms and concepts is made by our natural terms and concepts. There is nothing that our moral terms and concepts do with respect to the world that our natural terms and concepts cannot do. Therefore, moral properties simply are natural properties.

There is more to say about this argument, and reductionists disagree about how exactly it should be phrased and framed. But the essential idea is a strong one: there is a world seemingly simply composed of natural stuff. Can the moral be made out as different? No, because every distinction in the stuff that can be made using moral terms and concepts can also be made using natural terms and concepts.

This idea has been challenged and debated. Here is a worry. Let us grant for argument's sake that moral terms and concepts can be translated wholly into natural terms and concepts. Why assume that this means that moral properties just are natural properties? This seems to rely on the idea often called the 'coextension test for property identity'. What we have imagined is that whenever a moral term applies to some stuff (that is, some properties), then some natural term or terms apply to that stuff. Indeed, there is a necessary coextension between the two sets of terms: the moral terms and the natural terms we have recharacterized them as being. Further, it seems as if we are picking out two sorts of property: the moral and the natural. But, if the moral properties picked out using the moral terms are necessarily coextensive with the natural properties picked out using the natural terms, then surely the two sorts of property are, in fact, just one sort of property. If 'properties' are necessarily coextensive they are, in fact, identical and we have just one property here. Or, in short: if properties A and B are necessarily coextensive, then they are identical.

People challenge this last move, from necessary coextension to identity. That is, they hope to show that even if moral properties (and terms) are necessarily coextensive with natural properties (and terms), this does not mean that moral properties are natural properties. Here are two reasons why not. First, here is a quick challenge where using the test seems to cast doubt on it itself. The procedure works with the terms and properties 'being necessarily coextensive with' and 'being identical to'. Both these terms or properties seem to be necessarily coextensive. But, if that is true, and the test is correct, then both terms or properties are also identical with one another. Yet, this seems false since when we assert the test, it seems that we are referring to different terms or properties and making some interesting link between them. (This takes us back to the paradox of analysis from earlier, and defensive moves may be available.)

Second and more substantially, we can think of other examples where the test does not generate the right result. A common example – discussed on both sides of the debate – concerns triangles. Critics say that triangularity and trilaterality (for closed figures) are different properties that, nevertheless, are necessarily coextensive. One cannot have a three-sided (closed) shape without that shape having three angles, and vice versa. Yet, it is decidedly unclear that we would say that triangularity (or angularity in general) and trilaterality (and laterality in general) are the same properties. We seem to apply the concepts, and identify different properties, for different reasons. Angularity is concerned with the distance and relationship between two intersecting lines, and laterality is not. So, something has gone wrong with the test: necessary coextension is not the same as identity.

As I say, this point has been hotly debated. But, it is clear that the argument given by analytic reductionists does not go through smoothly. Indeed, even if they can answer this worry, there is another part of their position that often comes under criticism.

(ii) We might ask of the analytic reductionist why it is that they settle on certain features rather than other ones. How do we get to link certain moral terms and properties with natural terms and properties? (We can ask this of many sorts of theorists, of course.) For a synthetic reductionist this will be through massive and concerted empirical investigation. For the analytic reductionist they hope to make the link through analysis of our concepts alone, which requires knowledge of what such concepts mean and some limited knowledge of how they work. One way in which analytic reductionists make the link is through a procedure known as a 'network analysis'.

The point of a network analysis is to relate moral concepts to other moral concepts, and tell us how all of these individually relate to natural concepts. In doing so we work out the precise *role* that a moral concept plays, and from that are able to identify it with a natural property. In short, we hope to specify what the 'goodness role' is, for example, and from that work out which natural property plays that role. And, in creating a network analysis, we do not take just anyone's views about how moral concepts relate. We take the best views, perhaps of a community of mature moral language users.

So, for example, we list all of the key statements in which goodness appears and which tell us what role goodness plays in our conceptual scheme. Some of these statements relate goodness to other evaluative terms. Some other statements relate goodness to nonmoral, natural ideas. Such statements might be, 'the procedure "you cut, I choose" is a good one', 'the goodness of a thing gives us a reason to pursue it', 'goodness and rightness are different concepts', 'two things can both be good, yet one of these things can be better than another', 'pain is often not good', 'moral goodness is different from aesthetic goodness', and so on. There will, no doubt, be very many such statements, not just for goodness but for all other moral terms.

However, we then put all of the instances of goodness together in a sort of network, working out what exactly something needs to play the 'goodness role' in our conceptual scheme. Let us say, also, that we pick on 'goodness' as our chief moral concept. When we put all of our statements together, we remove all the other moral and evaluative and normative terms. We then work out which natural property (which may be quite complex, even disjunctively so) uniquely satisfies the description of goodness. And, once we have done this, we can retranslate and work out which natural property plays the rightness role, which one plays the kindness role, and so on, because we have an anchor in our system, for we now have a natural property that plays the goodness role. In short, we will have redefined all of the moral terms in natural terms and reduced moral properties to natural properties.

Various types of criticism have been advanced concerning this idea, although it undoubtedly has some strengths. I think that the overall position suffers from the worries I outlined just above, in (i). But apart from that, I worry that there is an assumption running through this position that is questionable.

In short, this analysis – and indeed the whole position – assumes there to be a clear division between the moral, the normative and the evaluative, on the one hand, and the natural on the other. Further, it assumes that we can discern this division. We translate vocabulary and terms and concepts from the one set into vocabulary, terms and concepts into the other set. How confident are we that there is a clear distinction? Certainly one can say that there are clear examples on both sides. Taken as concepts (and terms) or properties (or objects and relations), goodness, rightness and kindness, seem to be different from redness, knives, and unemployment. But, perhaps there are lots of concepts that lie in the middle and threaten to blur the boundaries such that any sort of analysis, and supervenience relation, may not work.

It may not be possible to capture everything that is relevant about a moral action in wholly natural terms. Imagine that Mark is on a bus and sees an old lady coming on, carrying heavy shopping bags. He moves from a seat to allow an old lady to sit down. But, that 'allow' might well be an evaluative or normative notion since it depends on social norms and conventions, and personal intentions; it does not seem naturalistic. Well, we could remove that word and concept, and just talk of Mark moving from a chair and the old lady sitting down. However, that description is compatible with two people coincidentally exchanging places, with nothing moral occurring. It misses the fact that Mark acted for a reason and with a certain intention, and that seems (for most people) to be part of what makes the action good and kind. At least, we need something that is sufficient to distinguish the action of coincidental exchange from an action that is good. Even deleting the 'allow' and saying 'Mark vacated his seat for the old lady', seems worrying: the fact that he vacated his seat *for* the old lady to sit on suggests a special sort of moral intention, which creates a type of moral action different from coincidental movement. Similar comments about 'allow' might work for many, many other concepts, terms and properties, such as one thing being 'better' than another, information being 'relevant' to a decision, one having 'sufficient' reason to act, one person 'refraining' from doing something, and so on. Some critics – including myself – suspect that when we try to analyse moral evaluative and normative notions, we will find that the moral (and evaluative, and normative) goes 'all the way down'. There may be no way of fully analysing a concept in nonmoral, naturalistic terms simply because a full analysis of any normative and/ or evaluative concepts will rely on other such concepts. This is partly a reflection of the difference between moral, evaluative and normative concepts, on the one hand, and natural concepts on the other. This is just by way of illustration. I think that there will be plenty such terms in our moral, evaluative and normative vocabularies. My suspicion has two aspects. First, imagine we do try to make goodness, for example, the anchor of our network analysis. We are asking a lot of this concept. Armed only with this and natural ideas we are able to determine what all the other moral, evaluative and normative words are, naturalistically. Indeed, with example such as that above, we can see how much work 'goodness' will have to do. Still we are speaking theoretically, and some reductionists will retain confidence. But, secondly and more fundamentally, are we so confident that there is a discernible difference between natural and nonnatural vocabulary? I am not as confident as reductionists, and many other naturalists are, that there is this difference. And if we do not have a clear division, then what hope have we to reduce and translate?

Does this last point threaten my argument above, in §3.8(c) about normativity? I don't think so. The challenge there was to say that the natural and the moral are quite different and you cannot simply say that the moral is the natural. This is supported by thinking about the normative. This intuition is supported by thinking about the very big difference between concepts such as goodness and unemployment. That big difference between *some* concepts is compatible with the claim that when we move away from these examples and think about other ones, there is less of a marked difference and, indeed, it is not so easy to discern any difference at all.

Reductionism – both in its analytic and synthetic forms – has many supporters. Again, its strength is to tap into our thought that the moral inhabits our everyday, natural world and, indeed, can be seen as an integral part of it. Its weakness is that it is difficult to make out how that can be done. Some problems may be practical, but others are more theoretical. Naturalists of all sorts will keep on bumping up against the concern that in some sense the moral is different: translating into a naturalistic vocabulary will leave things behind that change the nature of the moral too radically.

3.10   One last point

In this short section I simply connect the material in this chapter with one of this book's themes.

Cornell Realists are naturalists, and natural properties (we can assume) exist mind-independently. It seems sensible to assert that no matter what anyone believes or desires about the existence of *that* chair, the chair either exists or it does not. The same goes for the process of photosynthesis, the magnetic pull of the Sun, and electrons. All of these things, note, seem to be things that one can classify as 'natural'. But, that does not mean that Cornell Realists will automatically be advocating IMR. As it happens, some of them do. But, we should note that it is an extra step to link naturalism with IMR. Think of it like this. There is some form of identification (reductionist or not) between moral and natural properties. And, natural properties exist mind-independently. But, we have to ask what the status is of *the identification*, not of the thing that the moral is being identified with or being linked to. That is, if a naturalist wants to be an IMRealist, she has to do more than say that the property with which moral properties are identified is itself a mind-independently existing property. She has to argue that the identification is itself a mind-independent matter. After all, one could advocate the following theory: humans or best humans determine that *this* sort of (mind-independently existing) natural property should be conceived to be *that* sort of moral property. That does not look like IMR. A naturalist-IMRealist has to argue that the identification is something that humans can only discover, not make or stipulate. The identification is outside of human influence.

So, please be aware that naturalism and nonnaturalism and mind-independence and mind-dependence are two different distinctions. I return to this point yet again in Chapter 6.

3.11 Concluding remarks

In this chapter I have described and assessed a broad family, or two broad families, of moral realism. I have cast suspicion on both reductionist and nonreductionist varieties of naturalism. Some of the ideas introduced in this chapter will reappear again, such as the idea of patterns and disjunctive lists.

Before we examine nonnaturalistic views of moral realism further, we will profit by switching tack and considering two sorts of anti-realist or non-realist position. This is what I do in the next two chapters.

Further Reading

An excellent way into modern work on moral realism is Fitzpatrick (2009). There are excellent discussions in The Stanford Encyclopedia of Philosophy on 'moral naturalism' and 'moral nonnaturalism', listed in the bibliography respectively as Lenman (2012) and Ridge (2012).

The best version of Moore (1903) is the revised version from 1993 edited by Tom Baldwin, which itself has an excellent introduction. Frankena (1939) and Snare (1975) are two good discussions of Moore, but there are many! There are two excellent recent collections on Moore's philosophy: Horgan and Timmons (2006), and Nuccetelli and Seay (2007) (part III). The bibliographies in both are worth following up. Again, the Stanford Encyclopedia has a number of relevant entries; pertinent here is Hurka (2012), and Beaney (2012) (which is on analysis and has a small section on Moore and the paradox of analysis). Lastly, a super discussion of the very idea of reduction is Schroeder (2005).

The entry on ethical naturalism by Nicholas Sturgeon in Copp (2006) provides a clear, modern discussion of the position. Some of the points made in the section on Cornell Realism convey particular views of Sturgeon. It is worth reading other writers such as Boyd (1988) and Brink (1989) to get a flavour of the position as a whole. Copp (2003) is also well worth reading, especially if one wishes to think how naturalists might conceive of the normative. The debate between Harman (1985) and Sturgeon (1985) is a classic way into many of the issues discussed. The idea I call NN2 is not often noticed, but does lurk in some writings, for example Brink (1989), p. 157 onwards. For discussion of this idea and Cornell Realism generally, see Shafer-Landau (2003), chapter 3, especially pp. 65–72, and Miller (2003), chapter 8.

The Moral Twin Earth thought experiment is developed by Horgan and Timmons across a number of papers; their (1992) is representative. See also Copp (2000) for one response, then see Horgan and Timmons (2000) for a counter.

Some of the discussion of normativity stems from Parfit (2011), especially volume II, part six, chapters 24–27, and see also Dancy (2006). Copp (2012) is a good discussion of Parfit. From this last piece I take the idea of 'disciplinary' and 'criterial' conceptions of naturalism.

Synthetic naturalist reductionism is argued for by Peter Railton. Railton (1986) is the classic discussion of his view. Analytic reductionism is argued for by Frank Jackson. His view is best discussed in Jackson (1998). There he officially leaves it open as to what the moral reduces to, although it is clear that he endorses naturalism (or, strictly, 'physicalism'). The discussion of network analyses and the supervenience argument I give is roughly based on his thoughts. There is a good criticism of the supervenience argument in Shafer-Landau (2003), pp. 89–98, and Majors (2005), from which I borrow some of my concerns. Streumer (2008) is a response on behalf of Jackson. Brown (2011) is a good continuation of Jackson's argument. Ridge (2007) is also good on moral supervenience, and it criticizes some of the arguments in Shafer-Landau (2003).

4
Moral Error Theory

4.1 Introduction

Our focus shifts away from realism for a while. This is for two reasons. First, to get some sense of what realism is like it is important to understand who opposes it and why. Secondly, we have been thinking hard about realism for a while and the anti-realists need to be heard.

Recall that I have focussed on the metaphysical claims of realists, for realists believe in moral properties. Even if there is some muddying of the waters to come, that claim holds good for the most part. But, in this chapter, and especially the next, the purpose and character of judgements comes more to the fore.

In this chapter I detail moral error theory, which to my mind is a key position in metaethics. (Hereafter I mainly refer just to 'error theory'.) Despite its importance, it does not have many supporters. But amongst thoughtful people at large it may command more respect than philosophers think. Indeed, professional philosophers may find it hard on reflection to resist some of the charms – dangerous charms, perhaps – of error theory despite their reluctance to describe themselves as error theorists. We are dealing with powerful medicine here. That said, in this chapter I provide reasons to reject it.

I start by explaining what error theory is. I then examine arguments for it. I then, finally, consider what happens if one adopts error theory.

4.2 What is error theory?

(a) *General comments*: As I expressed in §1.2, moral error theory has a direct analogue with a more familiar idea, namely atheism. Here I refer to traditional atheism directed at traditional versions of Christian (and other monotheistic) thinking. So, in traditional Christianity there is a web of beliefs such as the belief that petitionary prayer can directly and literally help to influence the course of events, the belief that the world and universe were created and designed, and the belief in miracles. These beliefs seem to depend on another belief, a belief we can describe as key. This is the belief in the existence of a personal, intervening, loving God who is omniscient, omnipotent and omnipresent. Other beliefs will be at the core of Christian beliefs, for example the more general belief in the existence of some supernatural realm. But we will take the belief in God to be our example. As it happens, I know many Christians who reject some of the characteristics just given. But our focus is on ethics, and we are using theistic belief only as an example to aid understanding of the moral case.

The belief in the existence of God seems to be a non-negotiable commitment of traditional Christianity. Atheists will often direct their attention at the key belief about the existence of God and provide arguments against it being true. They figure that if they can bring this belief down, then the whole web of other beliefs will be shown to be false also. Of course, they may start by thinking about one of the other beliefs, such as showing that no prayer has ever had a direct and provable effect on anything. But that may not destabilize the core belief, and it is the destabilization of this that is the key task.

One can still talk of God and the magic of prayer after such a belief is shown to be false, but such talk will be fluff, insincere, or non-standard. There are, for example, some Christians who openly and sincerely embrace a sort of 'non-realist' or 'anti-realist' account of Christianity. Talk of God is meaningful and important, they think, but it is not literally true. For atheists, at least the ones we have been discussing, if one says this then one is changing the subject. Belief in a literal God is a non-negotiable commitment of traditional Christianity. Thinking as these non-realist theists think just shows that we have rejected traditional theistic belief. (Whether such believers are right to do so is no concern of ours.)

Atheism is a religious error theory. Moral error theory works in much the same way, and the points I have just sketched – such as 'changing the subject' – carry over to the moral case. So, in essence, moral error theorists claim there is one or a few core, non-negotiable beliefs amongst our everyday moral beliefs. Many other everyday moral beliefs depend on these beliefs for their importance, content or point. But, there is something troublesome about these core beliefs according to error theorists. They turn out to be false in some way and for some reason. Therefore, if these core beliefs are false, then all the other ones look as if they will be false. So, the whole of everyday moral thinking and speech is erroneous.

Let us set things out more strictly. An error theory consists of two main elements.

(A) The claim that there is at least one key, non-negotiable belief or commitment of everyday moral thought and language that is sincerely held and from which all the other everyday moral beliefs find at least part of their importance and point. Typically, these beliefs make some metaphysical claim.

(B) There is something wrong with this belief (and any other key ones) such that it can be seen to be false or unjustified, perhaps crazily so. Therefore, it is not just the case that any key belief is wrong, but also that the whole of moral thinking, as we know it to be or as we imagine it possibly could be, is wrong or unjustified.

(b) *Five notes*: I now make five points about this. The second one is the longest.

(i) To repeat, the end point of an error theory is to target an important belief whose importance lies partly in the fact that if this belief falls, so does the whole of the domain of thought of which it is a part.

(ii) I have expressed error theory in a general way. What sort of non-negotiable moral claims do error theorists typically focus on? They typically do not concentrate too much on beliefs such as 'Killing is wrong', or 'Respecting people is right'. True, these beliefs have widespread acceptance and have content that is fairly general, so we can expect that they will affect many more specific beliefs, such as '*That* killing *over there* is wrong'. But, if we were to show that these example beliefs and others like them are false, it would not seem to do the sort of damage that error theorists wish to do. It seems that morality could survive any argument that showed that 'Killing is wrong' is false. After all, to say that this belief is false would be to say that killing is right. This still leaves us with a moral rule or side-constraint that governs conduct towards ourselves and others. (I admit it seems strange to think that morality could survive such a change, although it seems less strange to say that morality could survive our rejection of beliefs such as 'All killing is wrong' and 'Many cases of killing are wrong'.) Error theorists do not hope to bring about only the downfall of moral beliefs as they are now, in their exact form. Rather, error theorists are hoping to cast serious doubt on any sort of thinking that could reasonably be described as moral. Think again of the analogy with religion. Atheists are not just hoping to prompt traditional theists into *redefining* God. They want to show that any such sincere God-talk is wrong-headed.

So, the sort of beliefs that error theorists focus on have to be of a different order. These beliefs have to be about or have implications for what morality's point is, how we come to form moral judgements, what conditions are necessary for morality's existence, and so on. Such beliefs should probably not specify first-order ethical content. A better example is one that reflects our previous discussions, especially those concerning IMR: 'There are mind-independent moral properties'. In this scenario, if error theorists cast doubt on this claim they are not attacking the belief that some things are wrong and that some others are right, say. Instead they are claiming that even if some killings are thought to be wrong, their wrongness cannot be mind-independently determined. And that may have important knock-on effects for how we view morality. (More on this below.) Indeed, this sort of belief, and variants of it, is a popular target of attack. Some error theorists suspect that many if not all of us routinely think that morality *is* based on the existence of mind-independent moral properties; they think we all get pulled one way or another to IMR. These error theorists think we are wrong to think like this since the idea of mind-independent values makes no sense. Often in this context you will see error theorists attack the belief that 'There are mind-independent moral reasons', 'There are categorical reasons applicable to all people', and an important favourite, 'There are objective prescriptions'. On some readings of properties, prescriptions and the like, these beliefs amount to the same thing: there is normative and evaluative stuff governing what we should do and be and that stuff is independent of all human desire and belief. (This is playing fast and loose with these categories, but here I am concerned only to give a flavour of possible targets.)

At first glance there does seem something strange about focussing on these beliefs. How many people explicitly and commonly think to themselves and express openly their belief in the mind-independence of moral properties? Probably hardly any, and I include philosophers here, at least in their everyday lives. So, if error theorists are to focus on these sorts of belief, they have to extrapolate a fair bit. They often assume, on the basis of things we ordinarily say or do, that we are committed to the sorts of belief I have offered as examples. So, they think that when ordinary people are saying things such as 'Killing is wrong', or '*That* killing is wrong', and when we trace through people's other beliefs and actions, they will be able to show that people are committed to some dubious conception or metaethical claim. This claim may be something of which ordinary people are unaware; it may be only implicit in what they think. But it is there, nonetheless, say error theorists.

I said in my two part characterization of error theory a few paragraphs ago (in (A)) that error theorists typically focus on beliefs that make some metaphysical claim. Furthermore, we often get some focus on the mind-independence of moral properties, in some form or another. So often do these sorts of belief get mentioned, that some writers think that these are the only sorts of belief that error theorists can challenge. Not so. Although it is true that such beliefs are a justifiably common target, error theorists can challenge other ideas. For example, it seems a common assumption (which again requires some extrapolation) that we are free agents and, further, that the purpose and nature of morality depends on our being free. If we really are not free, and all of 'our' actions and thoughts are determined outside of ourselves, then ideas such as praise and blame, punishment and reward seem to have little sense, or at least look radically different from how we routinely conceive them. So, attacking the belief that we are as free as we suppose might be a philosophically fruitful route for error theorists.

Indeed, commentators often construe the structure of error theory more narrowly than I have done, and claim that error theory is a combination of two things: a conceptual claim about what morality is or what it is based on, and an ontological claim (typically, 'No, mind-independent ethical properties *don't* exist') that reveals the error. It is true, as we will see, that the most famous and best forms of error theory are like this. But, it is not obvious that error theorists always have to attack some positive *ontological* claim that people make or are committed to. It may be essential for our conception of morality that we conceive it to be free from bias and social corruption. We may think that no one group in our community has in any way imposed its ideas on morality as a whole and, thus, does not seek to exert power over other groups. Error theorists might try to show these assumptions are false. But in doing so they wouldn't be disproving any ontological claim, or so it seems to me. What is at issue in this example is a socio-historic-political claim. We should, therefore, bear in mind that error theories can come in many guises.

(iii) It is important to understand exactly what error theorists can and cannot say in relation to moral judgements. First of all, they clearly cannot say simply that all moral judgements are false. Why not? Take again the belief 'All killing is wrong'. That seems pretty false; many sorts of killing are seen as morally acceptable, such as killing in self-defence. We could rectify this problem (ordinarily, ignoring error theory), simply by placing a 'not' at the start: 'Not all killing is wrong'. But, for error theorists that would not get anywhere close to solving the problematic nature of the claim that they were trying to point out by saying that the belief was false. Imagine, indeed, a whole society that went around believing things such as 'All killing is right' and 'Every act of charity is wrong'. Every moral judgement in this peculiar and unimaginative, homogenous society would be false. But, again, that would not get to grips with what error theorists typically want to say.

Error theorists may be happy to say that every moral judgement is false, but they wish to add that these judgements could not get to be true even if we fiddled around and negated them or changed the 'all's and 'every's to 'some's. Moral judgements are false because, for example, they assume the existence of properties that cannot exist because such things are silly and bizarre, or because moral thinking is based on a history of corrupt power relations that we choose to forget and ignore. This is why error theorists and other thinkers talk of there being a (supposed) *systematic* error. We could ratchet things up and say that error theorists believe that moral judgements are strongly necessarily false, false no matter how the universe turned out. (An analogy here would be a belief in square circles.) Some error theorists might want to go down this path, but others may not, arguing that all judgements are systematically false only in this universe.

That is one story to tell, and a decent one at that. But, it is worth pausing for a moment. Why run the position in terms of falsity when we are dealing with error theories that point to, or exemplify, an incoherent conceptual assumption? Judgements that seem to point out the existence of such things may appear to be truth-apt, that is they appear to be the sorts of thing that can get to be true or false. Yet, because of the ontological incoherence they may not even be (individually) false. Think again about the claim '*This* is a square circle'. Is that obviously, straightforwardly *false*? It appears as if it is the sort of thing that is truth-apt. But appearances can be deceptive. An alternative is to claim that moral judgements are all meaningless. They are not obviously meaningless in the way 'Take blue snod pring xxxxxx' is meaningless in English. But, because of the conceptual incoherence at their centre, moral judgements are meaningless nevertheless. Just as people can be in error by saying false things, so they can be in error if they take some strings of words to be meaningful (and true), which in fact are nonsense.

I take no view on this matter. My aim is to show only that error theorists have a choice here and that they need to pinpoint exactly what sort of claim they are making about everyday moral judgements.

(iv) However, falsity or the meaningless of beliefs may not be the only thing to think about. When I first set out (A) and (B) I also mentioned 'unjustified'. Most error theorists will aim to show that certain beliefs are false and hence that morality as a whole is erroneous. But it is important to acknowledge that there may be some error theorists who are trying to show only that there is no good evidence for believing the target belief (and perhaps some evidence against doing so), and hence there is no good evidence to believe that morality overall is in good shape. This is enough to expose some error in morality, for many typically do think it is in good shape, and we should be wary of our positive commitments. But, this sort of error theorist thinks that we should not therefore actively and completely disown everyday morality as definitely wrong. Rather, we should just withhold judgement about it.

There are a few writers who take this stance, although it is far more common for error theorists to try to argue outright that morality is false. In terms of our religious analogy, an error theory that talks of a lack of good justification instead of falsity seems to fit most neatly with a type of agnosticism.

(v) It is worth stressing that if we are talking of judgements being true and false, or justified and unjustified, we are talking about judgements that are an attempt to say what the world is like. The error supposedly comes with the fact that the world is not as described. This means that error theory contrasts with noncognitivism, which we consider in detail in Chapter 5. I will not labour the point here, but suffice it to say that whilst both theories are anti-realist, they differ mainly on what they take everyday moral judges and thinkers to be doing. Error theorists are cognitivists, as are traditional realists: everyday moral judgement is aiming to describe the world. Whereas realists think that people can be and often are successful, error theorists deny there is any success. As such they take a negative view of our moral activity. Noncognitivists, as I indicated in §1.2, take a more positive view of moral activity, even if they characterize it differently from how realists do.

(c) *Why be an error theorist?*: There is one final task in this section. We need to discuss the attractions of error theory.

There are anti-realist motivations that, I hope, are by now familiar. Morality seems an odd thing from the point of view of modern science and a naturalistic mindset. But, there is another idea that generally motivates error theorists. Put simply, they are aiming at what they think is true. Error theorists that I know do not take great delight in bringing down whole schools of thought. They typically have simple and honourable motivations. They, like many atheists, are convinced that the belief or beliefs they target are wrong, and that this has important repercussions that we would be unwise to ignore. Some error theorists argue, in addition, that the thought that morality is a good way of living has had terrible consequences for individuals and societies. Saying that people have to act in a certain way and criticizing them if they do not is something that can have detrimental psychological effects, for example. It can lead to worse behaviour than if one had tried to persuade in other terms. But that itself does not seem to be the first motivation. Error theorists are primarily interested in working out what is true and what is false.

4.3   Arguments for error theory

As with moral nonnaturalism and Moore, there is one philosopher we should discuss in connection with error theory. John Mackie's classic statement of his position comes in his 1977 *Ethics: Inventing Right and Wrong*. His error theory – what he calls 'moral scepticism' – is argued for in part 1. (Many philosophers do not read beyond this first part, but Mackie has interesting things to say about normative ethics and applied ethics.) Thus far I have abstracted from Mackie and other thinkers in order to distil the general essence of an error theory. In this section, however, I confine myself to summarizing and commenting on Mackie's two main arguments for error theory. These remain in my view two of the best attacks against the sort of moral belief he considered, although I think both are flawed.

(a) *Mackie's target:* Mackie was against the idea that there existed objective prescriptions, which he claimed were seen by mature moral thinkers to be a cornerstone of modern Western morality. We will discuss in detail later about what objective prescriptions are. For now, we can say this. A prescription is a demand for us to act, something that is stronger than a request or a piece of advice. It is something we must do. Often 'ought' and 'should' are used in this context also, although in everyday English these words can seem weaker than 'must'. This is often used by Mackie in connection with reasons: there is a reason that exists for you to perform this action, and it is not a weak 'merely' suggestive reason either. It is an important reason you should not ignore. Interestingly, although his official target is the belief in certain sorts of prescriptions and reasons, Mackie often talks of the 'objectivity of values' and illustrates his attack with evaluative properties such as kindness and cruelty. So, it is clear he is fairly liberal as to how his target should be characterized. Following on, objectivity can be used to cover a number of ideas; we encountered three in §2.4. Given what else he says Mackie often seems to use objectivity to mean mind-independence and has, I think, as his target what I have called IMR (or something like it), although as we will see, there are some philosophical niceties to work through. However, this should give us enough of an idea of Mackie's worry.

We now need to think about his two main arguments.

(b) *The Argument from Relativity*: Mackie begins with the (surely unarguable) claim that across societies and groups, and even within most societies, there is a variation in moral beliefs, principles and codes. In passing we can note that he sounds a more pessimistic note than some realists may do about the possibility of agreements and convergence. And, although he does not say it, we can also note the variations across individuals. He uses 'principles' and 'codes' a lot in this argument, presumably reflecting the thought that such things will specify the demands on us that supposedly exist.

He then makes his important philosophical move, which amounts to this: it is implausible to claim that this variation is a result of many people failing to grasp the objective moral truth correctly. It is far more plausible to say that people approve and disapprove of certain things *because* they happen to like or dislike doing those things. People do not participate in monogamous relations (his example) because they think it right, rather they think it right because they participate in this way of living. Mackie notes that disagreement can be found in many other areas of human life and thought, such as science or history. But such disputes are based on inadequate evidence or speculative inferences. Mackie thinks them structurally different from moral disputes. We can add that in many cases such disputes are resolved, which is not the case (Mackie thinks) in our moral lives.

Mackie does note a counter to his argument. Although there may be some difference at the specific level, at a more general level, and *contra* to his argument thus far, there is a lot of agreement, such as the thought that it is morally good to be kind to others and to respect people's lives. Even if we do not always act in accordance with these ideals, most people would readily sign up to them. Where we get disagreements are exactly how people should be respected and what it is to be kind: is it kinder to help the old lady struggling with her shopping bags, or kinder not to interfere so as to allow her to retain some dignity? So, the phenomenon that Mackie bases his charge on does not look as strong and concrete as he presents it.

Mackie reckons that this sort of argument on behalf of the 'objectivist' only partly answers his charge. After all, it will mean that only general principles and beliefs are objective. It is clear that the more fine-grained beliefs will be based far more on contingency and societal whim. Indeed, we should note, really, that most beliefs are based on such social-centred particularities, and that recourse to the general does not leave objectivists with much defence.

I think Mackie's first argument is weak, despite the obviously strong worry that the variation in some way does threaten an objectivist – or any realist – position. For a start, Mackie retreats to the thought that general moral principles could be objective, only arguing, surely controversially, that we focus more on specific moral principles and beliefs to guide our actions. Secondly, he introduces a suspect dichotomy, between (supposedly) objective principles and those that are contingent. The key combination that Mackie is ruling out is the idea that a thing cannot exist both contingently and mind-independently. But IMRealists, for example, are defending the view that the values that exist do so mind-independently. It seems possible that a value could depend for its existence on something else which itself is not necessary (and where its causing the value is not necessary), and that 'something else' not be anything to do with human minds. IMRealists could embrace this idea and not threaten their position. One can imagine Mackie trying to work through some details in order to convince us that the combination of contingency and mind-independence when it comes to values is hopeless. But, that will require some philosophical work. Furthermore, to turn our attention to the bigger argument, it is far from obvious that it is more plausible to think that our mores and ways dictate what is right and wrong than the other way around. The persistence of disagreements in ethics can in some cases be put down to inadequate evidence. Perhaps some moral cases in the medical sphere are like this. Also, it may be the case that some people and societies value kindness over respect, say, whilst other societies take the opposite view. If that is so, their respective moral views will clash, but this clash does nothing to show that (supposed) evaluative properties such as kindness and respect are not real and objective. What, however, it may well show is that we should be wary of there being objectively-determined *rankings* of such things.

So, in summary, there is some power to this argument, but this alone cannot put enough stress on the existence of objective prescriptivity. There needs to be a better objection.

(c) *The Argument from Queerness*: Mackie's second argument has attracted more attention than the first. In effect, he argues – or, some would say, just articulates the claim – that objective prescriptivity is a very strange notion, if not simply incoherent. We should not believe in it at all; claims that it exists are just false.

There are three main parts to this. First, Mackie thinks there is the metaphysical part. He says (p. 38 of *Ethics*), 'If there were objective values, then they would be entities or qualities or relations of a very strange sort, utterly different from anything else in the universe'. So, he claims that they would be strange, and part of this strangeness lies in them being unique. The second part is epistemological. If they did exist, how would we find out about them? Presumably, thinks Mackie, through some special faculty of perception or intuition again utterly different from our other ways of knowing things. Mackie goes on to deride the possibility of such a faculty, before noting that there could be a 'companions in guilt' strategy open to the objectivist, whereby other sorts of knowledge are listed as being the same as this characterization of moral knowledge. (Examples include knowledge of inertia, diversity, and causation.) Mackie's response shows his colours. One could try to construct an empiricist account of how we come to know about these things. But, if we cannot, we should ditch these other notions along with any supposed knowledge of objective prescriptions. The third part (occasionally portrayed as a different argument altogether) concerns the relationship between these objective prescriptions and the natural world that, supposedly, they should be related to. So, Mackie says, we often think that something is wrong because it is a certain natural way, because, say, it causes pain. But, what is the nature of this 'because' and how does it come about? Assuming that we allow some supervenient or consequential relation, then how can it be that we have this link? The place of the moral in the natural world seems mysterious. (We met the idea of supervenience in §3.9(c).)

Mackie's main ire is directed at the metaphysical part, and it is this that I concentrate on. Here a number of comments are worth dwelling on. He says that they would be unique. But this itself is no argument. Humans and our consciousness may be unique in the universe, but that does not mean we do not exist. It seems that his real worry is that such things themselves are strange. But why? Mackie argues (p. 40) that they would be like Plato's forms, '...such that knowledge of [them] provides the knower with both a direction and an overriding motive; something's being good both tells the person who knows this to pursue it and makes him pursue it.' That does seem strange. There is a property of an action that, if we know about it, will make us perform that action. We can go further than the Platonic illustration: perhaps there are properties that can magically cause us to act even if we do *not* know about them or acknowledge them. Some people would be prepared to defend the existence of such things against Mackie's worries, but for a moment let us agree that these properties are odd, as well as unique. Why exactly are they odd?

One ready answer is that on this view one could be made to act no matter what one's pre-existing desires and motivations. Simply by noting that a certain course of action was good or kind one would be motivated to act to perform it, even if one was not inclined towards such actions normally, or even if one did not care about being kind in general. It would seem odd that there is such a divorce between values and reasons for action, on the one hand and, on the other, the humans to whom reasons are supposed to speak and for whom values exist. It seems that Mackie is just incredulous that one would wish to combine objectivity (that is, mind-independence) with prescriptivity. How could there be demands without a demander? How can the universe decide what should be valued by humans?

One could challenge this way of looking at things by arguing that Mackie is quite scientistic, that is he is unduly prejudiced towards science. The idea of objectively existing values makes no sense in a scientific worldview, so therefore such things cannot exist. But, where is the argument that science is right?

I will not pursue this worry here although it is a common retort. Instead, I wish to point out a different concern with this argument.

Plato is not the only philosopher Mackie mentions. In the same paragraph I have just quoted he talks of Samuel Clarke's notion of fittingness, which is characterized by Mackie as the idea that somehow there are situations (that is, possible courses of action) that have a demand for such-and-such an action built into them. What is noticeable here is the mismatch between Mackie's presentations of Plato and Clarke. What is 'prescriptivity' supposed to be? Is it meant to refer to the idea that there is a demand to act? (That is Mackie's Clarke.) Or is meant to refer to the idea that there is a demand to act and that *in addition* anyone who knows of this demand is therefore motivated to act in accordance with it? (Mackie's Plato.) What exactly is Mackie's target?

Things get even more confused. So far I have interpreted Mackie's 'objectivity' to be synonymous with 'mind-independence'. There is good exegetical basis for this; it is clearly his standard line. But every so often Mackie says things that makes one wonder if his idea of demands being objective is best characterized in this way. Perhaps a demand for a certain individual can be objective if it has its basis in the ideas, desires and wants of other people and human-created institutions. That would mean that such demands would not be mind-independent, although they would be independent of the individual to whom the demand was directed. Even if Mackie would not accept that this notion partly characterizes his target, it is clearly a viable sense of objectivity.

Combining these two distinctions gives us four meanings of 'objective prescriptivity' that deserve further philosophical reflection. For example, mind-independently existing demands that both demand and motivate seem the most metaphysically extravagant and strange. But, it is not so strange to postulate the existence of demands for an individual (which may or may not motivate, depending on her psychology) where those demands occur and have legitimacy because other people make them. There are still worries with this second idea. Do such demands really have legitimacy, and if so of what sort? But they are not that strange, and are not strange enough to justify the sort of headline-level of importance that error theorists and others have given to Mackie's argument.

Let us pause and ask why we are talking about this. The point is not just that Mackie himself should have been clearer on his target, although he should have been. It is important for *any* error theorist to get their target correct: what exactly is the non-negotiable belief she is attacking? And with that question other points come back into focus. This belief has to be such that morality could not survive in anything like its current form unless this belief was true. In addition, it has to have widespread acceptance, explicit or otherwise. My suspicion – my strong suspicion – is that Mackie's discussion shows that he and other error theorists cannot satisfy all of the necessary desiderata. Beliefs important for morality – such as a belief in the existence of moral demands – may have a number of different interpretations and readings. Once one specifies a potentially worrying moral belief so as to show how odd it is, one may well lose the fact that is has common and widespread acceptance such that it remains as a non-negotiable commitment of morality. For example, Platonic, mind-independent, motivating demands do seem metaphysically queer. But, how many people implicitly or explicitly think that morality is committed to their existence? And how important is such a belief for the continuance of morality in anything like its current form? On the other hand, perhaps plenty of people are happy with the idea that demands exist and that their legitimacy stems from what other people (perhaps what wise people) think. Unfortunately for error theorists, that doesn't seem such a strange view.

So, I think there is a tension in error theory: it has to isolate a moral belief that is false but in doing so it cannot threaten the equally important claim that such a belief has key significance for morality. That is a hard trick to pull off. I do not say that it cannot be done, but it is difficult nevertheless.

For contrast, let us return to traditional Christian theism. Is the same tension at work? Probably not. There are many beliefs about God, and many ways of thinking about Him, not all of which actively appropriate capitalized male pronouns. But for traditional Christianity, the belief that there is a personal loving God with certain attributes such as omniscience is a key non-negotiable belief, and that has widespread acceptance. Indeed, it has 100% acceptance: such a belief seems to be the defining mark of being a traditional Christian believer. The same can be said about belief in witches. Witches are said to be those women that can perform literal magic, can fly on broomsticks, and so on. This is a widespread characterization that seems to many modern minds philosophically problematic. If there were a widespread belief that such women existed, an error theory could be on the cards. One could profess belief in 'white witches' and talk of wise women who heal using herbs, say. But that is really to change the subject.

So, error theories might remain for Gods and witches because there is a clear belief that helps to define the subject matter. Why doesn't the same work in the case of morality? Let me pull out one idea that might have gone by too fast earlier. What is driving my worry about moral error theory is that morality does not seem to have a distinctive belief or small set of beliefs that are non-negotiable, or if it does so they are at such a general level that one when specifies them to as to make them a philosophical target, one loses the sense that they receive widespread acceptance and are as core as one thought they were. In short, everyday moral thinking seems too messy and amorphous. Let me put this another way. Modern Western morality seems pretty much undeniably to have at its core the idea that there exist demands on people to act in certain ways. But, that is not philosophically problematic, or at least not *that* strange. Certain ways of understanding what those demands might be, and how they might exist and how they apply to people, do make such demands seem strange. But, then it is not clear that those specific and strange conceptions of demands are at the core of everyday moral thinking and help to define it. The more we specify the everyday moral claim in order to develop a target ripe for philosophical doubt, the more we may lose the sense that it is a widespread and non-negotiable claim of moral thought.

For further illustration, consider the earlier example about freedom and responsibility. Again it is undeniable that a belief that humans are free to act forms part of the basic picture of our moral thinking, and undeniable that certain views of freedom – that we are the complete and utter author of all of our actions – are philosophically very problematic; we may be psychologically or socially determined in certain ways. But, it is unclear that many people, on reflection, would advocate such an outlandish and immature view of freedom. Indeed, I think they would not. They may commit to more sensible views of freedom, praise and blame that help to sustain moral thinking. But, there are many different views of praise, freedom and the like across many people. Indeed, there is no reason to think that many people will be perfectly consistent across what they believe. So, there seems to be a mess of beliefs here, with no *specific* non-negotiable belief or beliefs at the core that help to define what moral freedom is.

Here ends the main thrust of this section. Let me tie up one loose end, though, and mention another. Part of Mackie's attack was directed at 'intuitionism', a position associated with Moore and others that in the late 1970s was unfashionable. The basic idea was encapsulated by Mackie: that we obtain knowledge of mysterious moral entities through some mysterious process (and that we know when our beliefs are true and justified). Recent work on intuitionism has shown that it is a lot more plausible than this short description suggests, and that the idea of gathering moral knowledge without inference or deduction from other beliefs is quite attractive, and if true is commonplace. I am not going to discuss the niceties of this position in this book. What I will point out is a rule of thumb in metaethics: the more plausible one's moral metaphysics, the more plausible one can make one's moral epistemology. Making the move as we did to show that many core moral views are not as strange as Mackie casts them may well help to defuse his epistemological worries.

Secondly, recall that Mackie worries about supervenience: what is the nature of the 'because' when we say that things are a moral way because they are a natural way? If we think the moral supervenes on the natural, then perhaps we can reduce the former to the latter, or at least wholly understand it in natural terms. We met this before, and we will briefly meet it again in Chapter 6 where I articulate a possible nonnaturalist view of the relation.

For now we should continue with error theory. Imagine that you still like error theory and are not convinced by any of the points I have raised against it. What happens then?

4.4 What if we accept error theory?

There are two topics in this section. First, if one is convinced of error theory, what attitude should one take to everyday moral thought and language in one's life? (I spend most of this section on this.) Secondly, if one is convinced of *moral* error theory, what implications does this have for the rest of one's thought?

(a) *Fictionalism and abolitionism*: What should one do with everyday morality if one is an error theorist? Well, just because one thinks like this, that does not mean that one should give up completely on morality. There is a significant group of thinkers who accept the truth of error theory and then further adopt a position called *fictionalism*. Think about what we tell young children about Santa Claus or the Tooth Fairy. We make up stories about them, make claims about what presents they will bring, ask children to make sure they are good or that their teeth are clean, and so on. As adults we do not believe that any of these claims are literally true: we do not believe in the existence of either Santa or the Tooth Fairy. Yet, we carry on doing this and see nothing wrong in it. In talking of either we are creating and indulging in a fiction. This may be a very useful fiction: it gets children to behave and clean their teeth. It can also bring them great delight; people have an appetite for stories and belief in magical things, after all.

Fictionalists believe that we can say the same about morality. The moral 'overlay' – the demands, values, or whatever is found to be troublesome – can be talked about and used because it is useful to keep it. Just as we can get children to do things by telling them stories that are in their interests, such as cleaning their teeth, so we can get everyone in society to act in ways that are for their, our and others' benefit. Moral talk can help to coordinate desires and interests more readily than other methods. But, to think there literally are objective prescriptions, say, is silly.

Fictionalists presently come in two main camps. The divide turns on niceties regarding communication and exactly what an error theorist can and should believe when she is giving voice to a moral statement. *Assertive fictionalists* think that error theorists can assert and argue that some things are right and demanded of us. It is just that they do not believe in such things when reflective. But, this style of fictionalism faces a major challenge: is it really possible for error theorists to maintain such a mental stance? In this scenario we both believe that there are no demands but, at the same time because we are taken to be asserting, we seem to have to believe in them when we voice our claims. This is worrying, and there are (possibly) two aspects to the worry. First, this seems to distinguish the norms associated with what it is to assert something and what it is to believe something, such that one can assert a claim and not believe it. Secondly, if one distinguishes in this way it may introduce too much psychological strain on someone to expect that they could be making a moral claim in something like a sincere fashion, and yet at some level not believe it. Indeed, such strain may indicate that distinguishing assertion and belief in this way is unwise. From these two points, many ask how useful it would be to retain the fiction that many did not believe.

Non-assertive fictionalists characterize the position of error theorists in society differently to show there is no problem here. As you might expect from the name, these fictionalists try to combine three things: a commitment to error theory, a lack of assertion when moral claims are made, and the idea that effective moral communication and argumentation is still possible. That seems odd: how can I communicate with others and get them to respond to and act on what I have said if I do not believe in the things I am saying? These fictionalists draw attention to the complex social nature of language. For illustration, perhaps Richard is playing a game with his children, and crawls around the floor saying in a gruff voice, 'I'm a bear'. Richard is not really asserting that he is a bear. If he were, he would be mad, and if we believed he were asserting, we would think him mad. Rather, he is pretending to assert he is a bear. On reflection, both we and he know this. Perhaps his children know it also, even if they cannot put it in these words. However, we can take his statement that he is a bear to be of use: he is helping to create the make-believe so that his children can have fun. He adds to this by talking in a gruff voice. Interestingly, for the children to enter into the spirit of the game they have to play along with Richard being a bear. They have to pretend to be scared or that they are riding a bear. If they do not it is no fun anymore. They could even spoil the make-believe by standing there looking unimpressed whilst contradicting his claim to be a bear. (Although doing that can sometimes be fun too; it changes the game.) So, in summary, Richard does not believe he is a bear and is not asserting he is a bear, but he can still communicate and interact with his children to some useful end as if he were a bear.

Non-assertive fictionalists think the same can be true of error theorists in a moral community. Imagine Dawn is an error theorist, and she says to a group of people, 'You shouldn't poke fun at that poor old lady struggling with her shopping bags.' As an error theorist she does not believe that there is a strong, objective 'should' standing behind this statement and that there is some demand she invokes. Dawn also does not believe that there is a demand at the time she makes her statement, hence avoiding the worry about her mental state that dogs assertive fictionalism. However, as the example of Richard's pretence shows, it is possible for others to interact with what she says and for her to argue with them.

This all sounds great. But, there are other concerns. The vision of social communication looks odd. We have a group of people such as Dawn who are taken to be speaking sincerely, but are not. If their systematic insincerity were to be found out, they would not be able to persuade others as they can do so now. Non-assertive fictionalists may not care since all they are trying to do is explain what it is like to be an error theorist in a community where there are likely to be few of them and they will not be found out. Yet, further, this seems quite divorced from the realities of communication and human psychology. When error theorists are communicating with others perhaps they may forget, even temporarily, their commitment to error theory and not have it explicitly before them. They may slip into old ways of thinking and really believe that there are moral demands and values. Talking with others who do believe in such things will encourage this. Even if non-assertive fictionalism is not subject to the psychological worry that afflicts assertive fictionalism, how many error theorists can maintain this stance? Indeed, in addition, some people think that if an error theorist is taken to be asserting by others, then they are asserting, no matter what the internal mental states and commitments the speaker has. Communication and characterization of a speaker can be dependent on both speaker *and* hearer. Is it theoretically plausible to say that fictionalists in this scenario are not asserting? (The debate about this is too complicated for me to detail here. See Further Reading below.) Finally, in the end are not error theorists motivated by truth? If they think that error theory is true, shouldn't they want *everyone* to be error theorists? If so, why bother making moral judgements and persisting in this underhand make-believe? Why not come out and get people to see the error straight off? This stance seems too cynical.

That last thought may not be strictly fair, since, again, fictionalists of both varieties may just be trying to explain how one can be an error theorist in a community where there are few. But, this challenge has some power since it seems as if fictionalists are losing sight of the big picture, which was to be motivated by the truth and, presumably, to share that with others. This leads to a different answer to the question of what we should do if we become error theorists.

Abolitionists explicitly advocate error theory to others, and in doing so try to purge thought and language of those moral elements that are found to be undesirable and erroneous. Not only do abolitionists point out that moral thought is in error, they disagree with fictionalists and argue that it should be jettisoned, either because its retention would not have any positive benefits, or if there are such benefits these are outweighed by the many disadvantages. In passing I have earlier mentioned the sort of thing abolitionists say. This moral overlay causes too much psychological distress to others in making them feel guilty for how they behave, and it can ratchet up the rhetoric to such an extent that opposing sides feel they cannot compromise.

If I were an error theorist, I think I would be an abolitionist. It is a clear position, and honourable in how it wears its philosophical commitment on its sleeve. However, it too faces problems. Some people think it creates too extreme a society: how on earth could we cope without moral thought and language, interwoven as it seems to be in what we do? Indeed, is it possible for abolitionists to jettison the way we think? Presumably they think it is good to compromise and not to make people feel guilty. How can they make that out without threatening their position? They cannot mean that such things are *morally* good. So, what sort of goodness is it? Surely if someone does not feel guilty then this will make them happier, other things being equal. But that idea seems to be a clear part of that classic moral theory, utilitarianism.

There seems to be a major stumbling block here, and it is something that provides some of the motivation for adopting fictionalism. It also echoes a criticism often given of Mackie. Recall that I said that only Part 1 of *Ethics* is devoted to error theory. In the rest of the book Mackie discusses – sincerely – topics in normative ethics and applied ethics. It is a constant worry that Mackie creates a view of morality that looks a lot like our own and that he frequently has to adopt moral terms in which to do this. As an error theorist, then, one has a choice: either one can keep the moral overlay and even encourage others to do so, and in doing so characterize one's internal mental states and language in a way that is both healthy and enables communication with others; or one can be open about one's commitment to error theory and be confident that one can convince others to live and think without moral terms and concepts. For many metaethicists, both options are unattractive.

(b) *Beyond moral error theory*: We have often mentioned demands and reasons. If a moral error theory shows them to be odd things, then what does that mean for the rest of one's beliefs? After all, in front of you right now is a book, in either paper or electronic form. You believe your senses are not faulty, and that everything else is fine. You should believe you are holding a physical book or are by a screen. That 'should' is a normative should: there is some demand on you to have a certain sort of belief. (We are not talking about some 'mechanical should' whereby if your eyes and brain are working properly we would expect you to form certain beliefs.) But, this 'epistemic should' does not seem at all dependent on my desire to form the belief, or anything else about me. Indeed, it does not seem to depend on what anyone else thinks and desires. Whether you like it or not, you really should believe that you are reading at the moment. But, can we really make sense of these objective epistemic prescriptions?

I hope it is clear that there is a nice challenge here for the moral error theorist, at least one who focuses on demands. If correct, error theory seems to prove far too much in a way that should make us challenge whether its advocates are correct to cast doubt on the existence of moral demands in the first place. Indeed, to twist the knife one last time, there are demands and reasons relating to thought and logic. If you are convinced by the arguments of moral error theorists then you should believe in moral error theory. But, if a Mackie-style error theory is right, and if we think it has implications beyond the moral realm that we must face up to, then how do we understand in a non-queer way the idea that we should believe in the error theory itself? Should we believe the conclusion of the error theory even if we are convinced the arguments are correct? What is the status of that 'should'?

4.5   Concluding remarks

In this chapter we first set out what error theory is and can be. We then examined two of the most discussed arguments for Mackie's version. We found both arguments wanting, and in particular voiced a tension that error theorists need to face up to. Having done that, we sketched what people should do about everyday moral thought and language if they become convinced it is erroneous in some regard. Again, we found difficulties.

In the next chapter we will examine another key group of anti-realist positions, namely positions that are noncognitivist. Unlike error theorists, noncognitivists do not think that deep down our moral claims are really attempts to state facts. Rather, something else is going on and, because of this, we cannot accuse people of speaking erroneously. However, as we shall see, noncognitivism also faces problems.

Further Reading

Joyce's (2012) Stanford Encyclopedia entry and Lillehammer (2004) offer good summaries of much of the whole topic.

The key reading for error theory is Mackie (1977). There are two collections that discuss his moral philosophy: Honderich (1985) and Joyce and Kirchin (2010). The latter also discusses error theory beyond Mackie's thought. It also contains Kirchin (2010a) in which I discuss the tension in moral error theory in more detail. The best recent lengthy defence of error theory is Joyce (2001); I take from him the phrase 'non-negotiable', and the bear example is also his (chapter 7). Joyce defends a non-assertive fictionalism. Nolan *et al.* (2005) defend an assertive kind. Garner (2010) is also from the Joyce and Kirchin collection and is the best recent defence of abolitionism. 'Moral overlay' is his phrase. See Olson (2011) also.

There are plenty of other pieces that are worth reading. Cuneo (2007) is a book-length treatment of the thought that Mackie's worries extend to epistemology, whilst Streumer (forthcoming), discusses the implication for belief in the error theory. Shepski (2008) is a great focussed piece on Mackie's Argument from Queerness. Wright (1995) is a classic paper about whether what is left in the place of morality looks an awful lot like morality anyway, and Miller (2003), chapter 6.6 offers commentary. For a good collection of articles on moral intuitionism see Stratton-Lake (2002), and also see Huemer (2006).

5
Noncognitivism

5.1 Introduction

I begin this chapter by reflecting straightaway on the relationship between noncognitivism and error theory.

Like error theory, traditionally noncognitivism is an anti-realist position. The arguments against realism that noncognitivists typically offer are similar to those offered by error theorists. Noncognitivists often point out the incoherence and queerness of moral properties, and the fact that the supposed supervenient relationship between the natural world and the moral world is dubious. However, unlike error theorists, noncognitivists do not seek thereby to convict everyday morality of error. Thus, if they are to look on everyday moral thought and language positively, then they have to offer something different. Error theorists such as Mackie take it that we are describing moral properties, but we are in error because there are no such things. In contrast, and in order to protect the integrity and non-erroneous nature of everyday moral thought, traditionally noncognitivists deny the existence of the presuppositions and commitments that error theorists focus on, or at least downplay their importance and deny that they are widespread and non-negotiable. In the next section we will see how typical noncognitivists characterize everyday moral thought and language.

Before we do that, two notes. First, whilst noncognitivists have traditionally been anti-realists, some noncognitivists, particularly in recent times, have talked more positively about the idea of moral properties and moral judgements being (properly) true and false. Indeed, one can even find defences of the mind-independence of moral properties! That can be confusing. Although I do not give an extended discussion here, the next section ends with some general pointers.

Secondly, a note on noncognitivism's history. I discuss noncognitivism ahistorically, but it is worth noting that noncognitivism held sway for a lot of the twentieth century, with early versions emerging in opposition to Moore. Earlier noncognitivists agreed that Moore was right to challenge naturalism, but did not like the nonnaturalistic moral properties that were assumed to exist instead. So, a new view of moral thought and language was supported, one that tried to encapsulate the difference between the moral and the natural. Until a revival of different forms of realism and Mackie's expression of error theory in the 1970s, noncognitivism was the chief metaethical view. It still has many adherents today, although as with many areas of philosophy, its supporters come in different varieties. Unfortunately we will be able to only sketch these distinct tribes in this book, but see Further Reading to get you started. In reading beyond this book you will see mention of 'emotivism', 'expressivism', 'prescriptivism', and other terms. I briefly define these below, but for the most part I use 'noncognitivism' as a catch-all term and assume it to be something fairly cohesive that can be contrasted with (traditional forms of) realism and other positions.

5.2   What is noncognitivism?

(a) *General comments*: I introduced noncognitivism in §1.2, but a repeat will not hurt. Noncognitivists think a lot about how moral language works. Recall the distinction between the ideas of surface and deep grammar. There is the (surface) grammatical way in which an utterance might work, and the way in which it can be used. These two things can come apart. For example, imagine Laurence is trying to hammer a nail into the wall so he can hang a picture. Unfortunately, he is no good at DIY. He slips and whacks his thumb. 'Aaarrrgghhhh!' cries Laurence as his thumb throbs. Yet, he has to get that picture up, so a few moments later he tries again. But, he does not learn his mistake and slips a second time. 'I've done it again!' he shrieks in dismay. Now, that second phrase functions descriptively, at least on the surface. It refers to a thing – an action in this case – that has occurred for a second time, or some similar idea. In contrast, the first utterance is not a descriptive phrase. 'Aaarrrgghhhh!' does not *describe* anything. Recall from §1.2 our simple test. In order for something to be a description (on the surface) it has to be able to replace p in the sentence 'It is true [or false] that p' and the larger phrase make grammatical sense.

The key thing here is that as I have described the situation Laurence's second utterance is also functioning, perhaps primarily, to express the pain he feels; it may also express his embarrassment and frustration. In other words, it is a more sophisticated version of 'Aaarrrrgghhhh!'. As we might imagine, words and structured utterances can be used in many ways. As well as describing and expressing, we can give commands, such as 'Do your homework', and we can ask questions and can name things, such as when someone is baptised. There are many other things we can do. As we have just seen, the distinctions between the functions of language are often not clear. Laurence may be both expressing frustration *and* describing a second action. (Perhaps he anticipates Carol, his wife, wondering what is going on and, sub-consciously, decides to share information with her about what has just happened.) Similarly, when Carol asks, 'Can I come in to look?' with a certain tone of voice and in a certain context she may be requesting and asking, but she may also be forcefully expressing her wish to come in. If she were to say to Laurence, 'I wouldn't do that if I were you' she may well not be merely describing, although she might be doing that. She could well be offering advice, and perhaps some criticism.

It is clear that we use many different ways of talking and thinking when we are talking and thinking about moral matters. No one can doubt the existence of descriptive ways of morally speaking and thinking, that is descriptive ways of morally speaking 'on the surface'. We often seem to be trying to represent the moral way the world is. But, that should not blind us to the fact that often people express things other than representations when they speak and think: they express demands, pieces of advice, their various desires and wishes, their disgust, their joy, and so on. Noncognitivists wish to argue that these non-descriptive functions are not just part of morality, but in fact give morality its distinctive character and, perhaps therefore, are the prime ways in which moral utterances function. And, it is this that sets noncognitivists apart from error theorists: if we are not really trying to describe some (nonexistent) moral reality, for example, then there is no error for us to be accused of.

The label 'noncognitivism' comes from the fact that desires, prescriptions and the rest are not, strictly, cognitive states of mind. Recall from §1.2 that 'cognitive' refers to states of the mind that can themselves carry knowledge: to cognize is to know or to become aware of something. When we describe something we are (supposedly) becoming aware of something that (supposedly) exists. And, what we say can be correct or incorrect, hence those 'supposedly' qualifiers. In the case of desiring something, we are not becoming aware of something outside of us, as it were. Rather, to express a desire is to express an attitude for something to happen. Similarly, when we issue a demand, we are not becoming aware of something. We are saying that the world should be changed or maintained by someone in a certain way. In the case of belief, we are reporting, or trying to report, that the world *is* a certain way.

Of course, demands, prescriptions, feelings and all the rest can themselves be objects of knowledge. I can note that Lisa has made a demand of me and that Darragh has certain desires. But that is just the same as me reporting that Laurence is in pain. These are descriptions or reports of demands and prescriptions, not expressions of them. This is a key point to understand about noncognitivism. I can report that Lisa has made a demand of me, and Lisa too can report that *she* has made a demand of me, just as Darragh can describe the desires he has. But, Lisa's reporting that she has made a demand of me is radically different, in surface form at least, from her making the demand of me.

I include the qualifier about surface form because, of course, when Lisa says to Darragh with a certain tone of voice and with me in earshot, 'I told SK to look at those essays three weeks ago', this could also function as a (frustrated) reissue of the same demand, not just a reporting of a previously voiced demand. Similarly, Darragh can respond by reporting a desire, 'I wish SK would look at those essays' and in doing so can also voice it. Further, he may be agreeing with Lisa if both utterances are taken as a desire for a certain state of affairs to come about. If they were both really just reporting, it would be odd to say there was any sort of agreement. There would be a coincidence in their two desires, but no significant meeting of them.

So, the key point for noncognitivists is that moral language, in whole or part, functions to do something other than describe aspects of a moral world that supposedly exist. It is worth noting in passing that whilst the messiness and variety of moral language can work in noncognitivism's favour, it does so primarily because one may enter into this discussion thinking that the prime or only function of moral language is to describe. Whilst we can now acknowledge that we can do lots of things with moral utterances, that should not blind us to the fact that we still describe. Indeed, even in cases where we say things such as 'Don't do that!', a realist who is encouraging us to think descriptively might argue that what is really going on with such an exclamation is the fact that the demander thinks she has noted a moral property or prescription that exists in relation to a possible action, and is pointing that fact out to whoever it is she is speaking with. So, although it is important to note the variety of language function, noncognitivists need to do more to motivate their position. We will look at how they do this in §5.3.

Before that, we need to think about the varieties of noncognitivism.

(b) *Some varieties*: Understanding these will give us some perspective on what we have just thought about. For a start, in its history some non-cognitivists have chosen to concentrate on desires, feelings, attitudes, and emotions. (I use 'desire' as a catch-all for now as I have done previously.) Earliest versions of this view were called *emotivism*. It was often termed the 'boo-hooray' theory of ethics. When we say something such as 'Charity-giving is good', what we are really saying is something such as 'Hooray for charity-giving!'. Despite the simplicity of this view, even its early advocates differed as to whether the expression or emoting of some desire was all there was to the moral judgement, or was just the main part of the moral judgement. There was also a difference as to whether the main point of moral language was to express the desires of the speaker, or whether it was to influence the audience into having the same desire. Other and later versions of noncognitivism focussed on prescriptions and demands, leading to the development of *prescriptivism*. According to prescriptivists, when I say 'Charity-giving is good', the only or main thing I am really doing is telling you to give to charity; I prescribe something for you to do, and in the moral sphere that is normally a demand and not just a piece of advice.

A recent version of noncognitivism is called *expressivism*. This has been very important since the 1980s. This view and term are prevalent, so prevalent that 'noncognitivism' and 'expressivism' are treated by some writers as synonyms, although, to repeat, I treat expressivism as a species of noncognitivism. Although expressivism comes in varieties, what unites all expressivisms is an important step. Positions such as emotivism and prescriptivism implicitly or explicitly were discussions of language, even if they mentioned states of mind such as desires and feelings. The emphasis was on moral utterances being types of speech act. If I say a certain moral thing, then the way in which I say it, the tone of voice with which I say it, the context in which it was said, and other things determine what sort of speech act it is: whether it is the expression of a desire or the voicing of a demand.

Now, despite my just using the word 'express', expressivism as understood technically is slightly different from this. Expressivism seeks to integrate language with thought. The emphasis is on the state of mind that one is trying to express or voice; expressivists go to a large amount of effort to get this right. Cognitivists think that moral judgements are attempts to describe the world. For cognitivists, a moral judge is in a state of mind which has – as it is called – a 'mind-to-world' direction of fit. In other words, the world is a certain way, and our minds have to meet it and fit with it if we are to capture it correctly. In this way, the world is the senior partner. In contrast, expressivists think that moral utterances come with states of mind that have 'world-to-mind' directions of fit. Our desires, attitudes, and demands, are a certain way, and the world must change or be changed or be maintained in order to fit with them. So, for example, when I express (rather than report) a desire, such as when I exclaim, 'Strawberries! I want *those* strawberries!', then I want the world to change such that I am given strawberries, and when I say, 'You should give to charity' I want you to do something that (presumably) you are currently not doing. What is nice about expressivist theories is that they tell us what moral utterances convey or what they involve, namely certain states of mind. In contrast, older noncognitivist theories focussed on what we were doing when we made the judgement. In this way, expressivism is similar to a moral realism combined, as it is often combined, with descriptivist accounts of moral judgement. Both positions can confusingly say that a moral judgement expresses something. But whereas descriptivists will say that the state of mind expressed is a representing state, and then typically add some moral realism to the position, expressivists will say that the state of mind that is expressed is something noncognitive that has a world-to-mind direction of fit.

I will continue to use 'noncognitivism' in this book, and often pass over the differences just made, although in the main I will have expressivism in mind, even when, for example, I use 'boo' and 'hooray' to explain certain points.

(c) *Relativism, objectivity, properties, etc.*: Before we look at the reasons for adopting noncognitivism, here is brief word on relativism. With mention of feelings and desires, and the silliness of boos and hoorays, you might be forgiven for thinking that noncognitivism is just extreme relativism by another name: I feel one way, you feel another, and that's that. Yet, that identification is a straightforward mistake. Noncognitivists of all stripes attempt to build on the base of various sorts of attitude one can take towards the (nonmoral) world: feelings, desires, plans, demands and similar such things, things that are not straightforwardly beliefs and representing states. From this it is open to noncognitivists to say that some ways of feeling or some demands are better than others, and mean these distinctions to apply across people and cultures in a way that extreme relativists will deny. Indeed, not only is it open for noncognitivists to do this, pretty much all modern noncognitivists do do this. Even if they make it clear that the materials they work with are noncognitive, modern noncognitivists typically try to build in notions of truth and knowledge into their positions. (So, occasionally you find noncognitivists rejecting the label 'noncognitivism', arguing that they can accommodate a *type of* cognitivist, knowledge-conveying set of utterances.) The embracing of a division between 'better' and 'worse' that has some wide or universal legitimacy marks them as different from extreme relativists. In short, then, they are trying to accommodate a type of objectivity, and often talk in terms of O2 from §2.4.

There are various ways in which they do this. They may speak of attitudes towards other attitudes, where often such things are combined with the idea that the better sort of attitudes find wider acceptance in a society and are longer-lived. (We will meet these ideas again, below.) Noncognitivists might also emphasize the nature and brute feelings that come with joy and pain, say. A huge amount of pain inflicted on someone who does not want it is typically a bad thing. Noncognitivists start from this point, rather than arguing for it. And, attitudes that boo such pain are themselves to be approved of, whereas positive attitudes to such pain are themselves to be booed. Many more complicated philosophical moves are forthcoming in this vicinity, but the general possibility, and initial plausibility, of the move is clear enough. The one thing we might challenge is the idea that we start from certain ideas, such that inflicting pain on people who do not want it is typically bad. Some matters may not be justifiable from outside a certain moral perspective. This issue will crop up again in Chapter 6.

What about moral properties? Every so often I have said that the waters will be muddied and that some anti-realists will try to adopt the language of moral properties. Here we can see how that can happen, although it can happen in one of two main ways. First, formally, all noncognitivisms have, at the core, claims about how moral language works and (sometimes) what sorts of mental state typically accompany, or are expressed by, such language. It is perfectly, logically possible to combine noncognitivistic views about language with a straightforward realist metaphysics. However, although possible, this has not proved very popular in the history of noncognitivism, simply because many noncognitivists were trying to undercut the motivation for straightforward realism by focussing on the way in which moral language could and does work. The idea seemed to be: 'If we can explain moral language and associated activity as being kosher without the need to postulate moral properties, why bother postulating them?'

Second and more intriguingly, if we can talk of better and worse attitudes, and if we can talk of a (sort of) moral knowledge, why not talk of moral properties of a certain sort? This seems like a perfectly acceptable stance to take, although noncognitivists will typically remind readers every so often that they are not straightforward realists. They may talk of '*quasi*-properties' or a sort of soft realism. The idea, however, is often the same. They are aiming to build up the ideas of truth, knowledge and property using traditional anti-realist resources. Some noncognitivists think that realists are too quick to claim all of these ideas and do not work hard enough for them, merely postulating the existence of a moral reality because they think this is the only way to secure ideas such as moral truth, objectivity (in the sense of O2), and knowledge. Some noncognitivists take a different view and wish us to think hard about what everyday moral judgements are like, and see what notions of truth and knowledge fall out from this. Similarly for moral reality: there is no moral reality we are aiming to represent in the way that realists typically mean, but we can talk of properties of a sort. Exactly how this idea is filled in will be up to individual noncognitivists, just as in the case of truth and knowledge. I don't discuss the idea here; it is enough to see the possibility.

One last point under this heading. Occasionally, some noncognitivists claim they can secure the 'everyday' idea that moral judgements are mind-independently true. A simple way of putting the move is as follows. When we ordinarily say, 'What makes cruelty to animals wrong is just that we take it to be wrong', then, according to such noncognitivists, we are making a *first-order* moral claim; we are *not* making a *second-order* metaethical claim. That is, this claim is on exactly the same level as, 'Cruelty to animals is wrong'. And, we can morally deny – in a first-order way – that claim about cruelty and our minds, for what makes cruelty wrong is the cruelty and the pain, not that we take a certain view about such matters. To say otherwise is to say something *morally* objectionable, as if simply changing our view could make cruelty and pain morally fine. And, of course, such noncognitivists will give a noncognitivistic analysis of what is happening, involving disapproval of such a thought.

Now, whilst this proposal is intriguing and has its merits, it seems obvious that in some sense typical noncognitivists – who do not wish to pursue the above logical possibility of combining their view with straightforward realism – have to deny mind-independent moral properties on some level. It is one thing to construct notions of moral truth and reality using traditional non-realist materials such as desire. It is another to create a full-blown sincere account of mind-independent moral properties out of such resources. In my view this sort of move is cheeky at best, but very confusing and confused at worst. (There is more to say here. See Further Reading.)

5.3 Why be a noncognitivist?

This explains what noncognitivism is. Yet, why should anyone be attracted to it? We can take it as read that there are negative reasons for the position: it is not committed to moral properties that are strange, and it is an attempt to make positive sense of what we are doing morally such that we are not convicted of any error. Aside from that, what counts in its favour? Here are three reasons.

(a) *Moral motivation*: Noncognitivism fits nicely with a certain view of moral motivation. I have mentioned this in §1.3, and we will discuss motivation more in Chapter 7. But here is a good place to summarize what is at issue. One key debate in metaethics is the relationship between moral judgement and motivation. Some people, **motivational internalists**, think that some appropriate motivation of some strength accompanies any moral judgement that is made. Indeed, they think that the motivational aspect is *part of* any moral judgement; it is internal to it. Note two things here. First, the motivation only has to be of some strength. It does not have to be the motivation on which we end up trying to act. It may be that when we judge we should give to charity on a particular occasion, we are only weakly motivated and, instead, have other stronger motivations that trump it, such as the desire to spend the money on ourselves. Such examples do not threaten internalism. Secondly, it does not matter whether the judgement is true or false. What matters is that someone makes the judgement and does so sincerely. So, as well as the example of charity-giving, we are also talking of cases where someone says, 'Kicking that small dog for fun would be morally acceptable'. We can still ask of this judgement whether appropriate motivation of some strength follows.

In contrast to internalists, **motivational externalists** believe that any link between a moral judgement and some motivation is a contingent matter; the motivation is external to the judgement. So, it may be that plenty of people do feel motivation of some strength to give to charity when they make the relevant judgement. But, some do not and the fact that they do not in no way threatens the claim that the moral judgements that are made are perfectly fine and legitimate as moral judgements. And, this is the key difference between the two camps. Imagine someone sincerely making a moral utterance that is grammatically perfect with a moral term or two in the right place and said in the right context. If that person feels no appropriate motivation to act on that judgement in some way, then there is a question as to whether it really is a moral judgement, or just a parroting of words or some other option. (This difference I mark with the word 'legitimate', which is here not the same as 'true' or 'justified'.) Internalists believe that such a judgement – or string of words – is not really a legitimate moral judgement, whilst externalists believe it is.

What of noncognitivism and this debate? If you are an internalist then you need to find some way of characterizing moral judgement so it is expressive of motivation in this way. Noncognitivists can seemingly do this easily. Noncognitive mental states such as desires, feelings and demands are intimately tied up with our motivations. Indeed, it seems right to say that 'desire' – even interpreted as a catch-all term for wishes, plans, commitments and the like – *just is* a state of being motivated. And, if I demand that you (or I) do something, then it seems pretty obvious that I want you (or myself) to do it. The general idea that noncognitivists push here is the thought that our moral lives are not just matters of reporting what the world is like. A key feature, perhaps the overriding feature, of our moral lives is that they are practical. Morality is all about people doing stuff and being a certain way. That often involves moving, both literally as well as metaphorically, from where we are to a different place. We need to capture that practical aspect in terms of motivation, desire and demand. Indeed, we should note that this general thought is part of what lies behind the attraction of motivational internalism also.

So: noncognitivists can nicely take account of the practical nature of moral judgement. One can think that morality is practical without being an internalist, of course, although if one is a convinced internalist, then noncognitivism seemingly slots nicely with it. With that said, internalism may well be wrong and some internalists are not noncognitivists. We will sort out these and other links in Chapter 7.

(b) *Moral disagreement*: A second reason for liking noncognitivism, say some, is that it makes sense of moral disagreement. To understand how, consider how extreme relativistic views explain – or fail to explain – disagreement.

Recall that relativistic Helen thinks that matters are at most 'true-for-her' and 'true-for-Edward' and 'true-for-[whoever]'. If talking about judgements of goodness, say, we can rewrite this as 'good-to-Helen', expressing the idea that things are good in (at most) her opinion. Imagine Helen is trying to explain a moral disagreement concerning abortion between Alex and Heather. Alex thinks that abortion is permissible, whilst Heather says it is impermissible. It seems to be a straightforward disagreement. Yet, how can Helen explain it? On her analysis, what Alex really means when we says abortion is permissible is that it is 'permissible-to-Alex'. Similarly, Heather is saying that abortion is 'impermissible-to-Heather'. When we put things like that we can see immediately that there is no disagreement here as Heather's claim is not the opposite of Alex's at all: 'impermissible' and 'permissible' clash, but 'impermissible-to-Helen' fails to clash with 'permissible-to-Alex'. This is often cast as the idea that two disputants end up 'talking past one another' on certain analyses.

Noncognitivists do not fall foul of such a worry, for they do not analyse moral judgements as being reports of anything. Instead, we have clashes between desires and attitudes that people hold. I boo one thing, say, and you hooray it. We are expressing attitudes about the same thing, so according to some there is a real connection, unlike in the relativistic analysis.

However, many people think this does not succeed at all in coping with disagreement. For them, disagreement really is a matter of two people using the same word in the same way, or roughly the same way, and there being a fact of the matter or some property that justifies one person as being correct and the other being incorrect. Talk of 'clashes of attitude' may well be some sort of tension, of course, but it is not disagreement.

Is this the only or best conception of disagreement? Or can noncognitivists seek to extend our notion of what disagreement can be and is, particularly in the evaluative sphere? I'm not sure. One point that noncognitivists can push home is they can nicely explain the long-standing nature of some disputes where there seems an impasse. For there we have fiercely held views that do not change, and the sort of passions that exist are captured by the fact that judgements are expressions of desire and attitudes, rather than matters of cognition. Indeed, if moral judgements were just matters of cognition, one would hope that disagreements might be resolved over time, as more things became known. But, say noncognitivists (and others), when it comes to some moral disputes, this does not seem to happen. So, perhaps we do need to widen our view of what disagreement is.

My own view about this topic, which I provide no argument for here, is that overall there is little to persuade us to adopt noncognitivism or its rivals from thoughts about disagreement. It is more likely that one's metaethical view will influence how one characterizes disagreement and agreement rather than the other way around.

(c) *The natural world again*: Noncognitivists are often thought to give us a nice explanation of the relationship between the moral and the natural. Recall from Chapter 4 Mackie's query as to what the status and nature of the 'because' is when we say that something is wrong because it is a piece of deliberate pain caused for fun. As well as raising negative points against moral realism, noncognitivists give a positive account of what is occurring. They typically explain how the moral is related to the natural by saying that what we have is the natural, nonmoral world, to which people then have attitudes, desires and other reactions. It is these expressed attitudes and desires that give moral 'character' to the world. And, all such expressed attitude can explain why the moral is normative and evaluative: we are expressing demands, suggestions, preferences, commitments, and the like. We can confuse ourselves by talking and thinking descriptively. But, at the base of all of our moral deliberations are certain noncognitive states of mind. Despite my point about mind-independence in §5.2(c), noncognitivists are committed, I think, to saying that something is wrong because of human feelings about and attitudes towards it. There is no real property of wrongness that we can pick out.

This fits with a naturalistic view of the world: for all there is is this world and our reactions to it. It need not be at all a straightforwardly realist position and so it is opposed to the various naturalisms we encountered in Chapter 3. However, like naturalistic reductionist positions noncognitivism seems to have an easy time of explaining moral supervenience: if we have two naturally identical worlds then the moral 'stuff' in both worlds is the same simply because of our reactions. Note the inverted commas: there is literally no moral reality for typical non-cognitivists. But they can and typically do try to secure O2 in some form so as to ward off extreme relativistic thoughts.

So, all three motivations, plus the problems of other positions and the attractiveness of the insight about moral language and thought, add up to a very appealing picture of what our moral lives are like. However, noncognitivism faces problems. I now detail two.

5.4 The Frege-Geach problem

One of the most talked about problems is the Frege-Geach problem. It begins, in official form, in an argument given by P. T. Geach in the 1960s developing ideas from Gottlob Frege. The fundamental worry existed before then, but Geach gave a crystal clear version of it and his name justly attaches to it.

(a) *Explaining the problem*: The problem is simply this. Whether or not moral judgements or utterances are asserted, they do not seem to differ in meaning. However, it appears that noncognitivists *are* committed to meaning changing dependent on whether or not a moral utterance is asserted. So, there is a huge tension. It seems that noncognitivists cannot make sense of everyday moral talk. In particular, much of our everyday pieces of moral reasoning employ and rely on our mixing asserted and unasserted moral utterances, and often the reasoning needs to preserve meaning for the reasoning to work. So, perhaps noncognitivists cannot explain everyday moral reasoning.

That worry, stated baldly and generally, may make little initial sense. We need to explain, amongst other things, what it is for a moral judgement to be asserted. When I say, 'Charity-giving is good' in normal circumstances (for example, I am not acting on the stage), I am asserting something, namely that charity-giving is good. However, there are plenty of contexts where I can utter this phrase and yet not assert it. For example, I can use it as the antecedent in a conditional statement, such as 'If charity-giving is good, then giving to *this* charity is good'. Or I can put forward a disjunction, perhaps as a choice, such as 'Either charity-giving is good or self-help is good'. In these and other such cases, our familiar phrase is embedded, embedded in larger phrases. And in each case, one can voice the larger phrase, perfectly sincerely and normally, and yet not believe *at all* that charity-giving is good. For example, both Dolly, the kind-hearted do-gooder, and Jasper, the mean-spirited charity-sceptic, can voice our conditional. We can imagine Jasper saying, "*If* charity-giving *is* good, then I should give to *this* charity. ... But I'm not going to, because it isn't good!" He isn't asserting that charity-giving is good in the first sentence. We can similarly imagine him putting forward our disjunction.

That can seem a little odd, at first. For we often imagine people speaking colloquially and using the conditional to assert that charity-giving is good, perhaps because of their tone of voice. Be that as it may, if our phrase about charity-giving is embedded it can be voiced perfectly normally and not be asserted at all. One can think of the phrase in the conditional as a supposition or a hypothesis. One is entertaining, as it were, the goodness of charity and then trying out ideas that may follow from it or are linked to it. One can put forward hypotheses without believing them at all. The same is true for the offering of choices: we simply wish to contrast one thing with another, or create a choice for someone, say. Indeed, all of this is true for all sorts of moral phrase. We need to think about the relation between the 'same' phrase when it is asserted and unasserted, when it is unembedded and when it is embedded.

So what? Imagine we have arguments in which people mix asserted and unasserted versions of the 'same' phrase. For example ('MP1' for moral premise 1, etc.):

MP1.   Charity-giving is good.
MP2.   If charity-giving is good, then giving to *this* charity is good.
MC.   Therefore, giving to *this* charity is good.

This seems a perfectly respectable piece of reasoning. It is a piece of modus ponens reasoning, and it has this form: P, if P then Q, therefore Q. Even if people rarely reason in this way explicitly, it surely is a nice formal way of characterizing what many of us do much of the time.

If one interprets matters normally, i.e. not noncognitivistically, there is no problem at all. We can ask how it is that 'charity-giving is good' means the same in both MP1 and MP2, such that we can make a 'connection' between them and, thus, license our conclusion. The answer is that the phrase 'charity-giving is good' is interpreted in a descriptive manner, and we can easily imagine what it would take for this utterance to be true or false; it depends on the moral nature of charity-giving. For a cognitivist, the meaning of a moral term is dependent on its description. 'Charity-giving is good' means the same in both MP1 and MP2, even though it is asserted in one and unasserted in the other. This change does not affect what these phrases describe or even alter whether or not they are descriptions. They simply are descriptions, so the meaning is constant. And, of course, these descriptions can be true or false.

It is important to see that this works in nonmoral cases also. For example, consider:

P1.   Thom writes many articles.
P2.   If Thom writes many articles, he must work very hard.
C.   Therefore, Thom must work very hard.

We have nonmoral phrases, but still the same structure and potentially the same problem: the 'same' phrase is both asserted and unasserted, and there is potentially a worry as to how this mixture can license the conclusion. But, there is no danger of us questioning how we can successfully reason in this way. The important thing to realize is how it is possible. Despite the same phrase being both asserted and unasserted at different points, meaning is preserved across the premises – that is, we assume that this phrase *is* the same – because we assume that it is a description, and thus something that is truth-apt.

From this we can see that noncognitivists are in trouble. For them moral judgements are not descriptions but expressions of attitude. We can clearly construe 'charity-giving as good' in MP1 as the expression of a positive attitude towards charity-giving, for it is asserted. But, when we come to MP2, we cannot assume at all that it is the expression of attitude, for we have an unasserted context. As we have seen (with Dolly and Jasper), one can put forward MP2 and not think charity-giving is good. For the noncognitivist this means one can put forward MP2 and not express any approval of charity-giving. So, our familiar phrase means something different in MP1 and MP2. We thus have the appearance of a valid argument, but in fact a crucial mismatch between our two premises. Because the 'same' phrase is not, in fact, the same phrase, we have no 'linking' between our premises and so the conclusion is not licensed.

This looks very bad. For, not only do we think that the moral example above is a good piece of reasoning, we typically think – so the argument goes – that moral reasoning is of a piece with other sorts of reasoning, such as that involving industrious Thom. But, noncognitivism makes moral reasoning quite different from other sorts of reasoning, and it looks as if we cannot get any sort of reasoning off the ground.

I have focussed on modus ponens arguments, as do many explanations of the problem. However, it is important to realize that this worry is a general one: how can noncognitivists explain the seemingly innocuous and straightforward way in which we use and manipulate the same moral phrase across different sort of contexts when we reason and think?

There are *many* responses that have been offered in answer to that question. Here are a few.

(b) *Some responses*

(i) First, and most radically, noncognitivists can say that if we reject the idea that moral utterances are descriptive and truth-apt, then we are revising what moral utterances are. In which case, if we are revising in this way – as all noncognitivists do – why not simply revise the idea of what moral reasoning is? In short, moral reasoning, if that is what it is called, is radically different from other sorts of reasoning, despite surface appearance.

Well, this is at least consistent. But, many people – most noncognitivists included – think this is too high a price to pay. After all, noncognitivism is radical enough, some think, so it is better if it can explain what happens in our everyday lives without worrying us unduly.

(ii) A second train of thought may be more profitable. We could embrace the idea that we do not have truth-apt parts of our reasoning, in line with one of the core claims of noncognitivism, yet emphasize that this need not mean there is no structure to our thought and no links in it. Another key piece of this proposed solution is to embrace the idea that not only can we express approval and disapproval of actions such as charity-giving, we can express attitudes towards other attitudes. (We saw this in §5.2(c).) For example, I can approve of your approval of charity-giving. And, having made this move, we can approve of combinations of attitudes.

This will help with our piece of modus ponens reasoning, which can be rewritten thus. (Note the inverted commas; philosophers normally pronounce MP1' as "MP1 prime".)

MP1'. Hooray for (giving to charity)
MP2'. Hooray for [Hooray for (giving to charity); Hooray for (giving to *this* charity).]
MC'. Hooray for (giving to *this* charity).

What does this represent? The 'Hooray for' operator now indicates that we are dealing with expressions of approval. (We can similarly introduce 'Boo for'.) In MP2' it is, strictly, not attached to two attitudes, but attached to the combination of two attitudes: one approves of those personalities or 'attitude sets' in which both of these attitudes are found. In essence, the whole piece of 'argumentation' reads thus: you approve of giving to charity, and you approve of those attitude sets that both approve of giving to charity and approve of giving to *this* charity, so you really should approve of giving to *this* charity.

In the normal case, a failure to advance C or MC justifies the claim that the reasoning is illogical or inconsistent. We cannot quite say that in this case, since we are not dealing with normal logic and consistency. But, clearly if you put forward MP1' and MP2' but failed to put forward

MC', then we could say that you had an odd set of attitudes. It would be strange of someone to put forward both MP1' and MP2', and to be indifferent to giving to *this* charity, or even booing it. Or so the train of thought goes.

However, there are problems. One of the most oft-cited is this. In the case where someone fails to have the attitude or desire expressed by MPC', and we criticize them, what are we doing? The claim is that the person has an odd set of attitudes. But what exactly is odd about this reasoning? We might criticize on moral grounds, perhaps, because we think that this person should have a different conclusion. But, indeed, we might be able to say that about *any* attitude which turned out to be (morally) wrong, no matter what the 'reasoning' or sets of attitudes that it was expressed alongside. What we really want to do is to be able to criticize the person logically: no matter what the 'content' of the conclusion, as it were (that is, no matter what the attitude expressed), there are certain types of conclusions that have to be drawn given other things that have been said or asserted and the structure that has been created or applied. But, it seems we are not able to do this on this account. We are not dealing with any sort of logical account now; we do not have the normal notions of consistency and logical structure in play. There are just collections of attitudes, say some critics. It may be odd to hold or express MP1' and MP2' and be indifferent to MC', but it is not logically bad.

This means we have a real gulf between this noncognitivist solution, on the one hand and, on the other, what seems to happen in both the example of industrious Thom and how descriptivist-realists typically characterize moral reasoning. In the latter two cases, the structure is important, and we can criticize logically, even if we agree with the conclusion drawn. Critics say that if we cannot judge and criticize moral reasoning in the way we judge and criticize nonmoral reasoning, then we have revised too radically.

The question of whether it is too radical a solution depends on the delicate question of how much we are prepared to stomach in order to accept some of the strengths that noncognitivism has. (Recall, again, my theme from the Preface concerning strengths and weaknesses of different positions.) Be that as it may, some noncognitivists accept that this is a worry, and devise other solutions.

(iii) So, noncognitivists could revert to our original way of understanding our moral modus ponens argument (MP1, etc., rather than MP1'), keep the format of the argumentation the same, but claim that the individual parts – the antecedent and the consequent, for example, – are now not truth-apt items but are themselves expressions of attitudes or desires, linked by certain logical means, such as the conditional.

A lot has been said about this sort of proposal – I am summarizing a complicated strategy – but the main worry with this is that it does not make sense to say that we have *normal* conditionals and *normal* statements, simply because such things are designed to work and connect with one another only if we have a 'truth-conditional semantics' as we had above in the case of industrious Thom and the moral case interpreted normally. Interpreting the antecedent and consequent as expressed attitudes that are not truth-apt and then assuming that all will be well is pie in the sky, according to many critics.

In short, we set up a dilemma involving this second and third strategy: either the format of the reasoning changes to accommodate the fact that we now have attitudes, or we keep the format the same. The problem with the former is that even if we can make sense of how certain connections work, this is too radical a revision of our reasoning processes. The problem with the latter is that normal reasoning between asserted and unasserted contexts works only if we assume that the things being linked have a truth value.

(iv) This suggests a fourth and final strategy. (A fifth is indicated in Further Reading.) What if we reconceive the idea of truth such that noncognitivists can talk with justification of expressions of some noncognitive state being truth-apt? This strategy seems promising, but is also, ultimately, very problematic.

Thus far we have assumed a correspondence theory of truth: roughly, there is some correspondence between the utterance and the world it is an attempt to represent. This theory of truth is pre-reflectively the most popular, and many philosophers defend it. But, it is not without its troubles. For a start, we need to work out the devilish detail of what the two *relata* are that are supposed to correspond to one another. (Do we pick uttered and written sentences, or the ideas that stand behind them, or what? And what is supposed to be the stuff that is being represented? Metaphysically construed facts or states of affairs? Parts of the world understood naturalistically?) But these details *may* be overcome with some cunning. Far more problematic is the fact that, in the end, we are assuming a correspondence relationship between two very different things. There has to be a certain sort of structure – grammatical, perhaps – to the things that carry truth values, and this structure has to be the same as the structure of reality, something that is not grammatically ordered. How *can* 'truthbearers' such as utterances correspond to reality? When put like that it is easy to see that there may be large problems ahead. This is by no means fatal to the correspondence theory. But it allows us to see why some thinkers are motivated to develop other theories of truth. One prominent family of theories or accounts is labelled 'deflationary' or, by certain thinkers, 'minimalist'. (These two labels are used synonymously by some writers, and used by others to pick out more specific and different types of account.) The main idea is this. The correspondence theory assumes some 'meaty', metaphysical or other connection between what we say (and think) and what there is, and it is this connection that determines truth and falsity. Or, as some people say, it is assumed that there is a special property of truth. Some utterances have it and some lack it. But, why assume that truth is a property? Some thinkers have claimed that the utterances 'the sofa is red' and 'it is true that the sofa is red' have exactly the same content and the same meaning. What would an assumed property of truth add to the latter?

There is much to be said about this sort of view. For our purposes, two points are significant. First, deflationists of various sorts still think that utterances can be true and false. They just have very minimal constraints on what it is for something to be true or false. What are these? Although there are differences, typically deflationists will say something like the following:

(ES) 'p' is true if and only if p

Where 'p' indicates some utterance or sentence, and p indicates something in the world. This is often called the 'Equivalence schema'. To give a concrete example:

'The sofa is red' is true if and only if the sofa is red.

Now, sometimes people claim that deflationists are not attempting to give a *conception* of truth that rivals the conception that correspondence theorists give. For the latter say, for example, that 'p' is true if and only if it corresponds with some part of the world, and then have to give further detail as to what 'corresponds' means. Deflationists do not insert a rival word or phrase instead of the 'corresponds'. Instead, all that deflationists are doing is indicating what it takes for an everyday person to have a decent concept of truth: she will have such a concept if she is prepared to accept all of the noncontroversial instances of ES.

The claim that there is no rival conception of truth offered can be a little confusing. What is true is that some idea of what truth amounts to falls out from this sort of discussion: the conception of truth developed by deflationists is simply that things get to be true if a competent user of some language accepts all noncontroversial instances of ES. The key point deflationists make is that ES gives us a condition – if not *the* condition – of truth.

Secondly, we can pick up on that last point. Some theorists, who may be sympathetic to deflationism in general, wish to add *further* minimal conditions for an utterance to satisfy if it is to be true, such as criteria relating to how to manipulate it logically and grammatically. For example, we might claim that some utterance is true only if it is assumed to be false once a 'not' is inserted at some suitable point. Again, there is much to say under *this* heading. For our purposes, we need not worry about these conditions. We are concerned only with ES.

No matter whether we add a few more conditions to the simple deflationism given, we can see why noncognitivists might wish to adopt it. (Indeed, many modern noncognitivists have done so.) We can categorize an utterance as true and others as false just in case we are prepared to assert it, and where there need not be some metaphysical connection between an utterance that is assumed to be an attempt to describe and some assumed existing property. Instead, assuming in a minimal sense that charity-giving is good, we can say that

(MES) 'Charity-giving is good' is true if and only if charity-giving is good.

Whether we analyse 'charity-giving is good' descriptively, or expressive of some noncognitive state, seems not to matter to its truth value. (I use MES to name this instance of the Equivalence Schema.)

A solution to the Frege-Geach problem now presents itself. If we can secure the idea that individual phrases can be minimally true, even if expressions of attitude, then we can show how meaning can remain constant between asserted and unasserted occurrences of the same phrase, even on a noncognitivist reading.

However, there is a very large worry, one so large that many think it insurmountable. Think back to MES. This gives us the (or a central) condition for what it is for that utterance to be true. The problem is that our moral phrase – 'Charity-giving is good' – is *embedded* in this larger phrase, it is an instance of the phrase when it is *unasserted*. That should set alarm bells ringing. Imagine we are trying to understand our moral modus ponens argument from above. We have to be able to say we know what it takes for our familiar phrase to be true in both MP1 and MP2 so that we can be confident that meaning is preserved and that we have a valid argument. So, we look to MES to see if the truth condition is satisfied. (Imagine us saying, 'Charity-giving is good' is true when.... what?) But, how can we understand MES and how can we understand if and how it applies equally to the phrase in MP1 and MP2? This may seem a strange question to ask. We do, I hope, ordinarily understand MES. What we are asking is whether, as noncognitivists, we can understand it. And, it appears, we cannot. For we need an analysis of how meaning is preserved and understood between asserted and unasserted instances, and between embedded and unembedded contexts. We have a phrase, in inverted commas, and that is true if and only if some thing is the case. But how are we to understand that phrase and the thing referred to? And how, if at all, do they connect with the phrase as it appears in MP1 and MP2? Strictly, there is no reason for us to say that there is a connection between the familiar phrase in MP1, MP2 and MES, for we are mixing asserted and unasserted instances of the phrase, mixing embedded with unembedded contexts. There is no reason for us to imagine that these phrases all mean the same, even if they all look like they mean the same. We have mystery here. In short, we need to solve the Frege-Geach problem *before* we can confidently adopt deflationism about truth.

Again, I encourage the reader to follow up on this worry in the Further Reading, as there are some possible retorts based on what exactly deflationists can assume about truth. But, I conclude our discussion of the Frege-Geach problem here. Despite the sharp nature of the problem, and the worry it still raises for noncognitivists, to my mind another problem bites deeper, partly because of something it points to.

5.5 The moral attitude problem

We have gone along with much of noncognitivist writing and said that moral judgements are to be analysed as an expression of some attitude or desire. Yet, surely more detail is required than this, otherwise noncognitivism may sound hollow or seem thin. What *is* this attitude?

Indeed, it is good to ask this question, for once we do a problem comes into view. Should the attitude or feeling (or whatever) be characterized in a moral way or a nonmoral way?

To see why this question bites and to see the importance of choosing one or other option, imagine first of all what happens if we analyse a judgement merely in terms of some approval. Imagine, again, our old lady struggling with her shopping bags. Oliver helps her. In the normal run of things, we say that we judge Oliver's action to be morally good and, further, kind. We analyse this as some expression of approval. Now, does 'Hooray for Oliver's action!' capture our judgement? It seems not. For argument's sake we can assume that we want something positive involved when we judge things to be morally good and kind. But, first of all, bare approval does not seem to be fine-grained enough to distinguish moral goodness from moral kindness. Just imagine if we had judged the action to be good but not kind. We would still have analysed it in exactly the same way, with nothing in our analysis to capture the difference that undoubtedly exists between our judgements. In fact, any positive sort of moral judgement will be analysed in the same way. So, all the range of moral concepts, such as goodness, kindness, justice, and courage, will get analysed in the same way. That is surely unacceptable. To add to the worry, perhaps *you* think that Oliver's action is morally good and kind, whilst *I* praise him aesthetically: he carries the shopping bags with such verve and style. Our judgements, which are obviously quite differently, get analysed by noncognitivists in the same way. Something has clearly gone wrong.

So, noncognitivists have to identify some way of characterizing attitudes such that they can account for all the divisions we think need to be made. Further, they need to do so without relying on any of our moral concepts. They cannot say, 'The moral judgement of kindness is to be identified as being that judgement that is accompanied by an attitude associated with a feeling that goes along with noting kind things'. That analysis relies on the concept we are trying to analyse, and is viciously circular. They also cannot invoke the idea of there being a moral property to which we have an attitude, for that will lead to the sort of realism that traditional noncognitivists wish to avoid.

Let us return to our question. Perhaps we give a characterization of the attitude in moral (or evaluative) terms. One proposal is to say that there is some distinct moral phenomenology or feeling or attitude that is part of or accompanies all moral judgements, and is not present when we make any other sorts of judgement. Similarly, the claim is that we have distinct feelings when we form judgements that something is kind, and different ones when we judge that something is brave. This is not subject to a worry concerning circularity: the idea is that these feelings occur prior to us forming any concepts. They are the raw materials from which an analysis of our concepts is formed.

Despite there being no worry about circularity, many commentators regard this option as outlandish. For a start, it does not ring true. Even if there are some moral concepts that seem to have some emotional or other sort of distinctive phenomenology, others do not. It may be that kindness could be one sort of concept of this type (although I doubt it), since it may have something to do with ideas that may feel distinctive, such as sympathy and empathy. Yet, when we judge that something is just, it does not appear that the (supposed) attitude that is directed to some situation or action has some distinctive character. Rather we look to whether a certain set of rules has been obeyed and look to the reasons for the action. The attitude that plays a part does not seem that distinctive.

The same sort of comment is made about the moral in general, partly as a result of doubts that certain moral concepts are distinctive. Is it really the case that there is something distinctive about the attitude applied in all and only all moral matters? Many just flatly deny this.

Despite these denials, this has not stopped some people trying. One proposal is to say that moral judgement is to be analysed thus: there are certain norms or rules in play about what we should do morally. If we transgress those rules, we feel guilty and if others transgress them we feel anger. It is the distinctive nature of these emotions – guilt and anger – that gives the moral its distinctive nature. Roughly, if and only if these emotions govern certain rules and norms, then our acceptance of the norms counts as a moral acceptance, and the norms count as moral ones.

There is a lot to say about this proposal. All I do here is express some general scepticism. First, there are all sorts of things that people feel guilty about and angry about for all sorts of reasons, and we would not wish to say in every case that the matter under discussion is a moral one. Sorting out the right sorts of psychology in the right sorts of circumstances, say, may be a lot harder than people think. Secondly, we need also to explain differences between different sorts of moral concepts and judgements. These emotions on their own will not be able to do that, I reckon. We will need to think hard about the details of the norms and rules that are in play. I will come to that later and in Chapter 6.

So, it appears difficult for noncognitivists to say that for every moral concept that we employ in a moral judgement there is a distinctive sort of feeling, and similarly difficult to make the more general claims about the moral generally.

What if noncognitivists characterize the required different sorts of approval and disapproval in a nonmoral manner? Here is discussion of a few options that pick up on some ideas from §5.2(c).

First, they might say that moral approvals and disapprovals are characterized by being stronger than aesthetic or epistemic approvals and disapprovals. But, this is clearly a poor move on its own. (As part of another strategy, it may help.) Here are two reasons why. For a start, sometimes people feel aesthetic or epistemic approvals very strongly. Just think how strong one's approval is when one is very confident that one knows the right answer to a question. Similarly, some people feel aesthetic reactions very strongly. And, anyway, this response on its own does not help us to distinguish the kind from the just, unless a noncognitivist makes a strange suggestion that approvals towards an action we wish to classify as just are always (slightly?) stronger than approvals towards an action we wish to classify as kind.

Here is a second option. We might say that moral approvals involve not just approving of something, but approving of others approving of something. So, we do not just hooray charity-giving, but we hooray all of those people who hooray charity-giving. In this way, moral attitudes are complex.

Yet, this sort of idea does not work, for many reasons. First, it is not so clear that every moral attitude works in this way. The thought that this sort of 'universal approval' is a necessary part of any moral attitude may strike some as controversial. Certainly there are some moral theories that require it, but not others. Secondly, and more importantly, this on its own does nothing to distinguish the kind from the just. Thirdly, and even more importantly, why think that this distinguishes the moral from the aesthetic? Isn't it often the case that when we judge something as beautiful or sublime, we think it very important, if not necessary, that other people think so too? Indeed, lastly, with mention of aesthetic approvals we can see that this analysis may well involve an infinite regress. We are trying to analyse the moral attitude that goes along with, say, charity-giving. But, when we wish to approve of other approvals of charity-giving, presumably we are approving of only moral approvals of charity-giving, not aesthetic approvals. So, we need some analysis of all of *those* moral approvals in order to make our analysis complete. But, that is just what we are trying to do right now. We clearly have a part of our analysis that can be filled in only by going back, and back, and back.

The worry that we cannot sufficiently delineate the moral from the aesthetic crops up again and again. Someone might say that the moral attitude is characterized as being the sort of attitude that remains stable under circumstances and is such that we wish it to remain stable under circumstances. No matter what happens, we think that people should approve of fair things. But, to my mind, we think the same about beautiful art objects and justified beliefs. Indeed, this sort of proposal does nothing to help us in capturing the difference between our judgements of kindness and justice, and surely both are judgements that we would like to be stable under all sorts of circumstances.

Similarly, invoking the idea of higher-order attitudes towards our attitudes need not do the required work here. Just because I hooray my (and your) hooraying, why think that this will be enough to do the required work? The same worries as before just seem as if they will crop up. So, I conclude that merely by focussing on the attitudes themselves, we will not be able to analyse things well. We need to be able to distinguish judgements that something is kind from judgements that something is just, as well as distinguish moral from aesthetic judgements.

However, the first sentence of the previous paragraph should give noncognitivists cause for hope. Why think that such divisions and distinctions have to be drawn solely by using the expressed attitudes? What about the nonmoral, natural features that these attitudes are expressed towards? Perhaps judgements of kindness are to be analysed as different from judgements of justice because of the nonmoral nature of the things approved of? Or, in other words, perhaps the rules and norms that are in play which we accept as governing our judgements can be captured nonmorally, and it is in these nonmoral characterizations that we find the differences we seek.

This is an important move. It brings us back to the patterns of nonmoral, natural features that we discussed and argued against in Chapter 3, with both NN2 and reductionist realism. In the next chapter I return to this idea again and show why noncognitivism fails and why a different sort of position fares somewhat better, despite some weaknesses.

5.6 Concluding remarks

As I have mentioned, noncognitivism was the dominant metaethical position during the middle part of the twentieth century, and therefore much was written in support of it. It still has a number of adherents today. There has been so much written about it, both in support and opposition, that I have barely scratched the surface.

Yet, I hope that I have done enough, both to indicate its strengths and its weaknesses. Its main strength, I believe, is to pull together a number of intuitions that we may have about the moral and, in doing so, it respects the naturalistic urge that many people feel. Its weaknesses are in how to account for reasoning and how to do justice to the way in which we judge. Behind those worries is the more fundamental worry that many of us who have realist inclinations that noncognitivists set their faces against. That takes us to the next chapter.

Further Reading

The best recent introduction to and exploration of noncognitivism is Schroeder (2010). He distinguishes, nicely, the various sorts of noncognitivism, and has in-depth discussions on the Frege-Geach problem, noncognitivism and truth, and other topics. (A few of the points made here I owe to this book.) Miller (2003) chapters 3, 4 and 5 is also very good.

Some classic statements of noncognitivism are Ayer (1946); Stevenson (1944); Blackburn (1984) – chapters 5 and 6 especially, (1993a) and (1998); and Gibbard (1990) and (2003).

As mentioned, there has been much written on the Frege-Geach problem. As well as Schroeder's book, the beginning student should read: Geach (1960) and (1965); Blackburn (1984), chapter 6.2 and (1988), which is also contained in his (1993a), and his (1993b) (from Blackburn I take two of the main solutions to the Frege-Geach problem); Hale (1986), (1993a) and (1993b); Schueler (1988); and van Roojen (1996). There are plenty of good things suggested by Schroeder and Miller also on this specific topic. Dreier (1996) is an excellent (critical) paper on whether the adoption of minimalism about truth can help solve the problem. Readers should note that although some of the classic noncognitivist solutions have focussed on modus ponens arguments, more recent (and technical) discussions have focussed on negation. Again, Schroeder (2010) is a good guide through this material.

Blackburn (1984) is a good place to start to understand theories of truth, as is his (2005). See also Kirkham (1995). But, should noncognitivists embrace minimalism about truth generally, aside from the Frege-Geach problem? See Smith (1994), and then Divers and Miller (1994). Recently a new sort of noncognitivism has appeared, namely hybrid theory. This may help to solve the Frege-Geach problem in a different way. For discussion of this see Ridge (2006) and Schroeder (2009).

There are other problems with noncognitivism. For example, some think it collapses into a type of one person descriptive- or realist-subjectivism. For more on this see Jackson and Pettit (1998), and for criticism see Smith and Stoljar (2003). Street (2011) and Zangwill (1994) are both excellent discussions of mind-independence; they relate to one part of Simon Blackburn's project, but their criticisms generalize I think.

Miller (2003) contains various discussions of how different noncognitivists have dealt with the moral attitude problem. Gibbard (1990) is the source for the idea concerning guilt and anger.

6
Sensibility Theory

6.1 Introduction

We now come to the last major metaethical position I consider. In this chapter I do a number of things. I sort out the two distinctions that have occupied us every so often, that between mind-independence and mind-dependence, and that between naturalism and nonnaturalism. I also think more about shapelessness. Lastly, a number of previously encountered issues crop up again in the form of problems.

These particular tasks are undertaken in service of a general aim, namely the articulation of a position I label 'sensibility theory'. As mentioned previously, I offer some guarded defence of it. Sensibility theory goes by other names, but I refer to it here in this way. No matter how we label it, the position I am interested in defending has the following features: it is realist (or at least, there is some justification in using that label), nonnaturalist, and is a mind-dependent position. From these ideas other things follow, such as the fact that moral utterances can be thought of as being truth-apt.

It is called 'sensibility theory' because much attention is given to the sensibilities – or complex psychologies-cum-personalities-cum-reasoning-capacities – that human beings typically have and which they bring to bear when forming moral judgements. We can talk of sensibilities when forming other such judgements, such as aesthetic ones, although my focus here will be on ethics. Chapter 7 will help to shore up support for this position by talking through two main issues in relation to motivation and judgement.

As well as defending sensibility theory, I indicate problems for it; in the end it does not have my unqualified support. Recall another of this book's themes, the fact that every metaethical position has flaws. It just so happens that I think this position has fewer, less significant flaws than other positions.

I begin by describing the view with reference to a famous analogy, and tie that to the discussion from §2.4 about objectivity and subjectivity. I then link this to a topic discussed in Chapters 3 and 5, namely the idea of multiple realizability. This leads me to summarize where we have got to, both in this chapter and the book, and indicate the attractions of sensibility theory. I then discuss some problems it faces.

6.2   Colours and ethics

(a) *Colours*: A nice way to introduce the details of sensibility theory is to think about colour properties. Properties and phenomena such as colours (and tastes, and sounds) are often contrasted with properties such as lengths and sizes. No matter what humans believe, this table has a certain length and Saturn has a certain size. The labelling and measuring of such things using inches and metres is a human-based activity, but that is another matter. In contrast, colours do not seem like that. Some object is red because of how I and other humans view and respond to it in certain lighting conditions. Indeed, as I have said earlier in this book, creatures different from us may see objects differently from how we see them and, to the best of scientists' knowledge, there is a range of different colour experiences and spectra across the animal kingdom.

From this and other facts a number of philosophical characterizations might be given of colour. Some writers think of colours in line with the account just given of length and size. Colour properties are to be identified with the combinations of (mind-independently existing) microphysical structures of certain objects in certain lighting conditions that react with the microphysical structures of eyes. These combined things together create the phenomenological feel and view of colours, but these feels and responses are themselves *not* the colours. Instead, the colours are to be identified with the microphysical structures of objects and/or the light wavelengths and other things. In short, we give a reductive account of colours.

Some people are sceptical about this first account because they think colours *are* essentially phenomenal; what seems odd about this account is that we get to the reductive analysis only once we have the feels and responses we have. Thus, surely any analysis should mention such phenomenology? Some people think it very important that the coloured way in which objects strike humans should be part of what it is for something to be a colour. Furthermore, the reductive patterns for colour phenomenology are not as straightforward as one might think: standing behind the different colours are light wavelengths, but these do not form the neat patterns one may initially assume, at least according to some colour scientists.

There is a lot more to be said about this first, reductive view of colour, but our focus is on sensibility theory in ethics, and a second view of colour is far more similar to that. This second view puts the phenomenology of colours centre-stage, and we talk explicitly of a response- or mind-dependent account of the colours. A first stab at an account or analysis of colours might go like this:

> Some object is red if and only if it produces the sensation of redness in some observer in some lighting conditions.

A moment's reflection should show us that this is a poor characterization of redness, for two main reasons. First, it suggests that an object is red only at the time it is being observed or responded to. But that seems crazy. Surely we would be uncomfortable saying that my red jumper stops being red because it is hidden away in a drawer. So, we get this sort of improvement.

> Some object is red if and only if it would produce the sensation of redness were some observer to observe it in some lighting conditions.

This is often called a dispositional analysis: something is the way it is *all the time* because it is disposed to do something in certain, important conditions, and we acknowledge that those conditions may not always be in place.

However, there is a second problem. This second version lets in any perception of redness. But, people may and do misperceive colours. Perhaps they see a white object as red because they are looking at it through red glasses or in red light. Perhaps they are colour-blind. So, in various ways philosophers taken with this general view typically include some conditions that mention some normative or evaluative term:

> Some object is red if and only if it would produce the sensation of redness were some normal/standard/best/etc. observer to observe it in normal/standard/best/etc. lighting conditions.

We have, in introducing some explicit reference to better and worse observers and conditions, implicitly said that there are, or there is the possibility of, better and worse responses.

Now note two things thus far. First, in previous formulations we had conditions of correctness, as it were. We are working out what it takes for something to be red. In all cases, we have O2. But, as we go through the formulations, we are developing more acceptable accounts of redness, versions that can cope with the obvious worries I have voiced. Secondly, note that we have redness being explicitly linked to human responses: one cannot get a handle on what redness is without making reference to how redness seems to (human) observers. This ties to S1.

There is one big issue for any theorist to work out. What counts as normal or best or standard in this case? We have a range of responses given by certain sorts of observer and we, for some reason, privilege some set. To put this idea differently, why think that the colour-blind are colour-blind and not just colour-*different*? (We met this question in passing in §2.4.) Why rule that their responses are worse? Why privilege normal daylight rather than red strip lighting?

Here is a brief response. First, there may be no way of conclusively arguing outside of the practice, and outside of the things that are routinely accepted, which sorts of response count as better ones. Things seen under red strip lighting stop certain wavelength bands from resonating with certain objects in certain ways, thus producing a distorted view of the objects for human beings. If you can't understand that *these* things are distortions then there may be no way to argue further with you. It is like arguing with an annoying child: 'But why are *these* sorts of lighting bad?', 'Well, because they give us a different sense of what the object's colour is compared to what it looks like in daylight', 'Yes, I understand that. But why are daylight conditions important and central?', 'Well....they just *are*!'.

The categorization of the colour-blind is slightly different. We might be able to categorize as faulty those people who fail to make *as many* colour distinctions as the norm. We can also, perhaps, categorize as faulty those people who swop certain colours such that contrasts between colours do not seem as bright as they do for other people, thus leading the colour-blind not to notice some things. But, some people labelled as colour-blind do not fall under either of these labels; they just swop colours around. It seems that their sight is regarded as faulty simply because they are in a small minority. But we needn't always defer to large majorities to get such a judgement. In many countries nowadays the estimated 10% of left-handed people are not seen as in some way faulty; they are seen as merely different. Interestingly, this is a change from recent history. In many Western countries one has to go back only 50 or 100 years to find severe cultural and educational prejudices against left-handedness.

I have not argued for this dispositional view of colours, nor will I. It is now time to think about the moral properties, whilst bearing in mind the points just mentioned.

(b) *Ethics*: Like the analysis of colours just given, sensibility theorists put the phenomenology of moral properties centre-stage: what is striking to them is their evaluative and normative nature. And, it is a nature that is linked with humans and our sensibilities: things are valuable for us, and things make demands on us.

So, how far can we push the analogy with colours? A straight translation to the ethical case, using goodness and replacing 'object', gives us this.

> Some action/situation/person is morally good if and only if it would produce the sensation of goodness were some normal/standard/best/ etc. observer to observe it in normal/standard/best/etc. conditions.

The reference to sensation jars a little. Perhaps the term 'response' would be fine for colour, and also for ethics. But 'sensation' brings out another point I want to make. A sensibility theorist is more likely to say the following.

> Some action/situation/person is morally good if and only if a normal/standard/best/etc. observer would judge it to be morally good in normal/standard/best/etc. conditions.

Why? Consider the nature of colour sensations and responses. Whatever we call them, they are immediately and directly caused in us by some combination of object, light and how our eyes work. Now, there is reference to our eyes, but in an important sense we have no control over how our eyes perceive objects. No matter how hard I try, I cannot but fail to see *that* jumper as red assuming that I view it in *these* lighting conditions. On reflection, I may judge that it is not really red, because I worry about the lighting conditions. But, if the lighting conditions and everything else are normal, then the sensation or response is something that simply happens, and in an important sense, it happens *to me.* Similarly, when a chair falls on my head, I feel pain, and the pain happens to me; it is not within my control, ordinarily, not to feel pain. In the colour case I may change the lighting conditions so as to cause a different sensation, but whatever sensation I have, it is something that is caused by factors affecting me and once those factors are in place, I have no control over the sensation. I cannot will things to be different, and my belief that there is no sensation typically has no effect at all.

That is not quite the case when it comes to ethics, and perhaps other sorts of evaluative and normative domain. It is certainly true, of course, that there are immediate and direct ethical responses. When I see Bob offering Jenny some strawberries, I may immediately think of him as being kind, and when I see Alan making fun of Edward's jumper I may be unable initially to think of him as anything but naughty. But, there is the possibility of more than this when it comes to ethics. I may reflect on my judgement and think about whether I was right to judge in this way. Perhaps Bob was not quite as kind as I thought, and perhaps I reckon that Alan's quip was made on the spur of the moment and I should not judge too harshly, as I often do. It is true that in some sense we can also reconsider our colour responses, for we can realize that our sensation was generated in the wrong viewing conditions and so disregard the sensation. But ethics differs from colours in at least two regards: first, it just seems more complex, for there seem to be more considerations for us to go through and reason about when judging our initial response, and secondly, there is the possibility of training ourselves and improving our pattern of responses through reflection (and, of course, we may deteriorate if we get it wrong).

Let me briefly talk though that last point. Perhaps as I feel myself getting angry at Alan on Edward's behalf I catch myself and decide that I am often too quick to judge this sort of action. Sometimes things that I perceive as massive embarrassments are nothing of the sort; I mistake childish play and banter for caustic criticism. I resolve to think differently about this situation and also to think differently about future, similar situations. Over time my initial responses can change as habits of thought, reasoning and confirmation of responses change. Importantly these are matters that I seemingly have some degree of control over.

With that point made, we can summarize thus. Normativity and evaluation can enter into the analyses for colour and ethics that I have concentrated on, for both mention phrases such as 'best response'. However, whereas there is no room for freedom and control in the case of colour sensation, in the ethics case it seems we can give an account – and should give an account – that both allows for the fact that human beings often develop their (immediate) responses consciously and which shows that human beings have some freedom over what concluding response or judgement they give. There is an important sort of normativity involved in the case of moral judgements, then, which is missing in the case of colour judgements. Once immediate sensations are given, in the moral case we can reason about them and from them, decide to discard or embrace them, and use them as bases for criticism of other things. Immediate judgements we have can themselves be changed over time partly by reason-governed judgement. Although we can privilege certain conditions and responses when it comes to colour, all such responses are automatic.

So, although ethics and colour – at least on some accounts – have a lot in common, it is important to recognize the disanalogy just given. This disanalogy is often summarized thus: whereas objects are said to cause certain colour responses, actions and situations are said to *merit* certain moral judgements. What does meriting mean? Whereas there is some freedom in the case of moral judgement, colour sensation is a type of causal or mechanical process – albeit one involving a sophisticated type of machine! We can come to appreciate how the situation should be judged morally, and we have reason-governed freedom to go right or wrong. This aspect is missing from the colour case, for colour responses just happen to us.

Despite these differences, I think it is important not to overplay matters as some writers do. To repeat, we have seen that even in the colour case we seek to prefer some set of response to other sets and build that into the normative and evaluative language used of the account, with its talk of best responses and standard conditions. In both cases we choose to privilege certain responses for certain reasons. Although, another difference may come into view. In the colour case, it seems that we choose certain responses because it is what the majority experience. That sort of option is not always taken in the ethical case and more complex, value-laden reasons might be given. We might choose a response because it is justified, or consistent, or noble, or kind, or whatever.

This brings an important point in view. We are picking responses because those responses themselves have evaluative properties, such as kindness. This reminds us that this position aims for a type of realism. So, this position is not just concerned with responses, it is concerned with responses towards things. A crucial element in sensibility theory is that we are picking out evaluative properties that exist: we are coming to form judgements about them. (This is also part of the idea of meriting: a situation merits or deserves a certain sort of judgement.) Some people can form good and correct judgements, and some do not. Our reasoning and sensing faculties, if they are working in the right way, should be able to point us in the right direction. (I return to this below.)

At this stage some overview would be good. Sensibility theorists think that moral properties exist. They are properties of objects. Yet, in giving a philosophical account of such properties – why they exist and what their nature is – essential reference has to be made to how humans judge these objects. One account of colour properties says that we cannot make sense of what redness is without essential reference to how humans experience the redness of objects. Similarly, we cannot make sense of what goodness or cruelty is without reference to how humans experience the goodness or cruelty of actions and people. But, no one doubts that colours are, in some sense, properties of objects even if reference has to be made to how humans experience these objects. It is not as if colour sensations are completely made up by humans and are fantastical creations: they strike us every day, in ways that we find inescapable. Likewise, even if we can question our judgements and change our pattern of responses somewhat over time, it seems inescapable that humans view the world in moral ways. Indeed, a different sense of objectivity now comes into view, which we can call O4:

> O4: Something (such as an object, or a property), is objective if it consistently features in the experiences of typical, mature human beings and whose reality is hard to ignore.

Sensibility theorists think that moral properties exhibit O4, just as colour properties do.

Let me give a quick example to illustrate a lot of the foregoing. Again, think about our old lady with her (constantly) heavy shopping bags. There are a number of features that constitute that situation. A judge will discern, in a way that is often opaque to her, which features are relevant to making a moral judgement and which not. A number of features then may become more salient than others at various times: the lady is struggling, but we remember that yesterday she did not want any help and appeared to be proud, but today her bags are heavier and she appears in some distress. We imagine various actions, and compare them with previous actions. Certain actions get classed as kind ones, and others as uncaring, and even callous, both by ourselves and by humans collectively. How do such collections of features stimulate or result in those judgements? Well, individuals' judgements will partly reflect the other times they have judged and ways in which they have been shown to judge by others (by family, friends, strangers, and so on). There are also, no doubt various broad patterns of reaction, and some specific responses, that are hard-wired into our biology. From these responses as a group we seek to reason about and justify certain ones. Certain views get reinforced in various ways. Certain patterns of natural features become standard examples of what kindness is and what cruelty is, for example. Throughout, it is how humans view these natural features that helps to determine which moral values and properties attach to which situations, actions and people.

This is only a sketch. There will be more on this in Chapter 7 when I discuss about motivation and judgement. But, I hope it gives us enough for now. Questions hang in the air, however. We need to think about a potential circularity. We need to ask which responses are important in the formulation. Lastly, we need to think how responses and properties are related, and whether the word 'property' is justified. These topics come later. Right now I return to two matters that have occupied us from time to time and show how they relate to sensibility theory: multiple realizability, and the distinctions between mind-dependence and mind-independence, and between naturalism and nonnaturalism.

6.3 Shapelessness and patterns

(a) *Other positions*: Many of the worries with the various forms of naturalism concerned the relationship between natural properties and moral properties. We saw that NN2 is explicitly the view that goodness, say, is multiply realizable by natural properties. We cast doubt on this in §3.8 by posing a dilemma: it either falls into reductionism or nonnaturalism.

The moral attitude problem for noncognitivism, discussed in §5.5, arises from the same general worry, and is worth spending time on. This is because many modern noncognitivists are quite close to sensibility theorists; it seems they 'cook with the same ingredients'. There is human judgement and response to the world. There is the sense that the normative and evaluative are different from the natural. There is some aim to secure O2 and similar matters. But, they end up in a different place: noncognitivists think that we have, at heart, a nonmoral world to which we express attitudes, whilst sensibility theorists conceive of the world morally. Why? And which to choose?

The challenge to noncognitivists was that we want to be able to pick out the moral judgements, and respect and analyse the divisions we make using nonmoral resources, but it appears we cannot. Some non-cognitivists think that we can mark those divisions by assuming a clear distinction between expressed attitude and nonmoral, natural features. Kindness is simply a certain, particular, unique set of natural features, whilst bravery has a different set. We might well find that such properties are analysed using the disjunctive list familiar from the discussions of naturalism. But, are we confident that we will get such an analysis? Will we fully encapsulate evaluative concepts naturalistically, and how confident are we that a division exists between moral, evaluative and normative concepts on the one hand, and naturalistic, nonmoral concepts on the other?

For the sensibility theorist this problem does not arise. Sensibility theorists wish to say that goodness is a real thing, something that can be cognized. It itself is the (nonreducible) pattern in the natural things, it is the property that joins all and only all these things together. This is how we can justify our applications of concepts: all our judgements of elegance go together because we are judging the elegant things, not because we have some positive attitude towards some natural things that form (reduced) elegant sets. In the previous section I emphasized that often we choose certain responses because such responses are justified, or kind, or noble, or whatever. Evaluative and normative properties can be picked out by judges in this account, but this resource is not available to noncognitivists. They just pick out attitudes, it seems, because they are the attitudes of such-and-such a nonmoral type that have been approved of. They approve of norms and rules specified in nonmoral terms.

But, why believe that moral concepts and properties cannot be reduced to natural, nonmoral concepts and properties? Here is a sketch.

(b) *Some justification*: I find it very appealing to think that moral concepts and properties are *irreducibly* complex with respect to natural concepts and properties. This idea can be referred to as 'outrunning': moral concepts outrun any natural characterizations of them. (Hence the horn of the dilemma posed for supporters of NN2: can you keep the '...and so on.'?) We may always come across an action with a set of naturalistic features never before analysed. We might then be unsure of what moral characterization to give of it, precisely because it has a new natural shape. It does not fit our analysis – it is new – and the analysis is all we have to go on to understand which things are and which things are not good, say. This idea is often phrased in another way: the moral is *shapeless* with respect to the natural. There is no natural pattern discernible in the set of natural things grouped as good things, say.

Of course, an obvious worry with this whole approach is that *many* things appear shapeless, and they are things that we would not decide are nonnatural. For example, as an exercise try to codify and analyse the concept of chair in non-chair and non-furniture terms. (It's hard.) Does this mean that chairs are nonnatural things? If it does, then surely something must have gone wrong. So, there must be something extra that moral concepts have or something they lack that sets them apart. Shapelessness may only point us to something. In brief, I think that three things matter here.

First, although supporters of NN1 might mount an argument to say moral properties cause and explain things, when we look hard at the things moral properties cause and explain, they seem to have different causal powers from other things. So, a chair occupies space and can cause me pain if it falls on my head. Kindness does not seem to be like that at all. But, in contrast, a chair cannot motivate me, on its own, whereas the kindness of a possible course of action can. This is not to say that kindness is not real. Rather, this is to question the move from 'satisfies the causal power criterion', to 'is natural': that move is quite some leap. (Think again, also, about God's causal powers.) This matters because we might say that even though the concept of chair and the concept of kindness are both shapeless, there is a difference because the way in which chairs interact with other things we accept as natural is different from the way in which the property of kindness does. Indeed, many, many things might be shapeless with respect to 'underlying' properties. Games, maps, currency and the like might all be subject to this phenomenon. We might say that they are natural in some broad sense. But that would be to disguise both the differences that exist amongst these things and the differences that exist between them and, say, chairs, plants, planets and electric currents in the brain.

However and secondly, are we caught in some hopeless circle? It seemed as if we were trying to explain the special nature of moral concepts (and evaluative and normative concepts) because evaluative and normative concepts are shapeless with respect to the natural. But now we might be tempted to explain why it is that moral concepts are shapeless with respect to the natural, or why it is that their shapelessness marks them as special, by pointing out that such concepts are evaluative and/or normative.

There is something to this charge – and this may be a weakness of the whole approach. (I do not deny that.) However, some things can be said here. As with some noncognitivists (see §5.2(c)), and when thinking about our annoying childish question concerning colour, one can state that we do not start from nowhere. There are certain patterns of appreciation, and ways of finding some things similar to other things, that are basic to what it is to be a human being, living in societies such as ours. The reason why this sort of shapelessness matters when it comes to trying to naturalize the moral is that the evaluative and normative do seem quite different from the natural. We have concepts that are used to mark preferences, demands and all the rest. It seems somewhat essential to human beings that we have these things. And, again, trying to naturalize these things will prove hard.

But, will it? Again, there is always the nagging doubt that we might well be able, in the future, to naturalize our moral concepts, or find natural properties that moral concepts refer to. Let me add one more thought, then.

Perhaps my optimism that the moral is shapeless reflects a prejudice. After all, it may be that we *cannot* go on all day adding new features and reordering existing ones. But, it *seems* as if we could, across many different examples. Just think of those run of examples I have given every so often to think through all of the kind things or the good things. And just recall the case of Peter, Delilah and the door in §3.8(b), where we imagined adding new natural features to the case and thus seeing the moral properties of the resulting overall situation change. The suspicion is that we can keep on adding, subtracting and changing natural features all day and never capture completely what it is wrong to do.

However, recall that I have said only that this *seems* as if it could happen. This brings out something epistemic. (The following idea colours everything to come.) We may, in fact, end up capturing a moral concept in entirely naturalistic terms. But, because it may seem to us that there is the possibility of outrunning occurring (and this thought surely should be in our minds), we can never be *certain* that we have successfully codified the moral in this way. That is, a reduction is not determined to be successful, even if it is, for we may always have some doubt in our minds. Or, in other words, if all we had was some naturalistic reductive analysis – if that is what we thought our moral concepts could be reduced to or what they referred to – then we should always worry about whether it will give out.

Yet, it is obvious that we typically do not have this sort of doubt in our minds. There is a certain level of confidence we have in our everyday use of concepts. We are not constantly worrying that we will not be able to go from one item to the next and worrying that we will not be able to apply concepts fairly faithfully. This is not to say that we will always classify correctly, only that there is some level of confidence we have that our concept-application is, by and large, in decent shape. Thus, there seems some mismatch between the mental state one might expect if we accepted that codification was correct, and what mental state and attitude we have towards our moral concepts and how we use them. Does this prove that the moral is shapeless in the way suggested? No. Moral concepts could be reducible and codifiable in the way envisaged. Indeed, in §3.9 I played with the idea that the boundary between the evaluative and the nonevaluative was not discernible, and even nonexistent. Perhaps I was being overly-optimistic there too. However, the various points put forward in that section and elsewhere in this book stand, I think, as decent considerations against which anyone who has reducing or reforming tendencies has to argue. It makes sense to treat the moral on its own terms: the positive case for codification is not made, and there are some reasons to be sceptical of it.

(c) *Tying up*: And so, in case it wasn't clear from above, the idea that we need the category of the nonnatural falls out quite easily from our thoughts on patterns and shapelessness. Even if every individual morally good action and situation can be captured in natural terms, so long as the goodness overall turns out to be shapeless with respect to the natural (because we are uncertain about future cases), then it itself cannot be a natural category. (This is a repeat of one of the horns of the dilemma that afflicted NN2.) We have to make out another category for it. This gives us nonnaturalism.

Indeed, multiple realizability gives us a connection with the natural world. Nonnatural properties need not ontologically separate entities that have no connection with the natural world. Goodness is realized by certain sets of natural properties. It is just that it cannot be reduced to them. Many theorists hope that this also responds to the issue of supervenience also: for this position is perfectly consistent with it. (We met supervenience in §3.9.) Goodness can be realized across many different sets of natural features. If there is a change in the moral feature then one would expect a change in the natural features. (But, this issue is fraught with challenges, so much so that some realists abandon supervenience and try for a different relation. See the end of Further Reading in Chapter 3.)

Let me tidy matters with two other positions. I do not agree with Mackie's error theoretic conclusion, for reasons explained in Chapter 4. However, I do agree with the general thrust of Mackie's argument from queerness. The types of moral property that are offered by IMRealists, and like-minded theorists, are queer. I find it hard to believe that there are evaluative properties, or prescriptions, or whatever, that are created and continue to exist mind-independently. No doubt some notion of objectivity is part of our everyday conception of what ethics is about. But that, I think, is satisfied by thinking harder about O2, and not by thinking that it can be secured only if we sign up to O1.

I have no further argument than this. In the end, I reckon that if people wish to believe in mind-independent ethical properties then they can. My, Mackie's and others' puzzlement at the postulation of such things is met by them with equal puzzlement as to how we could not believe in these things.

Why all this talk of shapes and patterns? Recall that a few paragraphs ago I spoke of patterns of response towards natural things. The idea is that sets of natural features are grouped together using a concept such as goodness only because humans respond to such sets of natural features in certain ways and, in doing, conceive them to be certain ways. And, to set this apart from noncognitivism, this is a cognitivistic ability; we can even stretch to say that there is a property of goodness shared by all and only all the sets of natural features deemed good.

This all sounds wonderful. Sensibility theorists promise cognition of (seemingly) real properties, with some standards to judge better and worse, and even true and false judgements. We keep evaluation and normativity because such properties are partly created by the creatures that respond to and understand values and reasons. We have some link with the natural world, for moral properties are constituted by patterns of natural objects that people respond to.

In the next section I return us to the two distinctions to cement this optimistic outlook. But, then we turn to look at some problems. It isn't all rosy in the garden.

6.4 Those two distinctions

I introduced two distinctions involved in realist writings: mind-independent and mind-dependent positions, and naturalism and non-naturalism. If we combine them we get four positions. Here are those positions, compared.

(a) *IMR and naturalism*: This is a perfectly possible position, but it introduces a wrinkle, one we have already met. This sort of IMRealist will say that moral properties exist and they do so mind-independently. These properties are also best conceived as being the sort of thing studied by the natural sciences. Recall my discussion from §3.10. Naturalism does not entail IMR simply because natural properties and entities, such as photosynthesis and Saturn, are assumed to exist mind-independently. We have to think about the 'identification link': we say that in some sense moral properties simply are natural properties, or *these* sets of natural properties are *those* moral properties, and it is a mind-independent matter that this is the case. In other words, it is not humans who have decided that moral properties are the natural way they are.

We have talked through the worries associated with IMR already. Our focus now is different: what is the wrinkle? Imagine someone is a thorough-going naturalist, not just a moral naturalist, and they think that every single property, fact and entity has to be explainable in terms of natural science now or in the future, say. Presumably they will have to naturalize the mind-independent fact 'these natural properties constitute (or are to be identified with, or. ...) kindness'. That is, they have to give a naturalized account of what it is for one thing to constitute another thing, or what identity is. That may be a tall order. It is often the difficulty in naturalizing these sorts of facts or claims – these conceptual and metaphysical claims – that create difficulties for naturalizing projects, or which result in people eschewing many such metaphysical claims altogether as obscure falsehoods. The alternative is to naturalize the moral, and other value properties, but refuse to naturalize nonevaluative facts. That stance would require an explanation, and that may also be difficult to give.

(b) *IMR and nonnaturalism*: An advocate of IMR combined with nonnaturalism may give different versions of their theory. First, they may say that the world is full of natural properties, but there are also some other properties, nonnatural properties, that (philosophically) co-exist with them and which exist mind-independently. This sort of position at least does not have to worry about the devilish detail of how it is that nonnatural moral properties interact with natural ones and how they inhabit a natural world. But, this is also a worry. The imagined properties do not really inhabit the, or a, natural world; the term 'co-existence' is telling. We have two distinct and different sorts of thing in the one world. These moral properties with no connection to our everyday properties and scientifically respectable entities inhabit the same space as them, in a broad way of speaking, and their existence is still in no way dependent on humans. To many modern minds, this brings out, or exacerbates, the queerness.

But, there is another way of combining IMR with nonnaturalism. We take the IMR naturalistic position from (a) and give it a nonnaturalistic twist. Natural properties exist mind-independently. Furthermore, it is mind-independently determined that *this* collection of natural properties is what constitutes kindness, for example. But, there is no naturalistic way of spelling out that pattern, nor the fact that *these* natural properties constitute *this* instance of goodness, say. So, we have a non-natural account of kindness.

That solves the problem from the previous paragraph at least, but this position will still be in Mackie's sights. Time to move to our third position, which develops this present idea.

(c) *Mind-dependent nonnaturalism*: I think it best to position sensibility theory here, all things considered. Ignoring other variations, the position I stake out is this. We have a world of natural properties and features, and combinations of them constitute moral properties. But, there is no full naturalistic account available of any moral property. And, this position involves the claim that what helps to determine the moral property of an action is human response, or best human response. Indeed, this is linked to the point about shapelessness. For the moral is shapeless with respect to the natural because of human views of the natural, and there is an assumption in this position that whatever 'human views' amount to, they also cannot be fully naturalized. Part of why they cannot be naturalized and predicted, part of why they are irreducible, is because humans can exercise freedom about which things constitute which moral things. This freedom is subject to constraints and rules – it is reason-governed – but these rules are also essentially normative. Recall my discussion of 'merits' earlier on. A certain object merits a certain response because of how it is. This is contrasted, tellingly, with a causal or semi-causal process. Part of why something gets to be the valuable way it is, is because humans have (freely) reasoned and judged it to be a certain way.

Compare this with the fourth position.

(d) *Mind-dependent naturalism*: This view claims that moral properties exist and do so mind-dependently. On the surface this seems like a straightforward type of position. But, all versions of it face problems, and these can be seen as problems of internal contradiction.

Consider, first, a fully reductive version of colour properties. In that case, we may perhaps have human phenomenology and responses as the 'trigger': if we did not have such responses, we would not care or know about the phenomena that we wish to explain and reduce. But, the feel of the responses and the responses themselves are no part of the explanation, partly because we do not think that colours are the responses. Colours are to be identified with the 'causal base': the structure of our eyes and the microphysical structure of things. There is no reference here to responses or freedom.

Think now about a reductive version of mind-dependent *moral* naturalism. Human judgements and responses are present, but they act only as a trigger for philosophical enquiry, perhaps. In the end we identify the moral properties with, or as, the causal base: the natural features of situations plus certain brain states.

Does this correctly capture the sense of 'mind-dependence' that we have worked with in this book? No. This leads us to see a possible internal contradiction. If we do away with all reference to responses and judgements, and see them just as triggers for analyses, as above, then there is no respect in which we as moral judges are now part of the creation of the moral properties. They are aspects of the world that happen to us. Of course, part of the causal bases will involve the sensory equipment of humans: how we automatically respond to various stimuli and perhaps the implicit, workings of the brain where we go from one stimulus to another. But this does not sit well with how we defined mind-dependence in §2.3. 'Mind-dependence' does not mean 'humans involved', remember. It means that, at the final point, humans can consider a situation or a something and what judgement they have in some way shapes the ethical nature of the thing. And, earlier, I stressed 'judgement' rather than 'sensation'. There is a strong presumption that ethics is a reason-governed activity, one involving normativity and evaluation. It is not a wholly automatic process in which humans are merely sophisticated machines that convert stimuli into sensation. We have freedom, governed by rules and values, to judge in one way or another.

We lose this when we have a reductive account, I think. And, the main point here is that we have a large clash, between the reductive-naturalism and the claim to mind-dependence.

We could, of course, characterize 'mind-dependence' (and mind-independence) differently from how I did in Chapter 2. I think we should resist this. A recharacterization along the lines needed would require us to understand in a quite different way all sorts of moral value, and the idea of a best response, and perhaps also the idea of freedom.

But, note that we do not have to embrace a reductive version of this fourth position. Imagine a mind-dependent version of NN1 instead. This may initially have more promise, but it still will run aground. One of my worries with NN1 was whether we could be confident in putting moral things together with (obvious) natural things in a broadened conception of the natural. Given the emphasis on freedom just given, and the normative notions that may be involved in a mind-dependent analysis of moral properties, I hope we can now see the force of this criticism even more. Photosynthesis and quarks will not receive analyses that depend at all on human freedom, or at least they seem unpromising. So, why group two such disparate sets of things using the label of the natural?

So: the position I stake out seems to look the most promising of these four options. But, as intimated, there are problems.

6.5 Problems and some responses

I discuss three main problems. There are others, but I focus on these three partly because they have attracted a lot of discussion and partly because they interlink nicely. Indeed, arguably one could say that they were aspects of one big problem concerning the relationship between humans, their judgements, and the properties they are supposed to be 'responding' to. One could order these worries differently, I think, but still end up with roughly the same challenge.

(a) *Circularity*: Consider two of the formulations from earlier.

> Some object is red if and only if it would produce the sensation of redness were some normal/standard/best/etc. observer to observe it in normal/standard/best/etc. lighting conditions.

> Some action/situation/person is morally good if and only if a normal/standard/best/etc. observer would judge it to be morally good in normal/standard/best/etc. conditions.

In the first we have 'red' defined partly in terms of a sensation of redness. Although we have two slightly different terms, it still makes sense to ask whether this sort of analysis of what red is is circular and, if it is, whether it is viciously so. We should admit that it is circular, but it need not be viciously so. The point of such an analysis is explicitly to encapsulate the idea that the property of redness or being red essentially depends upon how viewing subjects experience objects and upon their experience of redness. The analysis sets itself against those reductive views introduced earlier. But, the big task of such an account is to fill out what it takes for a response and the conditions to be normal or best. We can offer a few ideas. Perhaps some pragmatic ideas will be important, such as which lighting conditions more often than not result in us being able to make larger numbers of colour discriminations. We may also find some biological weaknesses in the eyes of the colour-blind. I said earlier that there may be no way of justifying 'from without', as it were, why certain factors are important and justify what we do. There may be no way of justifying why certain responses are better, for example. (Recall again our annoying, childish questioning.) Some things only make sense to those people who are already somewhat attuned to what it is to discriminate red things from green things, and why this sort of discrimination is important. This is a key part, I think, of any sensible account of colour and ethics that is analysed along these lines.

This is not to say that there may not be other worries with this account of redness. But – I am here being heroically bold – any difficulties do not crop up with regards to the circularity of the account.

What of the ethical case? Some sensibility theorists wish to say pretty much exactly the same thing. Yes, we define what it is for something to be morally good explicitly in terms of what it is for suitable judges to judge that something is morally good. But, this is the point of the approach. Indeed – a new point – other accounts think that one can analyse what it is for something to be morally good, say, without mentioning any sort of moral or evaluative or normative terms. That may not be circular, of course, but it may be a hopeless chase. For how on earth could one capture the moral and the evaluative and the normative in quite different terms? We have seen this complaint before.

So, let us leave aside circularity as such. I use this as a way to introduce problems – or aspects of the problem – that bite more.

(b) *Which responses? Which judges?*: There is an obvious question or two. Which responses are treated as the correct responses to plug into the analysis? Which judges are the best ones, or the standard ones? This is important, obviously, as we do not want just any responses counting.

First of all I think it very important, again, to remember that the best sort of analysis does not try to justify from without. We have to work from within. This shows us something important, particularly in the case of ethics. There may be no way of specifying what it is to be a good moral judge apart from in moral terms, using moral concepts. As well as the discussions about shapelessness and normativity, recall from §2.5(a) the point that we have a choice: either to describe a good judge in wholly nonmoral terms, or to describe the judge in moral terms, at least in part. There may be no way of understanding what kindness is unless one asks a morally decent judge.

Circularity again rears its head: 'a kind judge to judge which things are kind?'. But let us carry on granting that there is some virtue in this so as to press a different worry. Which judge do we favour? Whose ideas of what counts as a kind and morally decent just count?

This surely is a good challenge, and takes us back to Mackie's Argument from Relativity, perhaps. The phenomenon that Mackie is working with is simply that there are different ideas of what counts as morally good, or kind, or cruel, or whatever. Relativists, also, will lurk in the background. Perhaps sensibility theory – and its close competitor, modern versions of noncognitivism – are showing their true colours. Both say warm words about sophisticated attitudes and responses. Higher-order attitudes, responses towards responses. Stability. Trial and error. Patterns of basic human need, common to all. Justifications that appeal to other humans. And so on. But, in the end, we should recognize that there have always been moral and other differences amongst humans, and there always will be. So, says the relativist, you can define moral terms as you want to with this sort of approach. But in the end, stripped of the bells and whistles, you could be advocating a fairly localized form of relativism: 'something is kind if and only if the people that *we locals* judge to be kind deem it to be kind'.

Note that as well as relativists, IMRealists will be hovering. For, perhaps the only way to ward off the relativist will be to assume that moral properties exist mind-independently: no bias, no localization, universal authority.

Sensibility theorists will want to resist both IMR and relativism. How successful will they – and some modern noncognitivists – be in warding off the latter? That is, how much can they justify O2 with their materials? There is some weakness here. But, as with pretty much all positions, bar IMR, one can be as relativistic as one wants or not dependent on how optimistic one is that there is some measure of agreement across different people and peoples in moral matters. Most people in this world think that pain is bad, and that causing pain to innocents for fun is bad. Similarly, many people have similar ideas of what counts as 'innocence' and 'fun', although things do start to look more varied here. (Issues such as dress codes, prior action, family membership and so on can determine who is innocent of what, and there is cultural variability on this matter.) The more one can play up the universal nature of the human experience and the shared patterns of response, the more likely it will be that this threat of relativism recedes.

The full ambition, then, is to generate grounds for a universal sort of authority amongst humans. (We do not need to worry about Martians.) This may be too ambitious: there is surely enough variation to prick such an ambitious balloon. But, then, extreme relativists may have an equally hard time explaining away as mere coincidence all of those things people agree on. Recall from §2.5(b) that IMRealists press hard the ideas of agreement and convergence.

Just to wrap things up: the circularity worry is soothed the more one can be confident that people from within the moral system have substantial understanding agreement of what constitutes the various moral concepts. But, perhaps another worry bites.

(c) *Realism?*: Every so often I have pushed the idea that this position is realist. And, correspondingly, this position is supposed to be cognitivist and descriptivist. Can it make good on those hopes? This presses if there is some limited relativism involved.

Let us deal with the realism first. For a start, clearly we do not have the thought that we have mind-independent moral properties. In truth, some sensibility theorists may explicitly shun the label 'realism' because it has these connotations. They may often speak of their position as a sort of cognitivism, or as an 'anti-anti-realism'. I am going to put these worries aside here. I think that sensibility theorists can and should talk of properties. What matters is the characterization of what these properties are, and the sort of realism that is being espoused.

A deep problem comes into view. We can construct a dilemma: sensibility theory talk about responses, or judgements. Whatever we call these things, are they responses to properties that exist, or do these responses create the things that exist? One way lies a realism they eschew, the other lies something that looks like it has developed from types of noncognitivism. Although I have refrained from using the label thus far, people often talk of 'projectivism' in this light: we *project* our (noncognitive) responses onto a (nonmoral) world.

Sensibility theorists do not wish to take either view. A few thoughts in defence suggest themselves. First, it depends on who the 'we' is that is responding. The overall position is that humans as a group, in some very complicated, biologically-influenced way, have responded to the world they live in and helped to create patterns of justification and moral understanding, ideas that we now 'inhabit', think with, and use. Any individual person, or group of people, can go wrong since they just fly in the face of such things. We are somewhat programmed to avoid pain, and to rebuke those who cause pain to others without due cause. What counts as due cause has grown up over the years, establishing patterns of justification.

So, any individual response may not create a moral property, it does not bring it into being just like that. But, it is also the case that human responses are part of this story, just as in the case of the redness of objects. The natural world and humans play a roughly equal part of creating the moral phenomenology that we experience as an everyday part of our lives.

Secondly, however, we need to make sure that if this account is to keep its normative and evaluative element in the way I have pushed, we do not translate people's judgements as mere descriptions of how other people have judged: 'something is good if and only if those other people say it is'. That would be, I think, to offer a naturalized account. This is why I stressed the freedom earlier on. People are free to judge and reason differently, or to reason creatively. They have to work within the concepts handed to them, in order to justify and reach their judgements about something, which may often reflect what other people think. It is, of course open to them to use these concepts in new and creative ways, ways that help to change the moral landscape.

A third idea, to stress from earlier. Some sensibility theorists may say that the world is given shape – cognized and assembled into having objects, properties, situations and actions – because of the responses, judgements and conceptual apparatus of human beings. But, it is not as if they simply create these things. There are certain basic raw materials that help to shape things as well. It is a biological fact about humans, as we have evolved, that certain things can cause us pain, both physical and mental, and that such episodes are typically bad. This base fact is not something we have simply imposed on the world. That said, situation can get complex and we can reason about various features, bringing further considerations in. Sometimes causing pain can be wise (to embarrass a bully), or a necessary evil (such as what one might experience during dental treatment).

The responses given to these deep problems are just the start. But, I think there is good reason to be optimistic here. At least some of the strategy is to undercut some of the motivations that drive the challenges, and this undercutting can be both illuminating and justified. With that said, there are still flaws. First, we may have some limited sort of relativism, because of the inclusion of S1. Secondly, some people may not be convinced by what I have said about shapelessness, although I do think the whole matter is moot. Thirdly, this approach begins from and works within moral and evaluative phenomenology, assuming that it is essential that this is made central to any characterization of what the moral is. That is controversial, particularly for a reductionist, say. Lastly, I have based a lot of my characterization of sensibility theory on free will. Is such a thing an illusion? How does *that* fit into the naturalistic world? Whilst it is true that all positions face this sort of challenge, it may bite harder for sensibility theorists. They put the normativity and evaluative nature of moral properties and concepts at the heart of their position, because they both favour mind-dependence and, I think, a sort of nonnaturalism. Some work on expanding on and defending a notion of freedom has been offered by some sensibility theorists, but more needs to be done to convince on this score.

There are flaws I have not had space to discuss. (See Further Reading.) But, overall, I think that sensibility theory looks like a good bet in the metaethical field. In the next chapter, I add a little more in support of the sensibility theorists' cause.

6.6 Concluding remarks

In this chapter I have given a defence, albeit a limited one, of sensibility theory. It has its flaws, but these flaws are easier to deal and live with than the ones facing other positions, at least as far as I am concerned.

As I have just said, we now need to think hard about moral psychology, especially given that we have just been thinking so much about responses and judgements.

Further Reading

D'Arms and Jacobson (2006) is excellent on sensibility theory, and more critical than I have been. See also Miller (2003) chapter 10.

The two chief sensibility theorists are John McDowell and David Wiggins. Some of their chief publications: McDowell (1981), (1983), (1985), and (1987) (all collected in his (1988)); and Wiggins (1988), particular chapters 3 and 5, and his (1993a) and (1993b). Blackburn (1981) forms a debate with the McDowell paper from the same year. Similarly,

Railton (1993a) and (1993b) form a debate with the two papers by Wiggins. McNaughton (1988) is an overall defence of the position. There has been a great deal of critical commentary. See the bibliography of D'Arms and Jacobson above, and also Jacobson (2012). A good piece directed at McDowell (especially his (1985)) is Sosa (2001). Blackburn (1998) chapter 4 is very good on the interplay between some of the main positions I have been considering; he argues for a sort of noncognitivism recall, and the phrase about 'cooking with the same ingredients' is inspired by him. Shapelessness is a big theme in the writings of McDowell, and Blackburn. I discuss shapelessness in my (2010b). I also discuss the issue of thick concepts – evaluative and normative concepts such as kindness and macabre that are more specific than goodness and rightness – in my (ms). This provides a lot of analysis of the various sorts of noncognitivist and other proposals that seek to separate evaluation from nonevaluative conceptual content.

Philosophical discussions of colour spread out aside from metaethics. For a great overview see Maund (2012). See also Boghossian and Velleman (1989).

Recently some people have challenged what we mean by moral supervenience and questioned whether it is true, even assuming naturalism. On this very interesting topic see Sturgeon (2009) and Väyrynen (2009).

7
Moral Motivation

7.1 Introduction

We have spent most of this book thinking about metaphysics in a broad way. My language has focussed on properties and we have asked whether values exist and what they are like if they do. But, note that we have ventured every so often into talk of moral language and its function, and we have occasionally thought about the mental states that accompany language.

It is time to put the psychology of moral judges and agents centre-stage. Moral psychology is of great significance in metaethics. Indeed, in this chapter we will see that on reflection it is as central and important as the metaphysics. It is very plausible to argue, furthermore, that the metaphysical claims make sense only if one thinks hard about psychological claims and integrates the two. After all, perhaps one can speak of evaluative properties only if one situates humans' views in the explanation of why such things exist in the first place and what their nature is. This is clearly the case when it comes to any sort of mind-dependent view of properties. Even if one does not share this view, one has to think hard about how to characterize moral judgements if one thinks that such things play a purely epistemic role, allowing us to pick out the (supposed) mind-independent properties. Similarly, noncognitivists spend a lot of time thinking hard about the nature of the moral mental states that accompany typical moral utterances. And, I have discussed normativity every so often in this book. I have emphasized that some people do not just judge that a moral value or reason exists. They also care about the things they see as having value and are often motivated to act in certain ways because they think that they are subject to demands.

This chapter is fairly conservative in that it does not attempt to break new ground. What I say here is fairly standard and introductory to the main trends in recent material on moral psychology. But even if we stick to this we will see that there is still a lot to be said.

I first think about the relation between making a moral judgement and being motivated to act. Then I think about what moral mental states are or could be.

7.2   Internalism and externalism about moral motivation

In this section we are going to think about the link between making a moral judgement and being motivated to act. I have already introduced the main contours of this debate in §1.3 and §5.3, but a repeat will not hurt.

(a) *Preliminaries*: Here are five introductory notes. First, we are not concerned only with moral judgements that are true. The discussion applies to all judgements, true and false. Indeed, we are not really bothered about the niceties of truth-aptness. We just care about any sort of judgement, utterance, attitude, and the like. Thus, for our purposes a moral judgement is, broadly, a sincere expression of some moral view about some matter, where we remain neutral between expressivist, descriptivist, and other positions.

Second, the debate concerns the link between judgement and motivation to act, not between judgement and action itself. So, for example, I may be motivated right now to act to get some cake, but I am prevented from so acting because my dietician has pinned me to the floor in a vice-like grip. Whether I act may be something outside of my power, but my being motivated to act seems as if it can happen even if there is no external barrier. Third, we are talking of motivation of only some strength, not trying to link judgement with a judge's strongest motivation. So, for example, I might judge that the cake is tasty and I may feel some motivation to eat it. But, my judgement that I should keep to my diet links to a stronger desire, and this second motivation trumps the other one. However, my belief that the cake is tasty is still linked to a motivation to eat it.

Fourth, we are talking about sincere judgements in everyday contexts. So, we are unconcerned with both actors in character and liars, for example, and the moral judgements they (supposedly) make. Fifth and lastly, we are talking about a direct link between a judgement and some appropriate motivation. So, if I think the cake tasty, all sorts of appropriate motivations may follow: to eat it, to save it for later, to give it to someone I love, and so on. But, unless a justificatory story could be told, I presume that if we judge the cake to be tasty a motivation that would not count as appropriate would be a motivation to launch a Third World War. We cannot be precise here and give detailed necessary and sufficient criteria for 'appropriateness of motivation', but we should note that what counts as an appropriate motivation is a matter of both everyday and philosophical judgement.

Cakes are lovely. But let's focus on moral matters for a while. Some people think there is a conceptual or internal relation between making a moral judgement and being motivated to some degree to act in some appropriate way on that judgement. These people are called internalists about motivation, or just 'internalists'. They think that if someone makes a moral judgement then as a conceptual matter, as a matter of necessity, appropriate motivation of some strength will follow. In fact, internalists may say, and some often do say, that it is not as if we have *two* things that are linked necessarily. Rather, appropriate motivation is built into the whole idea of what it is to make a moral judgement: we have one thing, not two. But that is to get a little ahead of ourselves. The central idea is that there is some internal or conceptual connection.

There is a lot to be said for internalism, at least initially. In my opening comments I mentioned that when we reflect on moral thought we want to put the idea of caring in the spotlight: being motivated to act in appropriate ways is perhaps one of the key things that marks moral and other evaluative judgements as different from other sorts of judgement. So, it makes sense to think that moral judgements – all proper moral judgements – have to have some link with some appropriate motivation. Many people through the years have thought this. Just think of the many times when you may have judged something to be morally wrong, and how important you *felt* it was to prevent it. Or think of times when you have judged someone in distress and have been moved to do something kind for them. These and many other cases provide some support for internalism. Although note that not all internalists wish to base what they say on feelings. Sometimes I can be motivated to do something – such as to walk in the garden, or make a drink – and not feel anything much at all, there may be no distinct phenomenology. So, internalists often say that so long as one is disposed to act in a certain way, that is enough.

Despite the general attraction of internalism, externalists deny the specific claim of internalists. Appropriate motivation of some strength may accompany moral judgements. Indeed, it may do so often. But why think it has to be a conceptual constraint on making a moral judgement?

Before we proceed into this debate, a note on 'internalism' and 'externalism'. These terms are confusingly used to indicate a few different distinctions in philosophy. For example, some internalists about *justification* think, roughly, that in order for a person to count as knowing some claim C, that person has to know or have some understanding of why and how she is justified in believing C. Externalists about justification deny that this is a condition of knowledge. Other conditions have to be met, such as the belief being true, but not this one. Also, some internalists about *reasons* think, roughly, that something can be a reason for someone to do something only if it connects with or embodies in some way her commitments and desires. Externalists about reasons think there can be reasons for someone to do something no matter what her commitments. Our distinction here is different from both of these distinctions, although it has connections with the second.

Having contrasted these distinctions with that which we are interested in – internalism and externalism about *motivation* – let us think about the disagreement. Recall that there is some initial attraction to internalism, but once we start to think about some key examples, perhaps that attraction becomes less strong and externalism seems to look like the correct view.

In order to understand the examples we are really interested in, let's dispense with some examples seen as peripheral to the debate. A brief return to actors would be a good start. Imagine an actor in a play. In character he says, in a ham-fisted fashion, 'Let us give charity to this poor, miserable orphan, for giving to charity is morally good!'. Now, even if the *character* is then *portrayed* as feeling some motivation, the actor doesn't feel the motivation: he is just acting it out. What about his lines? Can we say that he is making a moral judgement? Well, what he says is grammatically fine, and it has a moral term in some suitable place. It *looks* like a moral judgement. But, perhaps it isn't, because it isn't been said sincerely. Even if the judgement is true, it would not be a *legitimate* moral judgement. (I introduced 'legitimate' in §5.3) The judgement or utterance has some of the hallmarks of a moral judgement, but it doesn't fulfil all of the criteria. For a start, even if the judgement itself may be true, it is said within a fictional setting and that may make us call into question its truth. And, furthermore, another condition that is not fulfilled is that no (proper) motivation comes forth, and so on this basis alone internalists will say this isn't a legitimate moral judgement, even if it *is* true.

'Legitimacy' may be hard to define in this debate. We are looking at judgements that have to be sincere, that have to aim at truth (or expression of some acceptable attitude, say, if one is a noncognitivist) and a few other things. The debate between internalists and externalists concerns whether 'necessarily motivates' is another condition moral judgements have to fulfil in order to be legitimate.

There are many other examples in this neck of the woods. Think about parrots. Imagine a parrot squawking, 'Giving to charity is morally good!' Perhaps it says this only because its owner is a philosopher or a charity worker. The parrot is different from the actor because it does not conceive of itself as acting a part. Also, crucially, it does not really know or understand what it is saying. It is, literally, parroting some words. Would we say that the parrot was giving a moral judgement? Almost certainly not, even though it, like the actor, is saying a perfectly formed English sentence that uses a moral term at some appropriate point.

Other sorts of cases can help us home in on what is going on. Imagine Sam is suffering from terrible depression. Much or all that he values (or, perhaps, only seemingly 'values') appears colourless to him, bleak, and at a distance. He can see and judge that he should give to charity, but feels no motivation to do so. Further, he is being sincere and is not acting, and unlike the parrot he understands exactly what he is saying.

In our previous cases we could pinpoint exactly the odd thing that was occurring. We had some pretence, or a lack of human understanding and consciousness. Here neither applies, and yet we have a judgement and no motivation. And, the judgement appears to be a legitimate one. We can drag ourselves back to the main debate and declare that we seemingly have a clear counter-example to internalism prior to any focussed criticism.

Perhaps we do. We will return to this example later. For now, however, we can note that internalists typically add a crucial clause to their claim. They are arguing not just for a conceptual connection between making a moral judgement and some appropriate motivation. If they did it would be easy to dream up counter-examples. Internalists are arguing instead that there is such a link only amongst those people who are *practically rational* (and who are also sincere). The example of the depressed person is not an example of a practically rational agent. So, it cannot count as a counter-example.

Can internalists say this? They can. But, only if they are able to rule that potential counter-examples such as Sam are not appropriate to the debate. In order to do this they have to provide good reasons, reasons that are not conjured up simply to defend internalism. Perhaps they can do that. We can rule out the actor because he is pretending and so not making a sincere judgement. Similarly, the parrot has no understanding of what it says. And Sam is *generally* depressed. By definition his whole psychology, and not just his moral psychology, is not working as it should. Internalists are concerned with agents whose psychology is working fine, and they argue that in such cases there is a conceptual link between moral judgement and motivation. So, although this paragraph started negatively, in fact we can see things slightly differently. A *strong internalist* will make the familiar claim about conceptual connection about all sorts of human beings, Sam and others. A *weak internalist* will make their claim only about agents who are practically rational, not to be cynical because they need to rule out Sam and others, but because they think that motivation and judgement are linked only when practical rationality is in play. With that said, however, we will return to Sam later. Weak internalists – and this is who I will talk about from now on with 'internalism' – still have to be confident that they can justify us ignoring Sam and other examples.

(b) *The debate itself*: With all of these preliminary comments made, I now turn to consider the debate between internalists and externalists itself. Here is another example. Gerald is a human being, not a parrot. He is sincere in his moral judgements and is not depressed. His psychology and his ability to will are as normal as you like. But, like Sam he has heard of various catastrophes, say, and thinks it is morally right, both in general and for himself, to give to charity. Yet, he feels absolutely no motivation whatsoever to give. (So, to underline a point from earlier, it is not just that he feels some motivation to help that is outweighed by some stronger motivation to do something else. He feels no motivation at all.) It *seems* that Gerald is a clear counter-example to internalism. Externalists think that Gerald's moral judgement is perfectly legitimate, whilst internalists do not. What can internalists possibly do to persuade us that they are correct?

In recent times many people have been thinking hard about a supposed phenomenon, one that can be illustrated by thinking about Janice and Dave. (I return to Gerald shortly.) Janice and Dave are discussing whether they should give to a particular charity. Janice is convinced that giving to this charity is morally good and is motivated to act appropriately. Dave is not so sure. It is not that he is a morally bad person, but rather he has doubts about how effectively the charity will use his money. Janice and Dave discuss matters and Janice manages to convince Dave that the charity will use his money effectively: it won't all be used to bolster the expense accounts of charity executives. Dave thus changes his mind – that is he arrives at a new judgement – and decides that giving to charity would now be morally good. Furthermore, he now feels motivation of some strength to give to charity. Some internalists think this illustrates a striking fact, namely that a change of judgement normally brings with it a change in motivation. It might or might not be the statistically predominant phenomenon. The key thing is that it happens a lot and seems important.

So what? Is it a mere coincidence that a change in judgement is accompanied by a change in motivation, every time? That hardly seems likely. Could it be something that is to be explained only 'locally', based on the psychologies of individual judges at particular times, as externalists typically suggest? Perhaps, but given that it both seems to happen so often and seems to be a significant part of our moral lives, then we may need to go beyond only local explanations.

How do internalists explain things? Given that they assume an internal connection between judgement and motivation, then it is easy for them to assert that one would expect a change in judgement to result in a change in motivation. In fact, the examples we considered earlier, where there is a lack of connection, are precisely the types of example that make trouble for internalists and which they see as abnormal. In contrast, the case of Dave fits – and exemplifies – their theory perfectly.

What about externalists? Well, they have a number of options. They can deny that there is this phenomenon. That does not seem like a promising strategy, since the phenomenon does seem fairly common. Secondly, they can admit that this phenomenon exists and even admit that it is common. But, they can also point out that they argue only against the necessity of the connection between judgement and motivation. They can allow that on occasion there can be a connection, and even that it is somewhat common. The explanation, then, as to why motivation can track changes in judgement has to do with the individual psychologies of the judges who judge. It has nothing to do with the nature of moral judgement itself and the conceptual constraints we put on it. The debate between internalists and externalists then seems to focus on how normal the case of Dave is and whether the sorts of case that internalists dismissed above really are abnormal. I say more on this later.

There is, lastly, a third interesting move for externalists, but one which may prove their undoing. Imagine that externalists agree that Dave's case is normal: a case where someone with normal-willing ability and psychology makes a straightforward judgement which leads to a change in motivation. In which case, externalists have to explain how there can be a reliable connection between judgement and motivation without committing themselves to internalism. How can they do that? The key move is for them, and us, to think hard about the character of the motivation that is linked to the judgement of something being morally good.

Up until now we have been dealing exclusively with judgements that something is morally good and appropriate motivations to do that particular something. That is the key internalist claim. The move externalists can make is to say that when judgements of the form 'this [something] is morally good' are made, a necessary connection does form. But, it is not the one that internalists insist upon. It is between this judgement and some standing motivation to do the morally good, or to bring about goodness, or some other wording. That is, we have a commitment to grand moral values. We see that this judgement involves goodness. We have a motivation to bring about goodness, and then this gets translated into some specific motivation to do the thing in question. If you like, we could say that under this explanation, externalists envisage judges in the normal case to be motivated to do The Morally Good, and they then cast around to see which things are good. In contrast to all of this, we have thus far, possibly, been imagining that when we make a judgement that something is good we are motivated directly to do the thing in question, which is a good thing. Talking in this way is often said to mark the difference between goodness *de re* (the things seen as good) and goodness *de dicto* (goodness itself).

So, to summarize: externalists who accept that this phenomenon is real and want to explain it can admit there is a connection in cases such as Dave's, but it is one that holds between judgements and motivations to do the good *de dicto*, not to do individual good things. The motivations to do the good things, motivations towards goodness *de re*, then come in the wake of the grander motivation, as it were. We have the judgement and we have some linked motivation. Hence, the reliability of the connection as shown in the case of Dave is secured. But, externalists can keep to their externalism because – as we *now* see – what internalists are really arguing for is a necessary connection between judgements that something is morally good and appropriate motivations to do *that thing*, and not a connection between such judgements and motivations to do the morally good *in general*.

What is so wrong with this? Internalists claim that it is always a 'fetish' to be motivated by goodness *de dicto* rather than being (directly) motivated by the good things themselves or, as is often the case, being motivated by the possibility of bringing about a good thing where currently there is none. We can see why they say this. Surely what we should care about are our friends and family, strangers in danger, the hurt that the old lady is feeling because of her heavy bags and how we might relieve her, and the many, many more things that motivate us every day. Talk of being motivated by goodness and rightness themselves suggests someone who is too interested in elevating and focussing on an ideal rather than the things that exemplify that ideal. In short, in explaining the link between judgement and motivation as they have, externalists make morally good, normal-willing people into people who fetishize an aspect, albeit a significant aspect, of the things that should really concern them.

To underline the fact, then, the charge against externalists is that they cannot explain the normal, central case of moral motivation. And, if they cannot explain that, then they must have a wrong-headed account of moral motivation overall.

This returns us to Gerald. The charge that internalists make is that although Gerald is being sincere in his judgement, he cannot be making a legitimate moral judgement because he does not feel any appropriate motivation. We are justified in saying this because externalism – the claim that motivation is not necessary for legitimacy of judgement – does not get the normal case correct. Gerald is not a literal parrot, but he may be like one. He may fail to understand exactly what his words mean and what implications they have, and this is shown simply because he feels no motivation.

Of course, it is open to internalists to put pressure on this sort of example as well as running the fetishism argument. Is it so obvious that Gerald will have no motivation at all, not even a passing flicker of commitment, or any sort of disposition to act? The example seems simple, but is it as common as externalists think? It may be simply a philosopher's story, dreamt up to fill a hole that has little or no foundation in reality. It is important to bring out something that has so far lain in the background. Gerald is judging that charity-giving is good; he is not judging or imagining that other people will find it to be good. That alternative judgement indicates some 'distance': it is a report of other people's judgements and psychologies. But, if Gerald judges that charity-giving itself is good, can there really be no motivation at all? To change examples again, when one judges that a cake is tasty – and not just that one can imagine other people finding it tasty – how often does one feel nothing, not even some passing temptation? Rare, I suspect.

However, before we conclude with a victory for internalism, we need to pause and go back a few moves. Are internalists correct to accuse externalists of fetishism? Just as we can chide such people for fetishizing an ideal, so we can praise those that care about goodness itself. As well as thinking of the prim and proper zealot with their head in the clouds (as we might imagine those accused of fetishization), we can admire the steadfast hero who cares about honour, liberty and truth. It is not so obvious that always being motivated by grand things, and being motivated by values such as goodness *de dicto*, say, is bad.

There is a fine balance here. It may in general be unproblematic to be motivated in this grand way when one is not called upon to make a direct judgement. Yet, what happens when one is in a situation and one has already made a judgement that one should, for example, help an old lady? At that moment it does seem a little odd to be motivated because one cares about goodness itself (or honour, or whatever), which then leads on to a specific motivation. Surely one should care about the old lady herself, having judged it good to help her, rather than care about the goodness of one's action.

As the reader may imagine, this debate about fetishism can – and has! – run and run, and I will not continue it here anymore. The key thing to ask when thinking about this debate is: when there is a change in motivation accompanying a change in judgement, what is required to explain it, and what is required to explain it plausibly?

Although I leave the material about fetishism there, we should return to an earlier part in the argument and whole debate. The fetishism argument has attracted some attention, but it is often put forward because writers think this is the only option for externalists. (If you don't appreciate that point, you may well wonder why we were talking about fetishism in the first place!) But, it is clear that there is another way in which internalism can be challenged, and we saw this earlier.

Is it so obvious that we are dealing with the (only) normal case here when we talk about Dave's change in motivation? Is Gerald destined to be cast as trying but failing to make a legitimate moral judgement? The debate here takes us through all of the cases we have so far considered: the actor, the parrot, and Sam the depressive. These cases get us to think hard about what counts as 'normal' and what the internalist is justified in classing as 'practically rational'. Recall that we cannot allow the internalist to define 'practically rational' such that it functions only to allow in all and only those cases that exemplify internalism, for then they would have secured only a hollow victory by mere stipulation alone. Yet, it does seem fair that internalists are able to rule out cases such as the parrot and the actor: one would not say that in these two cases we have proper and legitimate moral judgements.

The depressive is more interesting, I think. I let it pass earlier so as to get the debate underway. I said that we could class Sam as practically irrational because his whole psychology was abnormal. No doubt there are severe depressives who rarely if at all feel any motivation when they judge; there is some general mis-firing. But, many people may be classed as depressive who go through bouts of depression, and who have good and bad days, or even hours. Indeed, such people may feel a lack of commitment and spark about certain things (such as family or work), but more of a commitment about other things. The dividing line between severe depressives and Gerald, as he was first imagined to be, is wide. But, the dividing line between the more complicated sorts of depressive and Gerald may not be so great. Further to that, whoever said that Gerald failed to feel motivation most or all of the time? It may be that only occasionally he judges morally and feels no motivation. Some of those occasions may be to do with the fact that he is tired, say. But sometimes there is no explanation. Sometimes he simply feels no motivation.

So what? What I am trying to indicate is that the range of characters may be quite large, and people's 'practical rationality' may differ from time to time and context to context. Furthermore, I am indicating that there may be quite a lot more people than internalists imagine who are close to Gerald as originally sketched. We can ask again whether Gerald and others are practically rational only on those occasions when they feel some motivation. That takes us right back to the worry that internalists 'win' only by stipulation: Gerald's psychology is not normal simply because he feels no motivation. Hence, they don't win at all.

There may be no end to this sort of questioning. As in other philosophical contexts, a lot revolves around what is meant by 'normal', and many question-begging points may be thrown around. Perhaps a change of focus would help. I said earlier that Dave's case shows us something 'significant'. I myself have the strong feeling that this phenomenon *is* significant. Theorists should try to respect these interesting changes even if it does not happen in the majority of cases; often in life the normal case happens only occasionally.

But this change of focus may provide no help. Is there any way of spelling out how and why Dave's case is significant that does not beg too many questions against externalism? I doubt it. The prospects for a significant advance and decisive victory for either side may be slight, although I do think that externalists are better to engage on this ground than by trying to fight internalists about fetishism.

I offer no strong conclusion here, either for internalism or external-ism. By way of a summary, however, we can say that many people are convinced of externalism simply because it is too hard to hive off what are and what are not the normal cases in order to try to run something like the fetishism argument. In contrast, others hold fast to internalism because there seems to be something special and centrally defining about the case of Dave and people like him: if one is a psychologically normal agent, then appropriate motivations should follow moral judgements as a matter of necessity. Recall the point made every so often, that moral is practical and involves or embodies normativity: when we judge we care about what is happening and what can be done. Can one legitimately judge in a moral fashion and not be moved at all?

That last thought takes us to the next section.

7.3   Beliefs, desires, and besires

I said earlier in this chapter that we would integrate moral psychology with moral metaphysics. We haven't done that so far, but that is because the previous section was laying some groundwork for this section, and we now turn our attention to an issue that has direct implications for metaphysics.

(a) *Beliefs, desires and the neo-Humean model*: Let us begin with a division we have assumed and used every so often in this book, namely the division between beliefs and desires. Recall that these terms are often used by metaethicists as catch-all terms. Beliefs are those mental states that are aiming to represent some aspect of the world, and are often expressed using descriptive language. Desires cover a whole host of familiar ideas: attitudes, commitments, yearnings, wants, wishes, and so on. They can be deeply felt or weak. They can be long-lived or fleeting. What matters is that they are stances towards the world and they are in charge, as it were. Recall something I summarized in §5.3 The world may not fit with the desire in which case the desire may continue and the world may end up being changed through action. Or, if the world does fit with the desire – perhaps because one desires that the world be a certain way and continues to be a certain way – then action results to maintain the world on its current path. The different character of the desires may affect this relationship and other things: commitments are rarely fleeting and may be strong, whilst wishes may express a desire for the world to change, but one may also recognize that this matter is partly out of one's hands, unlike commitments and determinations.

Although there are clear differences within both groups, there is some appeal in putting them together in this way simply because there does seem to be a very general pattern of commonality. What supposedly distinguishes the two groups is that they have different directions of fit.

Desires have world-to-mind direction of fit, for the world must change (or remain as it is, or similar) in order to meet the desire, whilst beliefs have mind-to-world direction of fit since the mental state must match the world in some fashion for it to be considered decent, true, and correct.

Splitting our mental lives – at least the part of our mental lives relevant to morality and our motivation – into two broad groups of mental states has been an enormously influential way of thinking. Further to this other claims have been made that together constitute an important ingredient in contemporary metaethics.

The first claim we have just met: we have two sorts of mental states, beliefs and desires. It doesn't really matter what we call them so long as we assume a set of representational states and a set of desiring, attitudinative states. Secondly, there is the claim that the representational and motivational aspects of these two states are never mixed together in one mental state, at one and the same time. But, one can see various beliefs combine with various desires to produce action – in fact we see this all the time, think some writers – just so long as we remember that the beliefs stay as non-motivational representations, and the desires stay as non-representational states of being motivated. Thirdly, one typically sees the assumption that a belief cannot directly cause a desire, and vice versa. We should note, however, that many desires are *based on* certain beliefs: my desire to journey to the moon is based on the belief (explicit or implicit) that the moon is a place I could get to, for example. We can draw from these three ideas an implication, which is the thought that one could have, in theory, any combination of different beliefs and desires. In other words, there is possibility for a vast amount of 'mixing-and-matching', and the various combinations of beliefs and desires are typically seen as something that it is matter of local, individual psychology and, in the case of normal agents, something contingent: that is, again, any belief can go along with any desire.

This position, and variations thereof, is often called the Humean or neo-Humean account of motivation. It is based on the writings of David Hume, the eighteenth century Scottish philosopher. Whilst undoubtedly much of what Hume wrote can be seen as an inspiration for this position, there is some discussion as to the extent to which Hume himself was or would have been a neo-Humean. (I do not discuss this matter, but see Further Reading.)

How does the belief-desire model of motivation work? The thought is that both a belief and a desire are required for a directed action, although it is desires that are the senior partner. Imagine two different scenarios. First, you believe that a cake is in a cupboard but you have no desire to get it. So, we would not expect you to go to the cupboard to get the cake. (Indeed, the fact that you do not go to the cupboard indicates that you have no desire.) Secondly, imagine you have a very strong desire for some cake, but have no idea whatsoever as to where it is. A number of things could happen. You could end up searching the whole house because even though you do not have a strong and *precise* belief as to where a cake is, you have some *general* belief that there may be some cake around. But, the action would be lacking somewhat in point and direction. You might search frantically and frenetically, but get nowhere. Alternatively, we could alter things slightly and imagine you with no belief at all about where the cake was, plus some attendant thought that you will search only if you have a precise belief as to where the cake is. In this scenario you might well end up rooted to the spot: motivated to act but frozen in inaction.

In contrast, we can imagine a third scenario where you have a desire for some cake and a fairly precise belief about where some is. Assuming other things are equal – for example, you do not suspect that your dietician is spying on you – then you will go to the place where you think the cake is. So, both a belief and a desire are needed for directed action. But, as our previous examples showed, desires are the senior partner here. Desires simply are states of being motivated, and if they are not present you will not do anything relevant in relation to the belief, you will not search out any cake. In the first scenario it is clear you can go on and do other things because you have no motivation whatsoever to get some cake.

Yet, despite desires being the senior partner, it is clear that they require direction. In the scenario in which you stay rooted to the spot, we can see that there is some motivation to act, it is just that it finds itself with no vehicle. So, that is why neo-Humeans say we need both things: the desire, which just is the state of being motivated, and a belief or set of beliefs that help to guide the desire. Together they create a directed action.

Although I have talked through things in relation to cakes, again this applies to moral motivation. Neo-Humeans typically claim that their way of thinking about motivation and action can explain any sort of action. As we have seen, the key idea is that there are two types of mental state. Although the two types are to be kept apart in the sense that there is not a mental state that has both types of direction of fit, examples from the two sets can be combined in order to produce action.

There is some clear reason to like this model of human action. It has a simplicity about it, for a start. Secondly, it seems true that there are two directions of fit that can help to characterize a lot of our mental lives. Thirdly, thinking in this way does seem to help explain all sorts of action. Jonny and Fiona both have the belief that today would be a good day for ballooning. But, only Fiona has a desire to go ballooning so only she ends up in the balloon. If Jonny wanted to impress Fiona, he might end up in the balloon reluctantly. He might say, 'I don't really want to be here', but at some level – perhaps at some 'all-things-considered level' – his desire to impress Fiona might trump his fear of heights, and so his stronger desire would be to be in the balloon. Similarly, both Adrian and Miranda believe that the old lady is struggling with her shopping, but only Miranda has the desire to help her and so only she acts.

Whilst neo-Humeanism is influential and initially plausible, it has come under pressure. Some writers do not like it because of the claims it makes about moral psychology. Additionally, some of these writers, and others, do not like it because of what it means for other metaethical claims they hold dear. This then brings us to the idea of how psychology and metaphysics can be integrated. To understand why people do not like neo-Humeanism, I now do some theoretical carving by using some of the material from the previous section and other chapters.

(b) *A little bit of linking*: We are going to carve out three main positions, although the reader should be warned that these three broad options *do not* in any way exhaust the options: philosophers have attempted to position themselves in different ways to these options. But, it will do no harm to introduce them.

Imagine, first, that you think neo-Humeanism is roughly correct, and that mental states relevant to motivation and action come in two broad forms. Imagine also that you assume that moral judgements should be taken to be an expression of just one of these two forms. Which do you pick? Some people favour the idea that moral judgements are beliefs. Recall that the neo-Humean regards beliefs as utterly non-motivational.

Desires are required for motivation to occur since only these are states of being motivated. So according to this view when we judge that something is morally right or cruel, we are making fact-stating judgements that are highly similar if not identical in nature to judgements that a table is brown or that a balloon is high in the sky. Whether we do anything in relation to these moral beliefs – whether we act appropriately in accordance with them – depends on what desires you have. Some people will have such desires, and some people will not.

This sort of position fits nicely, I think, with naturalism and reductionism of various sorts. Advocates of these views may find it easy to plant their flag here because they typically claim that judgements are representational and, relatedly, that moral language is typically fact-stating. Behind these ideas stands the idea, already encountered, that what moral judgements pick out is not quite what some initially think they pick out: for example, they pick out moral properties that have been 'naturalized', or they pick out something that moral properties have been reduced to. Whatever detailed story is told, many such naturalists and reductionists will remove, or at least de-emphasize, the normative aspect of moral properties and with that, often, the motivational aspect. We do not need to worry too much as to how moral properties get us to act or make demands on us, for their ultimate nature is something not quite in tune with these aspects or ideas. Any motivation such properties or judgements about them carry is a matter of 'local' psychology, the psychology of individual judges.

I stress, however, that not all naturalists or reductionists situate themselves here. Indeed, those that do may still try to accommodate thoughts about normativity into their story. But, some naturalists and reductionists will find a nice home here, and many feel no strong need to worry about motivation.

A second sort of position also begins with an acceptance of the neo-Humean story, but it opts to identify moral judgements with desires. In doing so it seems to readily adopt internalism: the moral judgement simply is an expression of some motivation to act, so the internal or necessary connection is secured.

A number of types of theorists may occupy this position. From those theorists already encountered, the ones that come most readily to mind are noncognitivists. (Recall that 'desire' is a catch-all, so all sorts of noncognitivist will find it natural to place themselves here, no matter whether they deal in attitudes, prescriptions, or other things.) Normativity is placed easily here for, as we have seen, making a moral judgement is interpreted directly as a type of caring about the thing one is judging. But other problems loom, and these tend to revolve around the worry that the judgement itself may no longer be truth-apt or fact-stating or representational. We looked into this issue across Chapter 5.

Again, not all people who adopt neo-Humeanism and internalism will be noncognitivists. Also, some noncognitivists may choose not to embrace this position, or embrace it as readily as I have just indicated they can. But, we do have another neat connection that serves as an interesting start.

Just for the record, error theorists will probably not care that much whether theorists identify moral judgements as either beliefs or desires. Error theorists will seek to show that no matter what moral judgements are or are supposed to be, there is something bogus about them. For some error theorists, such as Mackie, the pull towards the belief-like property-representing nature of everyday moral judgements is in strong tension with their desire-like practical nature, and so the only rational conclusion is an error theory.

There is, of course, one sort of position that has so far not made an appearance in our little story. What of sensibility theory? Both of the main positions just canvassed embrace neo-Humeanism. Sensibility theorists do not wish to identify moral judgements with the non-motivational beliefs in the neo-Humean story. Why not? They wish to put normativity at the centre of their story too and, by and large, they embrace internalism. So, they do not wish to have moral judgements severed from motivation in the way that naturalism and reductionism may incline one too.

Yet, sensibility theorists do not wish to identify moral judgement with desires, at least as conceived by neo-Humeans, for they think that such judgements can be truth-apt and can represent, and what they represent are things that are deserving of the label 'property'.

How to resolve this tension? The solution is to challenge neo-Humeanism itself. There are a number of ways to do this. Here I concentrate on the most radical and the one that has generated the most comment in the past 20 years or so. The idea is to challenge the claim that we have just two types of mental state.

(c) *Besires*: Whilst we can acknowledge that there can be both beliefs that do not expression motivations and desires that are not representational, might there not be another type of mental state that is both representational and an expression of being motivated at one and the same time? Some people, including sensibility theorists and those influenced by them, think there could be and are such states. These states are often referred to as 'besires'. I return to sensibility theory explicitly after I have explained what besires are supposed to be.

Here are three introductory points. First, the adoption of besires as those mental states expressed by moral judgements leads one to see moral judgement and motivation as internally connected. We have a judgement that is also, at one and the same time, an expression of being motivated. So, the claim that moral judgements function to express besires commits one to internalism. Secondly, note that the challenge is not to say that there are no beliefs or desires as Humeans think of them. Rather, the challenge is simply to make out the existence of a third sort of mental state. To keep things simple, let us imagine that all moral judgements are to be identified with this third sort of state, although it is open to any theorist to muddy the waters further here.

Lastly, throughout I have used the phrase 'desire, which is a state of being motivated', or similar. It is now time to stress why. (Although, we have briefly met this point before, again in §5.3) Some people are (understandably) confused when they first approach all of this material for they think we have *three* elements in play: beliefs, desires *and* motivations. They may think, wrongly, that desires cause motivations. But, on quick reflection we can see that this is not the case, for desires are just states of being motivated: to say that one has a desire is simply a different way of saying that one is motivated. Why talk about this now? The point is that the present challenge to neo-Humeanism does not claim that beliefs also can cause motivations, but rather that certain sorts of representation can also be states of being motivated, and indeed that states of being motivated can be representational. The challenge is to mix the two directions of fit that neo-Humeans wish to keep separate.

With those points noted, we can ask some detailed questions. First of all, are besires possible? As mentioned, all sorts of desires might be in the mix here: desires to bring something about as well as desires that something continue. If we just restrict ourselves to the former, important example, we might think it impossible that a mental state can have both directions of fit: how can you both believe that something is the case and desire to bring it about? Does it already exist, or not? However, a moment's reflection shows that this contradiction is only apparent. A besire is not supposed to be a mixture of a belief that something is the case and a desire for that thing to come about. Rather, to put it in neo-Humean terms for a moment, it is a belief that a possible course of action is good, say, and a desire to do that thing. Or, it is a belief that a certain situation is good and a desire that this situation continue, expressed as a desire to defend it for example. And so on. The representational state is itself a state of being motivated in some way that links *appropriately* to the representation.

So, even if besires are possible, are they actual? Consider a non-moral example first. Karen is out shoe-shopping. She is not quite sure what she wants and trudges up and down the mall looking in various windows. Suddenly her eyes alight on a pair of banana yellow high heels. She stops and stares. She wants those shoes and nothing else matters. Describing the experience exactly may be hard and may be the sort of thing that only skilled novelists and poets can do. But, we can at least indicate a few things. She walks into the shop and nervously tries on the shoes. To her relief they fit perfectly and she can walk like a dream in them. She buys them and exits, full of excitement. Throughout this whole process other factors fade into the background: all the other shoes she had seen, the other shops, her ability to afford the shoes, and whether she had anything in her wardrobe that matched the shoes. All she wanted were the shoes. Only they were salient, only they were relevant. In short, Karen has the following besire, 'I ought to buy those shoes' or, if one prefers the language of values to 'oughts', her besire is 'Buying those shoes would be very good indeed, for they are awesome!'

I am confident that we have all had this sort of experience, even if not about shoes. Just think about the latest piece of electronic kit you have been desperate to get, or the book you wanted to read. The key question for our purposes is whether this is both a representational state and a state of being motivated. Well, it is clearly a state of being motivated. There is a strong desire for the shoes. But, we can also view it is a representational state. It represents the shoes, their position in the shop, and their possible position in Karen's life. The representation is not exhausted by the 'bare' sort of propositional claim, 'There are shoes in the shop window', because there is far more going on. Yet, this claim, and many others, can be drawn from the besire. The key move, behind all of this, is to see that we are no longer working with such bare propositions when explaining people's action. The move is to explore and bring to life the phenomenology of what it is to have a representational state, and show that such things might be complex, particularly if we are thinking about motivation and how motivation works.

In the case of Karen at least one thing is simple, namely that all other considerations fell away into the background. We could have made it more complex, and had her worrying every so often about how much money the shoes cost. To illustrate that, consider this moral case. Joshua is walking along the mall when he comes to a wine merchants. He sees in the window a bottle of a superb Merlot he has read about in the weekend paper, and it's on special offer. Luckily he has just enough money to buy it. He's going to a dinner party in the evening, and the bottle would be just the right thing to impress his friends. However, outside the wine merchants is someone collecting money for charity. It is a charity close to Joshua's heart – perhaps it is concerned with a disease that affected a close family member – and he is aware, as he sees the tin, that he has not given money to it for a while.

We can imagine that Joshua is caught in some practical dilemma: which should he spend his money on? He has two besires – 'I ought to buy the wine' and 'I ought to give to the charity' – and they clash. It doesn't matter to us how he resolves it although, as may happen in real life, we can imagine that he buys the wine but resolves to donate double the money next week when his monthly salary is due. What is key is that he may alternate in his choosing between one and the other before he reaches his decision. At one point he imagines how the wine will taste and he fleetingly recalls some of the choicer phrases from the newspaper review. At another time he thinks of his beloved friend and how his money may do more good if given to the charity than if it is was spent on the wine. But, he then thinks about his friends this evening. And so on. At one stage, certain factors dominate his thinking, at another stage others do. There are shifts in perspective, shifts in what he is attending to and thinking through. And, in the story he tells himself and the position he finds himself in, there is a clear tension, at least before he resolves it in the way indicated.

We could again draw out the non-motivational beliefs that Joshua has: a belief that the wine is in the shop, that it will taste nice, that it is a good deal, that the charity is deserving, that he owes something to his friend, and so on. But, the representations that are states of being motivated are, again, more than these beliefs. They are ways of presenting the various factors of the situation to himself, to show some factors as more important than others, and to show how various factors connect with, or are in tension with, other ones. In fact, the ways in which these factors present themselves to Joshua are expressions of how he is motivated to act. In the case of Karen, all factors bar one fade away or are 'silenced'. All that matters to her is buying the shoes. For Joshua, different factors come into view at various times, and this is itself an expression of the dilemma he feels he is in.

To cut a long story short, I think a case can be made for besires being real and there being more to our moral and other felt-experience than is captured by the neo-Humean story. It may make sense to think in terms of besires. But, does it make *as much* sense, or *more* sense, than thinking in terms of some belief-desire model alone? Or, in other words, whilst talk of besires puts the phenomenology centre-stage, is there any philosophical advantage to doing so?

I have already mentioned that the simplicity of the neo-Humean account is seen by many as an advantage: we have truth-apt representational states, and pushy, noncognitive states of being motivated. The introduction of besires seems to make things overly-complex and raise key worries. How is a besire such as 'I ought to buy those shoes' to be evaluated? Is it truth-apt? It seems so as it is supposed to be representational. Yet, at the same time it is an expression of a desire, and expression of how the person is motivated. So, perhaps it is not truth-apt after all?

No doubt the introduction of besires complicates matters, at least if one is thinking in neo-Humean terms. But writers introduce them because they wish to be faithful to the phenomena. It is often difficult to separate beliefs and desires in the way that neo-Humeans require. And, even if we can do so, perhaps in doing so we set-up a false philosophical dichotomy. If we adopt neo-Humeanism we get many of the problems that have afflicted us throughout this book. How can we reconcile the supposed normativity of the world with the idea that moral judgements are beliefs about that world? How can noncognitive states be truth-apt, and how can individual states be better and worse than other ones?

The point here is that although the neo-Humean picture is simple, in one respect, it ushers in a distinction that may, in the end, be our philosophical undoing. It creates tensions and questions, and gets us to see metaethical topics in a certain way that itself can be questioned. Being more faithful to the first person phenomenology (as I take it besire-talk is), may itself not be neutral and may introduce complexity, but it should give us pause for thought. It is not so obvious that the supposed simplicity of neo-Humeanism is an advantage.

Further to this, perhaps we understand everyday people *better* if we take seriously the idea of besires. We *can* explain Karen's directed action by listing a string of beliefs – such as 'The shoes are available to buy from this shop' and 'I can afford them' – whilst marrying them with a desire 'I want those shoes at all costs'. But, in so doing we may miss something, at least regarding certain people.

Consider Tim. Tim loves to climb mountains, indeed it is his main passion. Yet, he has often been injured whilst climbing. This has not dampened his enthusiasm one bit. He loves the possibility of danger, the uncertainty, the challenge. In this way, Tim echoes George Mallory, the famous mountain climber. Mallory replied to the question of why he wanted to climb Everest with the answer, 'Because it's there'. Now to some of us, certainly to *me*, the fact that a mountain is there and that there is some possibility of my climbing it is in no way a reason for me to climb it.

But for both Mallory and Tim the fact that there is this possibility *does* explain why they want to climb the mountain, despite the obvious dangers. This possibility is central to their lives: they feel intensely that there is something they have yet to achieve, and which they can achieve, and this is itself significant and highly relevant to their motivational state.

The point is that talk of besires not only enables us to start representing the phenomena more faithfully, but it enables us to appreciate the motivational outlook of an agent. Recall the fifth condition at the start of §7.2. We were concerned with appropriate motivation. I said that what counts as appropriate is a matter of judgement. I imagined that judging a cake to be tasty would typically not engender a motivation to start a Third World War. But, philosophy is full of surprising twists and perhaps some convoluted story could be told by the judge such that this motivation would make sense as something appropriate with regards to the judgement about the cake. Given what we know of humans, cakes and wars, this still seems an outlandish example, but less outlandish examples are possible that make the case strongly. For example, to take a famous philosophical example, we may think it odd that Michael desires to drink a saucer of mud. But, we can make sense of his desire by listening to how he describes the situation and possibility. Perhaps he is doing it for a dare. Perhaps he is curious as to what it tastes like, and he lists other strange things he has done out of curiosity. (And so on.) In the example of him being curious, we get a sense, as Michael speaks, that he is very curious, more so than the norm, and is driven to do many things out of curiosity. We can understand such motivations only if we get a sense of how Michael represents things to himself.

Furthermore, recall that a consequence of neo-Humeanism is that we can imagine odd or uncommon combinations of beliefs and desires. I am not challenging that claim itself. But when we do have such odd combinations there is typically some story to be told. When that story is told we should realize that there is often some explanation of why and how there are connections between the belief and desire, and why the belief happens often and the desires are strong.

To see this, think through how the neo-Humean might summarize matters with Tim: Tim strongly desires to climb the mountain and he believes that there is the possibility of him doing so, and he often brings this belief to mind. This last line gives the game away, I think. That fact that the belief often explicitly comes to mind, and is occasioned by some strong desire, should incline us to think that the beliefs and desires are in some way linked. And this might incline us to see beyond the neo-Humean model. The beliefs and desires are not separate things, but instead a way of representing things to oneself that can itself be an expression of how one is motivated. And if one is motivated to do something strongly, this representation will often appear, or never really go away.

To summarize, then: the neo-Humean model might, on the surface, capture all that we want about motivation. But, besires are not ruled out. And, if we really want to understand how people judge things morally we might do well to think of moral judgements as being expressions of desires.

There is more to say under this heading, as to whether besires are worth thinking more about. But I think the initial case is a good one. (See Further Reading for more on this matter.)

And if they are good things to think about, then this can only strengthen the case of sensibility theory. Sensibility theorists emphasize the ways in which we respond to the world and the way in which we can both represent aspects of the world yet that representation be evaluative and normative. Besires give colour to this idea: for we now see the possibility – and actuality – of a representational state that is also a state of being motivated. The two aspects are brought together in one thing.

But, surely there are problems with talk of besires? There are. Here, in brief, are three. First, clearly anyone who adopts the idea that moral judgements are expressions of besires will be an internalist. So, if one is convinced of the truth of externalism, one will want and need to dismiss thinking in these terms. We have seen that this is not so easy.

Secondly, despite besire-talk allowing sensibility theorists to show the possibility of something different from neo-Humeanism, it ends up with problems inherited from and shown up by this position.

This worry concerns authority, truth and description. Tim has a certain besire, that he ought to climb the mountain and that doing so would be excellent. But, he is clearly mad because he hasn't acknowledged the risks. He really shouldn't climb the mountain. Is there any basis for criticism? The answer is that there is on the sensibility account

for we talk of best judges and normal conditions, and all the other nor-
matively-construed criteria. The issue, of course, is whether we have
some form of relativism going on here and whether a basis can be
secured for authority of some sort that can show Tim to be wrong in
his judgement.

This is a real worry. But, I am strongly inclined to think that this is
not a problem with talk of besires as such, but is rather a problem with
sensibility theory. After all, the introduction of besires does nothing
to aid or help the thought that we can and should see people and their
judgements as better or worse than others. The introduction of besires
themselves is neither philosophically here nor there. What matters is if
we can secure standards by which people's views of the world and their
actions can be called to account. The fact that we base such standards
on a certain class of responses – be they beliefs, desire or besires – is
the key thing, not the character of those responses themselves. Having
raised the key worry in the previous chapter, I don't say any more about
it here.

A third and final worry does bite specifically for besire theory, but
has echoes in sensibility theory. There are, in the current metaethical
literature, a few ways in which we might combine or merge representations with motivations. Many of these keep representations as representations and motivations as motivations. That is, they keep to something
of the neo-Humean picture, I think, in imagining a whole mental state
that has, roughly, distinct parts that play distinct roles. Every so often
when explaining noncognitivism I have sneakily said things such as,
'the whole or main point of the utterance is to express an attitude'.
But, if expressing an attitude is only the *main* point, this implies (or
entails) that there must be *some other* point. Hence, some combination
of descriptions with expressions in one judgement.

Besires are not like that. They are imagined to be 'unitary' mental
states which are not fusings of separable parts – some representation
and some motivation. Rather we have *one* state that has discernible
aspects (as it were), not separable parts. We are imagining representations that are states of being motivated, not states that are partly representative and somewhat motivation. (I exaggerate for contrast, here.)
The worry with besires, say critics, is this is very strong. It seems that we
cannot pull apart these representations and motivations. But, surely we
want to be able to. Tim has a belief that it is possible for him to climb
the mountain and I have a belief that it is possible for me to climb the
mountain. Putting aside the fact that these judgements are indexed to
different people, surely these are the same belief. What distinguishes us

is just the difference in desire. This is not captured by talk of besires, because the link between beliefs and desires is inseparable. How can it explain this sort of case, and many, many others?

In brief, I think the way to diagnose this sort of case is to say that critics have missed what is radical about the idea of a besire. If one imagines that besires are just fusings of separable and pre-exisiting beliefs and desires, it does seem odd to explain how Tim and I can have the same belief or representation and yet different desires. The point of besires – in short – is to point out that Tim and I *do not* have the same representation. And this is shown, in the main, because we are motivated differently. Tim's representation and view of the mountain is different from mine, coloured by our different motivations towards it. We can – in English – represent the different representations using the same statement. But, as we often know, when Tim says that it is possible for him to climb the mountain this really means something quite different from me saying that it is possible for me to. At this point, our language may give out. What might appear to be the same representation may well be quite different.

To cement this, imagine a moral case. Imagine there is a party and Bill the bully and Samantha the Samaritan can both see Jimmy alone in one corner of the room, and surmise that he is lonely. Both wish to go over to him. Bill is motivated to take advantage in some way, whilst Samantha is motivated to be friendly. Both may note Jimmy's apparent loneliness, but it is perfectly consistent with besire theory to say that the representations of such loneliness by Bill and Samantha are different. Neo-Humeans miss out that this is what besire-theorists say, I think, simply because they are importing their view of what it is for something to be a representation. If one thinks only in terms of neo-Humean representations, much of besire theory makes no sense. But, it is this view that besire theorists are challenging.

7.4 Concluding remarks

In this chapter we have thought hard about two topics concerning moral motivation: the link between judgement and motivation, and the character of the judgement and motivation in play. As we have seen, this second topic in particular has implications for, and is affected by, the other metaethical topics we have encountered.

As I said earlier, this chapter has been meant to be a fairly standard description of two key topics in metaethics. In my final chapter I briefly discuss how we might play around with some of the ideas in this chapter amongst other matters. I then go on to question much of what goes on in metaethics.

Further Reading

Rosati (2012) is an excellent overview of the material covered in this chapter and it contains a super bibliography.

The modern *locus classicus* for much of this chapter is Smith (1994), especially chapters 3 and 4. The 'fetish' argument against externalism and much of my set-up is taken from him. He himself adopts neo-Humeanism and internalism about motivation although he is no non-cognitivist. Instead he is a cognitivist and a realist. He analyses moral judgements in terms of what we would desire were we fully rational. For more details see his book.

There have been a number of responses to Smith's argument against externalism. See, for example, Brink (1997), Dreier (2000), Lillehammer (1997), Miller (2003) chapter 9.9, and Shafer-Landau (2000). Simpson (1999) offers decent perspective on whether the whole debate between internalism and externalism is well-conceived.

A good paper on whether Hume was a neo-Humean is Millgram (1995). A good paper on noncognitivism and internalism that challenges the link I make in this chapter is Joyce (2002). I haven't spent any time discussing whether the direction of fit metaphor employed by Smith and others is any good. For more on this, see Copp and Sobel (2001), Humberstone (1992), and Zangwill (1998). Dancy (1993) chapters 1–3 is a good discussion of various challenges to the neo-Humean conception of motivation. The term 'besire' was introduced in Altham (1986). McNaughton (1988), chapters 7, 8 and 9 is also good on besires and argues for the same conclusion that I do. See also Van Roojen (2002) and Zangwill (2008). A more detailed treatment of sensibility theory and motivation than I give in this book is Helm (2001). For a sceptical treatment of the position see Kennett (2001).

8
Further Thoughts

8.1 Introduction

As advertised, this book has opted to lead readers through the main, standard questions and positions of current metaethics. I hope that much of what I have laid out has helped you think through various ideas and enliven other metaethical books and articles that you read. However, in this brief, final chapter I shake things up a little. There are some presumptions in metaethics, as in all areas of philosophy, presumptions that constitute the structure of the debates I have explicated. Presumptions and structures are good things to have, but that does not mean they cannot be questioned.

There are many things I could have picked on and discussed in detail in this final chapter. Here are a few, sketched. First, we could easily think harder about what naturalism is or could be. What is our definition of science? Are we confident that social sciences should be lumped in? Is unemployment that similar to a quark? Is the difference between normative and nonnormative stuff enough to give us a dividing line here and put the social sciences with the natural sciences? How easy is it to reduce the biological to the physical, and what does this mean, if anything, for reductionism generally?

Second, what is meant by normativity? How is it related to and differ from evaluation? How deeply entrenched and important is the idea of motivation to the idea of normativity? What is it for something to be a reason?

Third, we have hardly scratched the surface when it comes to naturalizing projects and thinking through detailed examples of what a naturalized psychology might look like in order to expose the strengths and weaknesses of moral naturalism itself.

Fourth, once we think hard about psychology and naturalization, we shall surely realize that there are many people whose psychologies differ from the norm. Not just the depressed, but the autistic, the highly-strung, the chronically tired, the mad, the overly empathetic, the psychopathic, the sociopathic, and many more. This immediately calls into question the truth of internalism, in a way that continues the main worry in Chapter 7. The normal case, as internalism has it, becomes more refined, special and rare. It is based on a privileged sort of person and psychology, more privileged than might have been apparent previously.

This then calls into question all of those positions that try to privilege O2 and try to combine it with S1. In order to get at our intuitive notions of which things are morally right and wrong, we are basing our notion of correctness on a way of thinking that may be less prevalent than some people think.

Well, this is a good and possible challenge. Relativism is, of course, in the air here. Some people think this sort of challenge is overplayed. Even accepting that psychopathy is more common and less extreme than one might think given how it is portrayed in books and films, it is still fairly rare. This whole issue can be settled only by extensive empirical investigation. What is clearly lacking is the philosophically-informed research that is required.

A fifth and final challenge picks up on another part of the previous chapter. Throughout I have said, as many others do, that the words 'belief' and 'desire' can be used as catch-alls for all sorts of mental state. Yet, are these things really useful 'catch-alls'? Although I have gone along with it for explanatory reasons, we should be suspicious when philosophers use one word to capture a whole host of phenomena. Generalizing and grouping can yield insights, but it can often also disguise.

For example, think of desires. I have mentioned yearnings, commitments, wishes and other things in passing. But, as I also mentioned, these are different things: wishes differ from commitments because in the latter but not the former, there seems to be a strong constraint relating to the possibility of the desired thing occurring, perhaps brought about by one's efforts. Similarly, yearnings may last longer than temptations. If one wishes to group together 'beliefs' and 'desires', based on some general direction of fit, one needs to investigate the idea of a direction in this context a lot more fully than I have done here. (There are three papers mentioned in Chapter 7's Further Reading on this.)

These are all important questions and debates. However, in the next section I focus on an issue that does not get the attention it deserves, but pervades the whole structure of metaethics and, I presume, other parts of philosophy also.

8.2   Metaethics and the generalizing tendency

(a) *Pretheoretical metaethical intuitions*: To get at the issue, I proceed in a number of stages.

First, consider the notion of a 'pretheoretical metaethical intuition'. I mentioned this in passing in Chapter 2, but it now comes to the fore. This idea seems as if it is an oxymoron, that is it seems as if it is an idea that is self-contradictory. Metaethics seems quite abstract and theoretical. How can it, therefore, be *pre*theoretical?

I believe that we have only the appearance of an oxymoron. Metaethics can often be quite abstract and may lack some of the direct punch of many issues in applied ethics. Yet, metaethics is not divorced from everyday debate and ideas. When writing about Duncan and Helen's debate in Chapter 1, I had in mind a real-life debate I have heard between two friends of mine who were not professional philosophers. Further, they drew out the metaethical implications themselves. And this is by no means an isolated incident. In my experience, when debating ethical matters (or aesthetic ones, or debates about etiquette, and the like) people will often catch themselves and wonder what the point of such a debate is and what the status is of what they are saying.

Let me develop this. I painted Duncan as a type of realist and Helen as a relativist. Imagine, further, that neither of them have done any philosophy, let alone studied metaethics. They may not even know the words 'realist' and 'relativist'. However, imagine that they are reasonably intelligent people. (For example, they may not know what a conditional statement is, nor know the word 'antecedent', but they can easily follow and discuss the formal piece of reasoning about industrious Thom from §5.4) Despite their lack of explicit philosophical acumen, they might well have philosophical thoughts. We do not have a great divide, I think, between many people and philosophers. What professional philosophers may bring is technical knowledge, knowledge of standard moves, dogged determination to get to the bottom of things, and (one hopes) some philosophical talent. But, there is no reason to suppose that Duncan would not be able to reflect on what he is saying and have thoughts that professional philosophers might label as being realist. Indeed, he may have such thoughts often. The same can easily be true of Helen. Indeed, in my experience this is often the case with people. Philosophical debates, of the sort I have outlined in this book, typically get started from everyday sparks of wonder, puzzles and questions that many people have.

It is these ideas, questions and patterns of thought that constitute pretheoretical metaethical intuitions, and I think it unarguable that they exist. Now for the second stage in mapping out the issue. There is no reason to suppose that Duncan is always a realist and Helen always a relativist, nor any reason to suppose the same is true of all real-life people. Of course, some people *are* quite hardened in their pretheoretical metaethical stances. And, perhaps reflection on such a strong conviction itself influences what stance some people take on how authoritative their view is, that is the extent to which it applies to other people and groups. There are certainly hardened realists and relativists around. But, it is often the case that people are realist or relativistic (or naturalistic, or. ...) about some issues, but take a different view or no view at all about other things. We may even be able to discern patterns across quite a few people concerning certain issues. For example, I imagine that typical Westerners and others are inclined to be moral realists about child murder, arson, and torture. However, although they may be confident about what they think, they may be less hard in their realism, and even relativistic, when it comes to thinking about how children and adults should address and treat adults in their everyday affairs.

Once we investigate the details of these two broad stances, things might become more interesting. Some people might emphasize the idea that child murder is wrong no matter what you think. Others may be more inclined to say, 'Well, yes, but it is wrong because this is the sort of thing that many normal moral people feel bad about', and seek to tie the moral value of acts to the judgements of people. We can imagine other people invoking social and legal rules that they have grown up with, and put to the foreground explicit agreements amongst people in a community. These emphasized claims and ideas are the starting points of a number of different metaethical accounts, as I hope you have seen. Crucially, we can imagine some people favouring different sorts of explanations and stances when it comes to different issues. Again, we might get a hardened, more metaphysically 'extreme' version of realism when we consider death and destruction than when we consider slighting and rule-bending.

I have emphasized mind-dependence, mind-independence and relativism thus far, but we can pick on other topics. For example, some people may be inclined to think that moral concepts that are emotionally charged, such as sympathy, can be reduced to natural phenomena, such as brain states. But they would find reductionism harder to think through – or, it just doesn't 'feel' right – when it comes to concepts that have hardly any emotional component, such as justice. (We have met this contrast before, in §5.5.) An extra layer is provided now with the thought that some people could think this means that naturalism is correct for some concepts and properties, whilst for others it is not, rather than trying to give an overall natural or nonnatural account of all moral phenomena. Similarly, there are some cases where we are clearly expressing some noncognitive state, and other times when we seem to be expressing, quite clearly, some cognitive view of the world. Further, ordinary people may catch themselves often, and reflect on these judgements and be able to sense some difference.

These are all suppositions, based on some experience. A really well-worked out position would have some decent empirical investigation behind it regarding people's pretheoretical metaethical intuitions. With that point accepted, let me draw things together thus far. The claim is that there appear to be quite a number of pretheoretical metaethical intuitions that people hold, across lots of different issues and in different contexts. Some people appear to be thorough and clear-sighted in their metaethical view, even if they cannot articulate it in the way philosophers do, whilst others are less so. Some people can be strongly inclined to a view at times, and at other times less so. Some people may be realists about some moral issues, but relativists about others, with many shades in between. The same is true for others aspects we have focussed on, such as moral language and the relation between the moral and the natural. In short, I think we can make the case for there being some variability across people's pretheoretical metaethical intuitions.

No doubt the claim I have just articulated can be justified in a deeper and richer way, and no doubt it can be challenged. The point thus far is simply to show the possibility of this phenomenon. So what? Now we come to the third stage that makes the issue explicit.

(b) *The generalizing tendency*: In metaethics all positions that we have so far canvassed adopt what I call the 'generalizing tendency'. Philosophers of all persuasions and in all fields of philosophy are trying to capture and explain the phenomena that they think constitute the area of life in which they are interested. That area of life may be the workings of the mind or brain, or how the law works in a society. Philosophers will have a particular view – metaphysical, epistemological, whatever – about that area. Importantly, that view may not be supported by or exemplified by all of the phenomena that they and their fellow thinkers believe constitute the relevant area of life. Or if it is (that is, if the philosopher thinks it is), it may not be obviously supported or exemplified and the philosopher may need to reinterpret or recharacterize what they think is (really) going on. That is, some phenomena may go against or seem to go against their philosophical view, and such examples require attention to show that they are no threat to the view being argued for.

Matters go a little deeper than this, of course. For it is not as if the area of life about which one should entertain a philosophical view is some neutral, wholly agreed upon item. A philosopher's view might itself shape the area. One may choose to downplay or de-emphasize some aspect so much that one can almost categorize it as peripheral to one's concerted study, if not ignore it altogether.

That was all very abstract, but this is required to bring out the generalizing tendency: there is a tendency to try to explain and characterize the area that constitutes some area of philosophical attention in such a way that it all conforms to one's philosophical view. For example, if you think moral properties exist, then they are standing behind all debates and judgements, ready to act as the standard of truth (or similar), and all are to be characterized in the same metaphysical way. Similarly, one may think that all moral language has the same depth grammar. Where there are some oddities, some strange examples, they are just that, odd (and rare). Finally, if a moral judgement is to be legitimate, then it must have *this* connection with motivation and psychology: either always necessary, or always contingent.

Further, picking up on a point given in the paragraph one before last, it may be that a certain naturalist will worry about normativity but not worry so much about motivation. Although not all naturalists take this line, it is open to them to de-emphasize the importance of motivation so much that they can treat it as only a secondary consideration when thinking about what the moral is.

There are good reasons to adopt this generalizing tendency, both in philosophy generally and in metaethics. I think through some later. For now, however, we need to complete this third stage and make the worrying issue explicit.

In short, if there is a variety of pretheoretical metaethical intuitions, then does that not cast doubt on how generalizing philosophers should be? Even if we accept that ordinary people can be wrong about what they are doing and how they should cast their moral activity, this worry may press the more varied we can show people's intuitions to be.

That is the overall thought. I now provide more detail. Think again about moral error theory. I characterized this as involving two explicit parts: a claim that everyday moral thought and language is based on some non-negotiable commitment, and an argument to show that such a commitment is wrong or unjustified. It is therefore incumbent upon error theorists to make sure they characterize everyday moral thought and language correctly, so as to be confident that they have got the first part correct. If they do not do this, then opponents may argue that the commitment is not present at all, or is not as central and non-negotiable as error theorists think, or is not quite as they cast it. Notice how I challenged Mackie's Argument from Queerness. If everyday moral thought and language is varied, and if the conception of a demand or a prescription itself varies, then this may spell doom for the pessimism of error theory. In brief, I floated the idea that although there are some conceptions of a demand that are queer, these are rare and morality can survive without them. Other conceptions of a demand exist, and may be quite common, but these are not obviously as queer as error theorists make out.

The general point is that error theorists are making a specific and explicit claim about what everyday moral thought and language exemplifies and, even, what everyday moral people think about it. In characterizing everyday moral thought and language, error theorists may just draw out some philosophical view based on how all people judge, talk and act. But, as part of this they will inevitably also think about the pretheoretical metaethical intuitions they hear voiced from time to time. Indeed, as I indicated, the interplay between these two things may be so common and complex that one cannot concentrate on one rather than the other. Some realists are realists about some issues because they have had realist-like thoughts previously.

Error theory is somewhat special, for the reference to everyday moral thought and language is explicit, more or less, in the position. It is designed to be a challenge to what goes on in everyday moral thought and language. Because error theorists say that there is sustained and systematic error, it is a deep and revolutionary challenge.

None of the other theories we have canvassed are quite like that. Realists and noncognitivists of various stripes can argue for their position and not seek explicitly and at length to confirm the pretheoretical metaethical intuitions that they detect or which they draw out. It is not essential to their position that they confirm or deny such intuitions. Yet, with that acknowledged, clearly realists, noncognitivists and others may well talk a lot about the character of our judgements and about our pretheoretical intuitions in order to support their respective views. Recall that in §2.2 I said that many realists begin by thinking about our phenomenology which they take to be realist-like, and then claim that any (decent) arguments for realism are really just counters to arguments against realism. The strongest argument for realism is that moral values seem real to us. Similarly, noncognitivists will think hard about what we do with our words and what we think we are doing with such words. I have suggested that naturalists seem to have a hard time in explaining normativity.

So, in short: all metaethicists should have recourse to the character of our moral lives, and also our pretheoretical intuitions about our moral lives. And, here I draw us back to a point made earlier. In part these intuitions help to create the area of our lives about which metaethicists debate. The view of Duncan that there is universal authority to his moral view (if true) helps to constitute for some people what we mean by 'the moral'. For relativists an aspect of the moral that deserves equal if not more attention is the intuition held by Helen and exemplified by her judgements that the authority of some people and their views cannot be applied to other people if their judgements and actions are not in keeping with such views at all.

The point being made at present is that although error theorists should clearly care about people's pretheoretical intuitions, so should many if not all other metaethicists. I cast error theorists as revolutionary since they take such a negative view and, we can assume, most everyday moral judges think there is some positive point to what they are doing; people typically do not think of themselves as being in systematic error. But, although error theorists are revolutionaries, we should note that all of the metaethicists we have encountered seem to be asking us to *revise some* of our (collective) pretheoretical intuitions. That is, a sensibility theorist will ask us to downplay any thoughts we may have that take us towards IMR: we need to resist the pull towards O1. Noncognitivists may say that some of our moral language looks as if it is trying to describe, but the deep function is something else. But what of those people who really believe in O1, or who really believe they are trying to describe something about the world? Amongst other things theorists may seek to draw out other commitments these people, or others, hold and show how they are in tension with the explicit beliefs.

Now, this is all part of metaethical and philosophical debate. What I am interested in here – and trying to get readers to reflect on – is why we have thought so little about an important position, a position I now turn our attention to.

(c) *Metaethical pluralism*: This position I call 'metaethical pluralism'. I do not advocate and support metaethical pluralism. (That would mark somewhat of a strange departure from Chapters 6 and 7.) But, I think it very important that we reflect on its possibility, even if we use it to reinforce a conviction that the generalizing tendency is not a wholly terrible thing.

Metaethical pluralists accept the description I have sketched that there is variety in our pretheoretical intuitions, and we can draw out different metaethical ideas from our everyday practices. Rather than seek to generalize, they seek to try to incorporate some of this variety. In short, they think that different metaethical views can be correct.

Notice straight away that I said that they try to incorporate 'some' variety. Assuming that people will contradict each other – in the way that Duncan and Helen did – any sensible metaethical pluralist is not going to say that we both should and should not be realists about the existence of moral values when it comes to state policies concerning family planning. Similarly, they will not advocate that a single moral judgement is both wholly descriptive (or expressive of some non-motivational representative state) and wholly expressive of some noncognitive, nonrepresentational state. I have no argument to show why they will not advocate such views, bar the thought that such views are flat-out contradictions. Anyway, a more interesting view is in the offing.

Pluralists can be inventive, but for simplicity's sake let us imagine that their core view will pick up on a theme mentioned earlier. They will try to carve out some areas within the moral – perhaps something to do with death, or something to do with inescapable demands, or similar – and argue that this area of the moral should be viewed in *this* metaethical way. And they may pick out other areas that should be viewed in *these other* metaethical ways. So, perhaps certain ways of speaking about certain issues really are best viewed as primarily or wholly expressions of some noncognitive state. Alongside these positive claims, it is open to them to argue wholesale against certain metaethical views: perhaps IMR is too extreme, and because we should vindicate morality to some extent, error theory is not on the cards.

To provide contrast with metaethical pluralism, consider *moral incoherentism*. Moral incoherentists agree that there is variety amongst our pretheoretical metaethical intuitions, and they think further that there are contradictions. They think there are so many and they run so deep that everyday moral thought and language is bogus and crazy (or similar). Moral incoherentists differ from error theorists because they do not think there are just one or a few commitments common across all everyday moral thought and language. But, their end point is pretty much the same.

Although I have only sketched these positions, I hope there is enough here to work with. So, should we adopt metaethical pluralism?

(d) *Against metaethical pluralism*: Here are three reasons not to. First, can we be confident that we can easily carve our everyday moral thought and language into areas? What should lead here? Should it be subject matter, such as death and child-adult relations? Or, should it be surface grammar of judgement? I can imagine there being a lot of 'mixing-and-matching': some cries and expressions of outrage at the terrible events we see unfolding, as well as fact-stating claims about how terrible they are. And, furthermore, it may be hard to demarcate subject areas. To motivate pluralism initially I have contrasted death and destruction with child-adult conversations. But, where do lying and thieving belong? Not as bad as death, perhaps, but worse than rudeness. Are such activities *somewhat* realist? (Does this idea make sense?) And, some types of destruction shade into theft, and vice versa. Similarly, the relations between children and adults at the dinner table, say, can be quite complex and may involve touches of deception. If we think such things wrong, does the metaethical status change? These look like pressing questions, which may be difficult to answer and take us into murky philosophical waters.

The second reason not to adopt metaethical pluralism stems from the first; it puts a more positive spin on matters. Just now we saw it might be hard to demarcate areas so as to support different metaethical views. But, besides that, we may well think that (metaethical) consistency and coherence across all aspects of our moral lives is a good thing. If we want to explain the three-way relationship between humans, values and the world, then we cannot do so by adopting metaethical pluralism, because the level of generality needed for such an explanation is lost. After all, we want to be able to communicate across the ethical areas and divides: we may see insights about demands and values in one situation that help us to understand them in other situations. If we postulate different metaethical positions across different areas, that may stop us from gaining such insights.

This idea, I take it, has a strong hold over us. (After all, there is a reason I began this book by introducing this three-way relationship.) However, whether this is a reason to reject metaethical pluralism is moot. After all, pluralists do offer a type of explanation: they say explicitly that such a question cannot be answered generally. The relationship is more complex than many metaethicists think.

That said, the first reason still stands, and it also leads to a third point. This point again may not cause us immediately to see pluralism as false, but it should give pluralists a lot to think about.

In short, people can be wrong, and often are wrong, about the status and nature of their own moral activity. This is obvious where they contradict themselves, either explicitly or if we trace through the implications of a number of things they say. We can, thus, form a question for metaethical pluralists. To what extent should pluralists privilege people's views? Is the pluralist just content with sorting out contradictions that individuals hold and contradictions between people? Or, does she go further and attempt to say that, although there is no contradiction in the various views held by people about a certain area, certain metaethical intuitions should be privileged more than others? And, in that latter case, what sorts of consideration are brought in? What role have metaphysical ideas, epistemological ideas and the like divorced (somewhat) from everyday people's intuitions? What life do they have outside of what ordinary people think?

Again, we have no reason to reject pluralism out of hand here. Indeed, these questions may prompt different shades of pluralism. But, they may do more than this. They are tricky questions to deal with and take us to the heart of philosophical enquiry: how much should we take from pretheoretical, everyday views? The history of philosophy says that we should take something, but not everything. There is the possibility of illumination and correction if we decide to privilege some intuitions above all others.

All in all, I think there are too many question marks against metaethical pluralism for it to be a plausible theory, or at least worthy of sitting amongst the other theories we have considered in this book. However, I also believe that we should be open to the possibility that a really neat and clever version could be developed that resolves some of these worries.

What is really interesting about metaethical pluralism is that it exposes us to the idea that there *is* a generalizing tendency. In turn we should reflect, finally in this book, on how metaethical theories treat pretheoretical metaethical intuitions. We saw just now that even pluralists may divide over this matter: do they merely sort out considerations, or do they privilege some over others because of other reasons? Also, earlier I cast error theorists as revolutionary with other metaethicists as revisionary. In a very important sense all of the main metaethical theories we have met in this book up until this chapter are prescriptive: they are telling us what to think about the status and nature of our moral activity, rather than (just) describing our views about it. The big questions that I end this section and book with are as follows. To what extent should metaethical theories prescribe in this way? How much store should they set by the pretheoretical intuitions they uncover? To what extent do these intuitions give all metaethicists the raw material with which they have to work? Do the intuitions of Duncan and Helen, say, mark the outermost boundaries of the moral? Do we have to take either seriously? If people have strong IMRealist tendencies, is it then incumbent on any metaethicist to treat such views seriously?

Working out answers to these and many similar questions may affect the structure and nature of the whole metaethical debate. They are certainly questions that, hitherto, many metaethicists have shown little, if any, interest in. I leave it to the reader to think more about these matters on their own.

8.3   Concluding remarks

This final chapter has been deliberately speculative. But, I hope that it prompts some reflection about the things we have discussed.

Metaethics has been one of the more fecund of philosophical areas, right from the start of the twentieth century through to today, particular so over the past 40 years. However, it will only keep our interest, and keep illuminating our moral lives, if things are pushed, puzzled over and shaken up. It is in that spirit that metaethical pluralism should be thought about, and perhaps other things that this book has prompted. When people construct metaethical theories, how important are the pretheoretical metaethical intuitions that are around us? To what extent should these ideas shape our reflective view of the nature and status of morality? What do these questions tell us about the point of the standard metaethical positions examined throughout this book?

Further Reading

Loeb (2008) puts forward a type of moral incoherentism. Gill (2008) and Sayre-McCord (2008) both reply. See also Gill (2009) for more on the background for the pluralism I sketch. Brady (2011) is a collection of excellent papers about new directions in metaethics. None discuss metaethical pluralism or metaethical intuitions, but all are worth reading.

Bibliography

The Stanford Encyclopedia of Philosophy is to be found at http://plato.stanford.edu All entries are referenced here as 2012. See specific details on the site for date of first posting and any revisions. I have listed all relevant entries in this bibliography; some listed here do not appear in any of the 'Further Reading' entries.
Entries with a * are also in Fisher and Kirchin eds. (2006), in part or whole.
Entries with a + are also in Shafer-Landau and Cuneo eds. (2006), in part or whole.

Altham, J. E. J. (1986). 'The Legacy of Emotivism', in *Fact, Science and Morality: Essays on A. J. Ayer's Language, Truth, and Logic*, 275–288, eds. G. Macdonald and C. Wright, Oxford: Blackwell.

Ayer, A. J. (1946). *Language, Truth and Logic*, London: Gollancz, 2nd ed.+

Beaney, M. (2012). 'Analysis', in *The Stanford Encyclopedia of Philosophy*, ed. E. Zalta.

Blackburn, S. (1981). 'Rule-Following and Moral Realism', in *Wittgenstein: To Follow a Rule*, 163–187, eds. S. Holtzman and C. Leich, London: Routledge and Kegan Paul.*

Blackburn, S. (1984). *Spreading the Word*, Oxford: Oxford University Press.*

Blackburn, S. (1988). 'Attitudes and Contents', *Ethics* 98, 501–517.* +

Blackburn, S. (1993a). *Essays in Quasi-Realism*, Oxford: Oxford University Press.+

Blackburn, S. (1993b). 'Realism: Quasi or Queasy?', in *Reality, Representation and Projection*, 365–383, ed. J. Haldane and C. Wright, Oxford: Oxford University Press.

Blackburn, S. (1998). *Ruling Passions*, Oxford: Oxford University Press.

Blackburn, S. (2005). *Truth*, London: Penguin.

Boyd, R. (1988). 'How to be a Moral Realist', in *Essays on Moral Realism*, 181–228, ed. G. Sayre-McCord, Ithaca and London: Cornell University Press.+

Brady, M. (2011). *New Waves in Metaethics*, Basingstoke: Palgrave Macmillan.

Brink, D. (1989). *Moral Realism and the Foundations of Ethics*, Cambridge: Cambridge University Press.

Brink, D. (1997). 'Moral Motivation', *Ethics* 108, 4–32.

Brown, C. (2011). 'A New and Improved Supervenience Argument for Ethical Descriptivism', *Oxford Studies in Metaethics* 6, 205–218.

Campbell, R. (2012). 'Moral Epistemology', in *Stanford Encyclopedia of Philosophy*, ed. E. Zalta.

Chappell, T. (2009). *Ethics and Experience: Life Beyond Moral Theory*, Buckinghamshire: Acumen.

Copp, D. (2000). 'Milk, Honey, and the Good Life on Moral Twin Earth', *Synthese* 124, 113–137.

Copp, D. (2003). 'Why Naturalism?', *Ethical Theory and Moral Practice* 6, 179–200.

Copp, D. (2006). *The Oxford Handbook of Ethical Theory*, Oxford: Oxford University Press.

188   *Bibliography*

Copp, D. (2012). 'Normativity and Reasons: Five Arguments from Parfit against Normative Naturalism', in *Ethical Naturalism*, 24–57, eds. S. Nuccetelli and G. Seay, Cambridge: Cambridge University Press.

Copp, D. and Sobel, D. (2001). 'Against Direction of Fit Accounts of Belief and Desire', *Analysis* 61, 44–53.

Cuneo, T. (2007). *The Normative Web*, Oxford: Oxford University Press.

Dancy, J. (1993). *Moral Reasons*, Oxford: Blackwell.

Dancy, J. (2006). 'Nonnaturalism', in *The Oxford Handbook of Ethical Theory*, 122–145, ed. D. Copp, Oxford: Oxford University Press.

D'Arms, J. and Jacobson, D. (2006). 'Sensibility Theory and Projectivism', in *The Oxford Handbook of Ethical Theory*, 186–218, ed. D. Copp, Oxford: Oxford University Press.

Darwall, S., Gibbard, A., and Railton, P. (eds) (1992). *Moral Discourse and Practice*, Oxford: Oxford University Press.

Divers, J. and Miller, A. (1994). 'Why Expressivists about Value should not Love Minimalism about Truth', *Analysis* 54, 12–19.*

Dreier, J. (1996). 'Expressivist Embeddings and Minimalist Truth', *Philosophical Studies* 83, 29–51.

Dreier, J. (2000). 'Dispositions and Fetishes: Externalist Models of Moral Motivation', *Philosophy and Phenomenological Research* 61, 619–638.*

Enoch, D. (2011). *Taking Morality Seriously*, Oxford: Oxford University Press.

Firth, R. (1952). 'Ethical Absolutism and the Ideal Observer', *Philosophy and Phenomenological Research* 12, 317–345.+

Fisher, A. (2011). *Metaethics: An Introduction*, Durham: Acumen.

Fisher, A. and Kirchin, S. (eds) (2006). *Arguing about Metaethics*, London: Routledge.

Fitzpatrick, W. (2009). 'Recent work on Ethical Realism', *Analysis* 69, 746–760.

Frankena, W. (1939). 'The Naturalistic Fallacy', *Mind* 48, 464–477.*

Garner, R. (2010). 'Abolishing Morality', in *A World without Values*, 217–234, ed. R. Joyce and S. Kirchin, Dordrecht: Springer.

Geach, P. T. (1960). 'Ascriptivism', *Philosophical Review* 69, 221–225.

Geach, P. T. (1965). 'Assertion', *Philosophical Review* 74, 449–465.

Gibbard, A. (1990). *Wise Choices, Apt Feelings*, Oxford: Clarendon Press.

Gibbard, A. (2003). *Thinking How to Live*, Cambridge, Mass.: Harvard University Press.

Gill, M. (2008). 'Metaethical Variability, Incoherence, and Error', in *Moral Psychology, volume 2*, 387–401, ed. W Sinnott-Armstrong Cambridge, Mass.: MIT Press.

Gill, M. (2009). 'Indeterminancy and Variability in Meta-ethics', *Philosophical Studies* 145, 215–234.

Gowans, C. (2012). 'Moral Relativism', in *Stanford Encyclopedia of Philosophy*, ed. E. Zalta.

Hale, B. (1986). 'The Compleat Projectivist', *Philosophical Quarterly* 36, 65–84.

Hale, B. (1993a). 'Can there be a Logic of Attitudes?', in *Reality, Representation and Projection*, 337–363, ed. J. Haldane and C. Wright, Oxford: Oxford University Press.*

Hale, B. (1993b). 'Postscript', in *Reality, Representation and Projection*, 385–388, ed. J. Haldane and C. Wright, Oxford: Oxford University Press.

Harman, G. (1985). 'Is there a Single True Morality?', in *Morality, Reason and Truth,* 27–48, ed. D. Copp and D. Zimmerman, Totowa, NJ: Rowman and Allanheld.

Helm, B. (2001). *Emotional Reason: Deliberation, Motivation and the Nature of Value,* Cambridge: Cambridge University Press.

Honderich, T (ed.) (1985). *Morality and Objectivity,* London: Routledge.

Horgan, T. and Timmons, M. (1992). 'Troubles on Moral Twin Earth: Moral Queerness Revived', *Synthese* 92, 221–260.*

Horgan, T. and Timmons, M. (2000) 'Copping out on Moral Twin Earth', *Synthese* 124, 139–152.

Horgan, T. and Timmons, M. (2006) (eds). *Metaethics after Moore,* Oxford: Oxford University Press.

Huemer, M. (2006). *Ethical Intuitionism,* Basingstoke: Palgrave Macmillan.

Humberstone, L. (1992). 'Direction of Fit', *Mind* 101, 59–83.

Hurka, T. (2012). 'Moore's Moral Philosophy', in *The Stanford Encyclopedia of Philosophy,* ed. E. Zalta.

Jackson, F. (1998). *From Metaphysics to Ethics,* Oxford: Oxford University Press.+

Jackson, F. and Pettit, P. (1998). 'A Problem for Expressivism', *Analysis* 58, 239–251.*

Jacobson, D. (2012). 'Fitting Attitude Accounts of Value', in *Stanford Encyclopedia of Philosophy,* ed. E. Zalta.

Joyce, R. (2001). *The Myth of Morality,* Cambridge: Cambridge University Press.+

Joyce, R. (2002). 'Expressivism and Motivational Internalism', *Analysis* 62, 336–344.

Joyce, R. (2012). 'Moral anti-Realism', *The Stanford Encyclopedia of Philosophy,* ed. E. Zalta.

Joyce, R. and Kirchin, S. (2010). (eds) *A World without Values,* Dordrecht: Springer.

Kennett, J. (2001). *Agency and Responsibility: A Common-Sense Moral Psychology,* Oxford: Oxford University Press.

Kirk, R. (1999). *Relativism and Reality,* London: Routledge.

Kirchin, S. (2010a). 'A Tension in the Moral Error Theory', in *A World without Values,* 167–182, ed. R. Joyce and S. Kirchin, Dordrecht: Springer.

Kirchin, S. (2010b). 'The Shapelessness Hypothesis', *Philosophers' Imprint* 10, 1–28.

Kirchin, S. (ms). *Thick Evaluation.*

Kirkham, R. (1995). *Theories of Truth,* Cambridge, Mass.: MIT Press.

Lenman, J. (2012). 'Moral Naturalism', in *Stanford Encyclopedia of Philosophy,* ed. E. Zalta.

Lillehammer, H. (1997). 'Smith on Moral Fetishism', *Analysis* 57, 187–195.

Lillehammer, H. (2004). 'Moral Error Theory', *Proceedings of the Aristotelian Society* 104, 93–109.

Loeb, D. (2008). 'Moral Incoherentism: How to Pull a Metaphysical Rabbit out of a Semantic Hat', in *Moral Psychology, volume 2,* 355–385, ed. W Sinnott-Armstrong, Cambridge, Mass.: MIT Press.

Mackie, J. L. (1977). *Ethics: Inventing Right and Wrong,* London: Penguin.* +

Majors, Brad (2005). 'Moral Discourse and Descriptive Properties', *Philosophical Quarterly,* 55, 474–494.

Maund, B. (2012). 'Color', in *Stanford Encyclopedia of Philosophy*, ed. E. Zalta.

McDowell, J. (1981). 'Non-cognitivism and Rule-Following', in *Wittgenstein: To Follow a Rule*, 141–162, eds. S. Holtzman and C. Leich, London: Routledge and Kegan Paul.*

McDowell, J. (1983). 'Aesthetic Value, Objectivity, and the Fabric of the World', in *Pleasure, Preference, and Value*, 1–16, ed. E. Schaper, Cambridge: Cambridge University Press.

McDowell, J. (1985). 'Values and Secondary Qualities', in *Morality and Objectivity*, 110–129, ed. T. Honderich, London: Routledge and Kegan Paul.* +

McDowell, J. (1987). 'Projection and Truth in Ethics', Lindley Lecture, University of Kansas. *

McDowell, J. (1988). *Mind, Value and Reality*, London: Harvard University Press.

McNaughton, D. (1988). *Moral Vision*, Oxford: Blackwell.

Miller, A. (2003). *An Introduction to Contemporary Metaethics*, Cambridge: Polity Press.

Millgram, E. (1995). 'Was Hume a Humean?', *Hume Studies* 21, 75–94.

Moore, G. E. (1903). *Principia Ethica*, Cambridge: Cambridge University Press. Reprinted 2nd ed., ed. T. Baldwin (1993) Cambridge: Cambridge University Press.* +

Nolan, D., Restall, G. and West, C. (2006). 'Moral Fictionalism versus the Rest', *Australasian Journal of Philosophy* 83, 307–330.

Nuccetelli, S. and Seay, G. (2007) *Themes from G. E. Moore*, Oxford: Oxford University Press.

Olson, J. (2011). 'Getting Real about Moral Fictionalism', *Oxford Studies in Metaethics* 6, 181–204.

Parfit, D. (2011). *On What Matters*, Oxford: Oxford University Press.

Railton, P. (1986). 'Moral Realism', *Philosophical Review* 95, 163–207.* +

Railton, P. (1993a). 'What the Non-Cognitivist Sees the Naturalist Must Help Us to Explain, in *Reality, Representation and Projection*, 279–300, ed. J. Haldane and C. Wright, Oxford: Oxford University Press.

Railton, P. (1993b). 'Reply to David Wiggins', in *Reality, Representation and Projection*, 315–328, ed. J. Haldane and C. Wright, Oxford: Oxford University Press.

Ridge, M. (2007). 'Anti-Reductionism and Supervenience', *Journal of Moral Philosophy* 4, 330–348.

Ridge, M. (2006). 'Ecumenical Expressivism: Finessing Frege', *Ethics* 116, 302–336.

Ridge, M. (2012). 'Moral Non-naturalism', in *Stanford Encyclopedia of Philosophy*, ed. E. Zalta.

Rosati, C. (2012). 'Moral Motivation', in *Stanford Encyclopedia of Philosophy*, ed. E. Zalta.

Sayre-McCord, G. (ed.) (1988). *Essays on Moral Realism*, Ithaca, NY: Cornell University Press.

Sayre-McCord, G. (2008). 'Moral Semantics and Empirical Enquiry', in *Moral Psychology, volume 2*, 403–412, ed. W Sinnott-Armstrong, Cambridge, Mass.: MIT Press.

Sayre-McCord, G. (2012a). 'Metaethics', in *Stanford Encyclopedia of Philosophy*, ed. E. Zalta.

Sayre-McCord, G. (2012b). 'Moral Realism', in *Stanford Encyclopedia of Philosophy*, ed. E. Zalta.

Schroeder, M. (2005). 'Realism and Reduction: The Quest for Robustness', *Philosophers' Imprint* 5, 1–18.

Schroeder, M. (2009). 'Hybrid Expressivism: Virtues and Vices', *Ethics* 119, 257–309.

Schroeder, M. (2010). *Noncognitivism in Ethics*, London: Routledge.

Schueler, G. F. (1988). 'Moral *Modus Ponens* and Moral Realism', *Ethics* 98, 492–500.

Shafer-Landau (2000). 'A Defence of Motivational Externalism', *Philosophical Studies* 97, 267–291.

Shafer-Landau, R. and Cuneo, T. (eds) (2006). *Foundations of Ethics*, Oxford: Blackwell.

Shepski, L. (2008). 'The Vanishing Argument from Queerness', *Australasian Journal of Philosophy* 86, 371–387.

Simpson, E. (1999) 'Between Internalism and Externalism in Ethics', *Philosophical Quarterly* 49, 201–214.

Sinnott-Armstrong, W. (2012). 'Moral Skepticism', in *Stanford Encyclopedia of Philosophy*, ed. E. Zalta.

Skorupski, J. (2009). *The Routledge Companion to Ethics*, London: Routledge.

Sosa, D. (2001). 'Pathetic Ethics', in *Objectivity and Law and Morals*, 287–329, ed. B. Leiter, Cambridge: Cambridge University Press.*

Smith, M. (1994a). *The Moral Problem*, Oxford: Blackwell.* +

Smith, M. (1994b). 'Why Expressivists about Value should Love Minimalism about Truth', *Analysis* 54, 1–11.*

Smith, M. and Stoljar, D. (2003). 'Is there a Lockean Problem for Expressivists?', *Analysis* 63, 76–86.*

Snare, F. (1975). 'The Open Question as Linguistic Test', *Ratio* 17, 123–129.*

Stevenson, C. L. (1944). *Ethics and Language*, New Haven, CT: Yale University Press.

Stratton-Lake, P. (ed.) (2002). *Ethical Intuitionism*, Oxford: Oxford University Press.

Street, S. (2011). 'Mind-Independence without the Mystery: Why Quasi-Realists Can't Have It Both Ways', in *Oxford Studies in Metaethics* 6, 1–32.

Sturgeon, N. (1985). 'Moral Explanations', in *Morality, Reason and Truth*, 49–78, ed. D. Copp and D. Zimmerman, Totowa, NJ: Rowman and Allanheld.* +

Sturgeon, N. (2006). 'Naturalism', in *The Oxford Handbook of Ethical Theory*, 90–121, ed. D. Copp, Oxford: Oxford University Press.

Sturgeon, N. (2009). 'Doubts about the Supervenience of the Evaluative', *Oxford Studies in Metaethics* 4, 53–90.

Streumer, B. (2008). 'Are there any Irreducibly Normative Properties?', *Australasian Journal of Philosophy* 86, 537–561.

Streumer, B. (forthcoming) 'Can we Believe the Error Theory?', *Journal of Philosophy*.

Van Roojen, M. (1996). 'Expressivism and Irrationality', *Philosophical Review*, 105, 311–335.

Van Roojen, M. (2002). 'Humean and Anti-Humean Internalism and Moral Judgments', *Philosophy and Phenomenological Research* 65, 26–49.

Van Roojen, M. (2012). 'Moral Cognitivism v. Moral Non-cognitivism', in *Stanford Encyclopedia of Philosophy*, ed. E. Zalta.

Väyrynen, P. (2009). 'Normative Appeals to the Natural', *Philosophy and Phenomenological Research* 79, 279–314.

Wiggins, D. (1998). *Needs, Values, Truth*, Oxford: Oxford University Press, 3rd ed.+

Wiggins, D. (1993a). 'Cognitivism, Naturalism and Normativity', in *Reality, Representation and Projection*, 301–314, ed. J. Haldane and C. Wright, Oxford: Oxford University Press.

Wiggins, D. (1993b). 'A Neglected Position?', in *Reality, Representation and Projection*, 329, 338, ed. J. Haldane and C. Wright, Oxford: Oxford University Press.

Wong, D. (2006). *Natural Moralities: A Defense of Pluralistic Relativism*, Oxford: Oxford University Press.

Wright, C. (1995). 'Truth in Ethics', *Ratio* 8, 209–226.

Zangwill, N. (1994). 'Moral Mind-independence', *Australasian Journal of Philosophy* 72, 205–219.

Zangwill, N. (1998). 'Direction of Fit and Normative Functionalism', *Philosophical Studies* 91, 173–203.

Zangwill, N. (2008). 'Besires and the Motivation Debate', *Theoria* 74, 50–59.

Index

Some Examples

Topics